Foreword by
ALLAN H. ANDERSON

A Theology of

CONTEXTUAL PERSPECTIVES in KOREAN PENTECOSTALISM

Sang Yun Lee

WIPF & STOCK · Eugene, Oregon

Wipf and Stock Publishers
199 W 8th Ave, Suite 3
Eugene, OR 97401

A Theology of Hope
Contextual Perspectives in Korean Pentecostalism
By Lee, Sang Yun and Anderson, Allan Heaton
Copyright©2018 APTS Press
ISBN 13: 978-1-5326-6327-7
Publication date 7/12/2018
Previously published by APTS Press, 2018

Praise For

A Korean Theology of Hope: A Conversation with David Yonggi Cho and Jürgen Moltmann in the Context of Korean Pentecostalism

Sang Yun Lee provides with this monograph the definitive *theological* apologetic for the "blessing theology" of contemporary Korean Pentecostalism, both by contextualizing its main tenets within the historical, political, and economic history of the Korean peninsula of the mid-to late-20th century and by engaging with the main themes of the predominant theologian of hope—Jürgen Moltmann—of the present time. Along the way, what emerges also is a set of important constructive proposals to ensure that the Korean blessing—and hope—theology will be pertinent not only for the 21st century East Asian context but also for any theological vision aspiring for global relevance in the third millennium.

Amos Yong, Professor of Theology & Mission, Fuller Theological Seminary

Sang Yun Lee's sustained account of the Threefold Blessing taught by Pastor David Yonggi Cho, Korean Pentecostalism's iconic leader, offers a unique insight into the man, the movement, and especially the context which gave birth to the phenomenon.
This is a compelling case study of how social and cultural forces shape religious movements, and the challenges facing them when the context changes. Cho's teaching on prosperity illustrates that a doctrine is never a generic one-view-fits-all but must be evaluated within its context.

David A. Reed, Professor Emeritus, Wycliffe College

Sang Yun Lee sets forth an authoritative theological account of the Threefold Blessing in Korean Pentecostalism. Developed by Pastor

David Yonggi Cho, its iconic leader, this volume offers a unique insight into the man, the movement, and the context which gave it birth. This is a compelling case study of the social and cultural forces which shape religious movements and the challenges facing them when the context changes. Cho's Threefold Blessing—especially the theme of prosperity—illustrates that a doctrine is never a generic one-view-fits-all but must constantly be interpreted and evaluated within its own history and context.

Wonsuk Ma, Distinguished Professor of Global Christianity, Oral Roberts University

Lee introduces and reinterprets a theology of hope for the Korean context in vivid conversation with Jürgen Moltmann, David Yonggi Cho, Pentecostalism, and the proclamation of the Threefold Blessing. Engaging the reader in the historical, soteriological, pneumatological, eco-theological, and socio-theological perspectives of a revitalized Korean theology, this book calls for a broad renewal of the role of the church as a catalyst for social transformation that changes the way we see salvation, prosperity, and healing.

Wolfgang Vondey, University of Birmingham, author of *Pentecostal Theology: Living the Full Gospel*

This book by Sang Yun Lee deserves serious and widespread attention as a significant achievement in theology and modern church history, especially as it relates to Korean Pentecostalism. On one level, this is a provocative theology of hope that takes up the challenge of Rev. Yonggi Cho's message of salvation, healing, and prosperity. On another level, this is a breathtakingly thorough treatment of the Korean context for doing theology. Anyone interested in either Pentecostal or Korean theology cannot afford to ignore this important work. I learned much from it.

Frank D. Macchia, Professor of Christian Theology, Vanguard University of Southern California, Associate Director, Centre for Pentecostal and Charismatic Studies, Bangor University, Wales (UK)

Publisher's Preface

We are pleased to offer this fourth volume in our APTS Press Monograph Series. This is the publication of the author's doctoral dissertation done under the mentorship of Dr. Allan H. Anderson at the University of Birmingham in the United Kingdom. The purpose of this series is to give our readers broader access to good scholarship that would otherwise be unavailable outside of the academic community. This is part of our ongoing commitment to discipleship through publishing.

The other three titles in this series, *Theology in Context: A Case Study in the Philippines,* by Dave Johnson, *Leave a Legacy: Increasing Missionary Longevity*, by Russ Turney and *Understanding the Iglesia ni Cristo*, by Anne Harper, are all available at www.aptspress.org. If you have any questions, you can reach us through our website. We would be happy to hear from you.

We hope you enjoy this book.

THE PUBLISHER

Contents

Preface	*ix*
Foreword by Allan H. Anderson	*xi*
Acknowledgments	*xv*
Tables	*xvii*
Abbreviations	*xix*
Glossary	*xxi*

PART 1   1
INTRODUCING THE THREEFOLD BLESSING IN THE KOREAN CONTEXT

Chapter 1	The Historical Korean Context	3
Chapter 2	Previous Studies of Korean Pentecostalism and the Threefold Blessing	7

PART 2   13
THE HISTORY OF KOREAN PENTECOSTALISM

Chapter 3	The Arrival of Christianity as the *Silhak* Legacy in the Chosŏn Dynasty	15
Chapter 4	Christianity Becomes Rooted in Korea	21
Chapter 5	The Influence of Early Protestant Missionaries and Bible Translations	25
Chapter 6	Korean Revivals and the Birth of Korean Pentecostalism	33
Chapter 7	Korean Pentecostal Revivals and the Development of Korean Pentecostalism	43
Chapter 8	Early Pentecostals and the Quickening of Pentecostal Hope	53
Chapter 9	The Establishment of Korean Pentecostalism	59

PART 3   69
THE CONTEXTUALIZATION OF PENTECOSTALISM IN KOREA

Chapter 10	*Hananim*, the Name of God for Korean Christians	71
Chapter 11	*Minjung* and *Han*: The People of God in Suffering	79
Chapter 12	The Influence of Korean Shamanism on the Contextualized Hope of the Threefold Blessing	95
Chapter 13	Korean Pentecostalism and the State	103

PART 4   109
THE THREEFOLD BLESSING AND HOPE IN THE KOREAN CONTEXT

Chapter 14	Yonggi Cho and the Threefold Blessing	111
Chapter 15	The Threefold Blessing in the Korean Context	123
Chapter 16	The Hope of the Threefold Blessing	135
Chapter 17	The Threefold Blessing and Moltmann's Theology of Hope	141
Chapter 18	Theologies of Hope and the Kingdom of God	149

PART 5   155
THE SPIRITUAL BLESSING OF THREEFOLD BLESSING

Chapter 19	Spirit Baptism and Infilling in the Threefold Blessing	157
Chapter 20	Prosperity and Hope in the Threefold Blessing	173
Chapter 21	Healing and Hope in the Threefold Blessing	177
Chapter 22	Kerygma in the Threefold Blessing	181

PART 6   187
THE THREEFOLD BLESSING IN PRESENT AND FUTURE PERSPECTIVES

Chapter 23	Changing Contexts: Current Korean Pentecostalism	189

Chapter 24	Renewing the Threefold Blessing in the Current Context	197
Chapter 25	Recontextualization of the Threefold Blessing	203
Chapter 26	Observations and Recommendations for Contextualizing the Threefold Blessing Into the Current Korean Context	219

Bibliography	223
Appendix A. Interview with Dr. Jürgen Moltmann	247
Appendix B. Interview with Dr. Young Hoon Lee	253
Appendix C. Interview with Dr. Amos Yong	261
Appendix D. Interview with Dr. Vinson Synan	267

Preface

This book examines the Threefold Blessing: salvation, financial prosperity, and healing as a contextual hope in the Korean Pentecostal context. Ironically, hope always begins in hopeless situations. It will not function as hope unless it is renewed in a context related to a current lack and deficiency.

The Threefold Blessing was the most urgent and eager hope for desperate Koreans in the post-Korean War context because it contradicted socio-economic and political situations. It successfully contextualized into the Korean context, became deeply lodged into Korean Pentecostals' lives, and influenced the growth of strong Korean Pentecostal churches.

As Korea's contexts change, the Threefold Blessing must be reinterpreted and theologically recontextualized. The original Threefold Blessing emphasized the spiritual, physical, and prosperous life of individuals. The new Threefold Blessing must expand its theological perspectives to include social and ecological matters. This book examines the Threefold Blessing as a Pentecostal hope in the Korean context and suggests ways for its recontextualization for present and future Korean Pentecostals

Foreword

*I*t was my privilege to supervise Sang Yun Lee's PhD research at the University of Birmingham a few years ago. The strength of this study is that it comes from an insider of the now famous Yoido Full Gospel Church in Seoul, South Korea, where the author serves on the ministerial staff and knows the teaching of the church inside out. David Yonggi Cho (1936-) led this congregation for fifty years (1958-2008). South Korea has gone through several crises and transformations during this time. Sang Yun Lee takes the context of this large congregation seriously. He advocates a "theology of hope," essentially different from the Moltmann version on which the idea is developed. Lee shows how Cho's message, particularly in its promise of a "saved" healthy, happy and prosperous life (the "Threefold Blessing"), was the antidote to the events that had ravaged the Korean peninsula in the 1950s. Of course, Korea has had a terribly fraught history during the twentieth century, after centuries of being the "hermit kingdom" standing between the great powers vying for influence: China, Russia, and Japan. The first half of the twentieth century saw the Russo-Japanese War, after which Korea was annexed by Japan and was oppressed until Japan's defeat by the United States in 1945. Then came the Korean War in 1950, also aggravated by the ideological conflict between the superpowers the Soviet Union and the United States. Although it ended three years later with a divided Korea that exists to this day, this was only a truce and the two Koreas are still technically at war. At least three million died in the conflict, which left many Korean people destitute and in deep despair, known to the Korean people as *han*. It was into this context that a young Yonggi Cho began preaching hope to his people.

This was the beginning of the most remarkable growth of a congregation ever recorded in recent Christian history. Cho and his future mother-in-law, Jashil Choi (1915-89), in the aftermath of the devastating war began a small tent church in a slum area of Seoul in 1958 with five members. By 1962 this congregation had grown to eight hundred and by 1964 had a sanctuary seating two thousand people, the second venue for this congregation. In 1969 the church bought property in Yoido before it became prime real estate, and he dedicated a new 10,000 seat auditorium there in 1973. This Full Gospel Central Church (as then known) was now receiving international attention. By 1982 the Korean Full Gospel (Assemblies of God) churches were the third largest Protestant group with over half a million members, half of whom were in Cho's church, which became Yoido Full Gospel Church (YFGC) in 1984. Cho became chairman of the World Pentecostal Assemblies of God in 1992, and the church planted churches all over Korea and internationally. By 1993 the YFGC reported 700,000 members under 700 pastors and was the largest Christian congregation in the world. By the year 2000 the Assemblies of God, with over a million affiliates, was by far the largest Pentecostal denomination in Korea. When they joined the Korean National Council of Churches in 1999, it was the first time any national Assemblies of God church had entered an ecumenical council of churches.

The context of Korea has affected the appeal of the message of Yonggi Cho. Although his writings are devotional and inspirational rather than theological, those writings that deal with Cho's own context illustrate how his implicit theology may be regarded as "contextual" and a theology of hope. This is what this book is all about. It is true that Cho's publications are mainly about his understanding of the Bible and his own experiences as a pastor, but he also refers to the context in which these experiences and understandings were developed. His books abound with biblical illustrations and teaching, but he develops his theology in a particular context of suffering and pain. For Pentecostals in different parts of the world, the "freedom in the Spirit" allows them to formulate, often unconsciously, a theology that brings hope to people in different life situations, and Cho's theology is a leading example of this. Pentecostalism has taken on a distinctive form in Korea, quite different from that found in the West. Observers who have tried to emphasise the "American" nature of Pentecostalism throughout the world or the "Americanization" of Christianity in Korea and elsewhere often miss this important fact. Creative innovations and the selective transformation of foreign symbols are constantly occurring and, naturally, a synthesising process takes place as a new form of Christianity like Pentecostalism interacts with older Korean religions like shamanism and Buddhism. For example, the well-known prayer mountain movement in Korea is a culturally relevant form of Christian practice that reflects the ancient spirituality of the Korean people. Similarly, Korean people suffering from their accumulated grief or *han* seek healing and "blessings" from traditional shamans to alleviate their deep pain, such as in the years following the Korean War or more recently, during the International Monetary Fund crisis in the late 1990s. The fact that a prominent part of Cho's message is to proclaim that God brings "blessings" and healings is a contextual message for Korean people that is readily accepted. This is a theology of hope for people who need it. Those who censure Korean Pentecostals for their alleged "shamanism" often fail to see that the parallels with ancient religions in these practices are also continuous with the biblical record. Furthermore, these Pentecostals define their practices by reference to the Bible rather than to shamanism, but see their activities as creative adaptations to the local context. So we are dealing with both a continuous and a discontinuous relationship with the past.

At the same time, Asian Pentecostal scholars might also need a greater appreciation for both the diversity and richness of their cultural and religious past. Demonizing this past does not explain the present attraction of Pentecostalism for peoples deeply influenced by their ancient religions and cultures. But one conclusion that is incontrovertible is that Korean Pentecostals have found both culturally and biblically acceptable alternatives to, and adaptations from, the practices of their ancient religions and are seeking to provide answers to the needs of their own context. I live in the western world and my understanding of religious phenomena outside my context will always be partial. There are unanswered questions about Cho's theology that are better debated by Koreans themselves. But Pentecostal theology in countries like Korea should not be a reflection of a theology born in the totally different context of the western world, even though cultural radiation from the USA has influenced South Korea for over a generation. A theology of hope made in Germany, the USA or any other place, whether Pentecostal or otherwise, is a form of cultural colonialism. I believe that Asian

Pentecostals must develop a theology that speaks with a different perspective of the voice of the poor, a theology of hope for a suffering people, a genuinely contextual theology. The good news, Cho declares, is that God meets all the needs of believers, including their spiritual salvation, physical healing, and other blessings for material needs. East Asia, like Africa and Latin America, also has the phenomenon of mass urbanization, and the Pentecostal churches have provided places of spiritual security and personal communities for people unsettled by rapid social change. As Korean churches becomes more relevant to their cultural and social context, they become more able to serve the wider society.

I do not plan to repeat what the author has outlined so well in this book. Sang Yun Lee also brings out the very important need for the changes to the message of hope to include changing social and environmental concerns. He speaks of flexibility and change, how a theology of hope must keep up with contemporary needs and contexts. It is always offering hope in the midst of contrary indications and circumstances that suggest there is no hope. I commend this study to you warmly. Read on . . . .

Allan H. Anderson
University of Birmingham, England

Acknowledgments

"The Lord God has given me the tongue of the learned, that I should know how to speak a word in season to him who is weary. He awakens me morning by morning, He awakens my ear to hear as the learned." Isaiah 50:4 (NKJV)

I read this prayer every early morning and at night while I wrote this book, which is based on my PhD studies. Thanks and glory to God who heard my prayers and strengthened me. This study would not have been achieved without the consistent support and guidance of my supervisor, Professor Allan Anderson. My special thanks goes to him. I am grateful to all teaching faculty members of the Theology department at the University of Birmingham, especially to Dr. Andrew Davies, who helped me during the first year of my study. I would like to express my gratitude to Dr. Wonsuk Ma, Dr. Julie Ma, and Dr. Sangin Han for their continuous encouragement and words of wisdom during my stay in England. I appreciate all the research participants including Sean Huh, who voluntarily offered their time to be in this study. Thanks to Dr. Moltmann, Dr. Synan, Dr. Yong, and Dr. Young Hoon Lee for their interviews. I am also indebted to the following people and churches for their financial assistance. Because of them, I was able to continue my study: The Yoido Full Gospel Church, Dongbu Full Gospel Church, Rev. Soonyeol Seo, Rev. Wookeun Kang, Rev. Jaeman Park, Deacon Kwangho Choo, and Deacon Youngsam Park.

Lastly, I cannot thank enough my wonderful wife Sarah Nayung for her patience through many journeys and adventures with me, even in the midst of her own studies. My love also goes to my sweet children: Teresa, Chara, and Christopher. Their sacrifices will not be forgotten.

Tables

Table 1   62
The Statistics of Pentecostal Churches and Membership in Korea during 1934-1941

Table 2   88
The Rate of Korean Churches' Growth (1969-1982)

Table 3   90
The Participants of '80 WEC-Here's Life

Table 4   107
Growth of GNP Per Capita and Pentecostalism

Table 5   118
Comparison Between the Four/Fivefold Gospel by Classical Pentecostals, the Four-Fold Gospel by A.B. Simpson and the Five-Fold Gospel by Cho

Abbreviations

AG Assemblies of God

APTS Asia Pacific Theological Seminary

AJPS *Asian Journal of Pentecostal Studies*

KAG Korean Assemblies of God

CTCCA Commission on Theological Concerns of the Christian Conference of Asia

IMF International Monetary Fund

ITI International Theological Institute

JPT *Journal of Pentecostal Theology*

PCCNA Pentecostal/Charismatic Churches of North America

PFNA Pentecostal Fellowship of North America

YTI Yeongsan Theological Institute

YFGC Yoido Full Gospel Church

Glossary

Abouji: Father
Amateras: The Japanese heavenly goddess
Cheong-Bi-Sa-Sang: The idea of honorable poverty
Che-Sa: The Confucian ancestral worship
Chonju: The lord of heaven
Chosŏn WhangJo Silrok: The Annals of The *Chosŏn* Dynasty
Chukbok: Blessing.
Gidowon: Prayer Mountain
Gut: Shamanic ritual
Haet Byet Jeong Chaek: The Sunshine Policy
Hak-Gyo: School
Hangŭl: Korean Language
Han: Accumulated feeling of unresolved resentment
Hanmoon: Chinese composition
Hananim: One Supreme Being
Haneunim: Heavenly One and Supreme
Han-puri: The resolution of *Han*
Jang Lo: Presbyterian
Jaju: Self-support
Je-Joong-Won: House of Universal Helpfulness
Jesu: Jesus

Jesu Sŏngkyo Lukabokum Jyunsŏ: The Book of Luke of Jesus Christ
Joeushin Hananim: Good God
Joong-In: The middle-lower class
Kookga Jochan Gidohoi: The National Prayer Breakfast
Kwang-Hye-Won: Widespread Relief House
Mi Gam li: American Methodist
Minjung: A group of ordinary people
Oh-jung-bok-eum: The Fivefold Gospel Pentecostal: Korean Pentecostal unless otherwise specified
Sam-jung-chuk-bok: The Threefold Blessing
Silhak: Practical Thought
Tao: The great ultimate in Confucianism
   The Chosŏn Dynasty: the last dynasty of Korea before Japanese occupation (1392-1897 A.D.)
The *Daehan Jeguk*: The Korean Empire (October 1897 - August 1910 A.D.)
Tianzhu shiyi: The True Teaching of the Lord of Heaven
Yangban: The upper class Koreans

Part ONE

INTRODUCING THE THREEFOLD BLESSING IN THE KOREAN CONTEXT

The Korean context has birthed and shaped a unique form of Pentecostalism that stands in agreement with and in contrast to other global Pentecostal movements. Korean culture, politics, religion, and economic factors continue to influence the current Korean Pentecostal movement. In particular, the Threefold Blessing of Yonggi Cho—a Pentecostal promise of salvation, healing, and prosperity (blessing) which emerged in the middle of the twentieth century—needs to be re-examined, recontextualized, and reapplied to be relevant to Korean Pentecostals in their contemporary context.

CHAPTER 1
THE HISTORICAL KOREAN CONTEXT

By the time Christianity arrived, Korea had isolated itself from the Western world. Confucianism provided the foundation of the cultural, socio-political, and religious lives of Koreans. It was the most crucial persecutor of and became the most significant contributor to the beginning of Korean Christianity.

Confucians practice ancestor worship. Koreans combined that Confucian filial piety with Korean shamanic beliefs: fortune and misfortune were dependent on how they served their ancestors. Ancestor worship was not considered optional. Many believers were persecuted and martyred by the government due to their rejection of ancestor worship.

Nevertheless, Confucianism contributed significantly to the advent of Korean Christianity. Korean neo-Confucian (*Silhak*) scholars introduced Christianity to the country in the eighteenth century before the arrival of Western missionaries. These scholars also translated the Bible into the Korean language. Some *Silhak* scholars wanted to transform the nation through "practical studies and thought"[1] and, consequently, became interested in Western civilization as well as Christianity. With the government's implementation of a closed-door policy, their hopes of reform could not become a reality.

Through the Treaty of Kanghwa in February 1879, (also known as the Korea-Japan Treaty of Amity, an unequal treaty imposed by force), Korea opened her ports to trade with other countries. After the treaty was signed, Korea became subject to Japan and the whole nation plunged into chaos.

With the fall of the Chosŏn Dynasty and Japanese rule, the influences of Buddhism and Confucianism declined. During the Kabo-

---

[1] *Silhak* is a compound word: *Sil* means "practical" or "actual" and *hak* can be translated as "learning" or "studies" in English. From the late seventeenth and early nineteenth centuries, *Silhak* developed with the metaphysical nature of neo-Confucianism and became a social reform movement with practical approach to statecraft in Korea. It denied following Confucian teachings without criticism. See "Practical Learning School, Korean Silhak," in *Britannica Encyclopaedia of World Religions*, (London: Encyclopaedia Britannica Inc., 2006).

Ulmi Reform movement (1894-1895), Confucian society carried out one of the biggest changes in its five-hundred-year history in Korea. In December 1895, a reform cabinet led by Hong Jip Kim promulgated new laws to modernize the country. These included the "Short Hair Act," the use of the solar calendar instead of the lunar calendar, the abolition of slavery, the prohibition of child marriage, and the permission of widow remarriage.²

According to Confucian teaching, 身體髮膚受之父母不敢毀傷孝之始也 [*Shinchebalboo Soojiboomo Bulgamheisang Hyojisiya* - the body is from the parents, so causing no damage to it is the beginning of filial piety], Koreans traditionally did not cut their hair their entire lives, adopting the topknot. Because of the "Short Hair Act," they had to cut off the topknot, which symbolized Confucian society as well as male authority in Korea's patriarchal society. This new decree caused many small-scale revolts by Confucian scholars³ because the topknot had been a sign of their integrity for hundreds of years.⁴

The use of the solar calendar was also a significant social transition and a symptom of the decline of Confucianism. Farming, ancestor worship, marriage systems, and the registration of birthdays and anniversaries had been based on the lunar calendar.

In 1905, Korea became a protectorate of Japan and five years later, its sovereignty was turned over to Japan. In 1910, it became a Japanese colony by force.⁵ By the early 1930s, the Japanese enforced the practice of Shinto worship in Korea.

For thirty-five years (1910-1945), Koreans suffered socio-political repression and religious persecution. Their properties and family members were taken by the Japanese government for the wars that Japan carried out in Asia and the Pacific. Most Koreans were deeply frustrated by these tragic and shameful events. In their desperation, they found little

---

²Keith Pratt and Richard Rutt, *Korea: A Historical and Cultural Dictionary* (Richmond Surrey: Curzon Press, 1999), 194-95.

³James Hoare and Susan Pares, *Korea: An Introduction* (London and New York: Kegan Paul International Ltd., 1991), 47.

⁴Pratt and Rutt, *Korea: A Historical and Cultural Dictionary*, 479.

⁵Hoare and Pares, *Korea: An Introduction*, 50-53.

consolation or hope for the future in their socio-political or indigenous religious systems.

Korea was liberated from Japan in 1945. Five years later, the Korean War broke out and devastated the country. During the three-year war (1950-1953), innumerable people were killed or went missing. Millions of families were divided and their properties destroyed.[6] Most Koreans suffered severe poverty and disease in the aftermath of the war. To survive, many were reduced to eating the bark of trees.

In this post-Korean War context, Yonggi Cho introduced the theology of the Threefold Blessing during the early days of the Yoido Full Gospel Church (YFGC, around 1958-1959). The eschatological hope of the Kingdom metamorphosed into an emphasis on the Kingdom of God in the "here and now." For Koreans affected by the war, the Threefold Blessing summarized the hope they placed in God: salvation for their souls, prosperity to overcome absolute poverty, and divine healing for their diseases.

Scholars inside and outside of the global Pentecostal and Charismatic movements have studied the Threefold Blessing in terms of the Korean shamanistic influences on Korean Pentecostalism or as one of the factors behind the explosive church growth of Korean Pentecostalism, but not as the Pentecostal hope in Korean contexts.

---

[6]*A History of the Korean People* (Seoul: Hollym International Corp., 1988), 377-378. The Korean War was the biggest national tragedy. During the war, most of the industrial facilities and foundations were destroyed. Although many people survived the war, they were still victims. Their houses were destroyed, and most of them lost family members.

CHAPTER 2
PREVIOUS STUDIES OF KOREAN PENTECOSTALISM AND THE THREEFOLD BLESSING

A new study of the Threefold Blessing requires an interdisciplinary approach which combines theology with a sociological analysis of the context in which it emerged. The Threefold Blessing has to be understood not only in terms of the influence of indigenous Korean religions but also the socio-economic and political contexts. Then we can discover why Koreans enthusiastically accepted the messages of the Threefold Blessing and how the Threefold Blessing needs to be recontexutalized into the contemporary Korean context.

This book will examine the Threefold Blessing from soteriological, pneumatological, eco-theological, and socio-theological perspectives. Its three theological tasks include a systematic study of the soteriology, Christology, and doctrine of God in the Threefold Blessing; comparing the Threefold Blessing and Jürgen Moltmann's theology of hope; and explicating the contextual hope of the Threefold Blessing in the Korean context.

Scholars inside and outside the Pentecostal and Charismatic movements have researched the beliefs and practices of Korean Pentecostalism in religious and cultural perspectives, including the Threefold Blessing.[1] However, the influences of Confucianism on Korean Christianity and Korean Pentecostalism have been largely overlooked. Some have emphasized the relationship between the Threefold Blessing and the influences of Korean shamanism on Korean

---

[1] Boo Woong Yoo, *Korean Pentecostalism: Its History and Theology* (Frankfurt am Main: Peter Lang, 1988); Walter J. Hollenweger, *Pentecostalism: Origins and Developments Worldwide* (Peabody, MA: Hendrickson Publishers Inc., 1997), 99-105; Sung Hoon Myung and Young Gi Hong, eds., *Charis and Charisma: David Yonggi Cho and the Growth of Yoido Full Gospel Church* (Oxford: Regnum Books International, 2003); and Allan Anderson, "The Contextual Pentecostal Theology of David Yonggi Cho," *Asian Journal of Pentecostal Studies* 7, no. 1 (January 2004): 101-123; Harvey Cox, *Fire from Heaven: The Rise of Pentecostal Spirituality and the Reshaping of Religion in the Twenty-First Century* (Reading, MA: Addison-Wesley Publishing Co., 1995), 213-41; Young Hoon Lee, *The Holy Spirit Movement in Korea: Its Historical and Theological Development* (Oxford: Regnum Books International, 2009), 13-14.

Pentecostalism from a religious perspective.[2] Korean Pentecostals, the nature of God for Pentecostals, and the negative and positive influences of shamanism as primal religiosity on Pentecostalism will be discussed in terms of the contextualization of Pentecostalism in the Korean context.

Boo Woong Yoo explores the roots of Pentecostalism in Korean history and culture in *Korean Pentecostalism: Its History and Theology*.[3] He compares the unique historical and theological characteristics of Korean Pentecostalism with American and European Pentecostalism from the perspective of *Minjung* theology, without dealing with the Threefold Blessing as a theology of Korean Pentecostalism. Ig Jin Kim assesses the religio-social context of Korea, the doctrines of classical Pentecostalism, the influences of the American Assemblies of God on Korean Pentecostalism, and the life and theology of Yonggi Cho in his book, *History and Theology of Korean Pentecostalism: Sunbogeum (Pure Gospel) Pentecostalism* (2003).[4] In *The Holy Spirit Movement in Korea: Its Historical and Theological Development* (2009), Young Hoon Lee focuses on Cho's biography, his theology, and the history of the YFGC.[5] As the senior pastor of the YFGC following Yonggi Cho, he also presents rich empirical information about how the YFGC engages in social works and world missions in other developing countries.

Stephen Bevans has addressed external factors including "historical events, intellectual currents, cultural shifts, and political forces" and internal factors such as "the incarnational nature of God," "the sacramental nature of reality," and "the understanding of the nature of divine."[6] However, Bevans overlooks other fundamental factors: "people" as the subject of contextualization; the specific nature of God for the people; the primal religiosity and the ethical emotion of the

---

[2]Cox, *Fire from Heaven*, 213-41; Young Hoon Lee, *The Holy Spirit Movement in Korea*, 13-14.
[3]Boo Woong Yoo, *Korean Pentecostalism: Its History and Theology* (Frankfurt am Main: Peter Lang, 1988).
[4]Ig Jin Kim, *History and Theology of Korean Pentecostalism: Sunbogeum (Pure Gospel) Pentecostalism* (Zoetermeer, Netherlands: Uitgeverij Boekencentrum, 2003), 202-209.
[5]Young Hoon Lee, *The Holy Spirit Movement in Korea*.
[6]Stephen B. Bevans, *Models of Contextual Theology* (Maryknoll, NY: Orbis Books, 1997), 5-10.

people; the socio-political, economical, and religious contexts; and the way Scripture is contextualized.

Other research has focused on the history and theology of Korean Pentecostalism as well as the history of the YFGC and Cho's theology.[7] In *An Introduction to Pentecostalism: Global Charismatic Christianity* (2004), Allan Anderson discusses the theology of Cho and Korean Pentecostalism through the lens of global Pentecostalism and contextual theology.[8] Harvey Cox examines the relation between Korean shamanism and Korean Pentecostalism from a religious, rather than theological, perspective in *Fire from Heaven: The Rise of Pentecostal Spirituality and the Reshaping of Religion in the Twenty-First Century* (1995).[9] Although these books are not monographs focused solely on Korean Pentecostalism and its theology, they provide an important understanding of Korean Pentecostalism from theological, historical, and religious perspectives.

Previous studies tend to downplay the influence of socio-economic and political contexts on the development of the Threefold Blessing. Anderson, however, shows the importance of the post-Korean War context and Cho's personal suffering from poverty and illness for the emergence and popularity of the Threefold Blessing.[10]

Moltmann's direct approaches to the theology of the Threefold Blessing and his theology of hope provide rich insights for understanding the Threefold Blessing in terms of hope.[11] His theology of hope, his Christology, and his soteriology are compared and contrasted with the theology of the Threefold Blessing. Moltmann wrote several articles for the *Journal of Pentecostal Theology*.[12] "The Blessing of Hope: The Theology of Hope and the Full Gospel of Life" examines the contextual

---

[7] Jae Bum Lee, "Pentecostal Type Distinctives and Korean Protestant Church Growth," (PhD diss., Fuller Theological Seminary, 1986); Sung Hoon Myung, "Spiritual Dimensions of Church Growth as Applied in the Yoido Full Gospel Church," (PhD diss., Fuller Theological Seminary, 1990).

[8] Allan Anderson, *An Introduction to Pentecostalism: Global Charismatic Christianity* (Cambridge: Cambridge University Press, 2004).

[9] Cox, *Fire from Heaven*.

[10] Anderson, "The Contextual Pentecostal Theology of David Yonggi Cho," 101-123.

[11] Jürgen Moltmann, "A Response to My Pentecostal Dialogue Partners," *Journal of Pentecostal Theology* 4 (1994): 59-70; *Journal of Pentecostal Theology* 9 (1996): 3-15; "The Blessing of Hope: The Theology of Hope and the Full Gospel of Life," *Journal of Pentecostal Theology* 13, no. 2 (2005): 147-161.

[12] Moltmann, "A Response to My Pentecostal Dialogue Partners," 59-70; Moltmann, "A Pentecostal Theology of Life,", 3-15; Moltmann, "The Blessing of Hope," 147-161.

commonalities between his theology of hope and Cho's theology as well as the biographical similarity between himself and Cho. However, Moltmann's theology of hope cannot be fully applied to the Korean context without understanding the contextual Korean backdrop.

Cho's sermons in the new millennium show some theological transitions in the Threefold Blessing, including changes in his soteriology and extended perceptions of healing, social-theology, and eco-theology. I conducted face-to-face interviews with Jürgen Moltmann, Vinson Synan, and Amos Yong and had email discussions with Young Hoon Lee (senior pastor of the YFGC since Yonggi Cho's retirement.)

The following questions guided this study of the Threefold Blessing:
- Is it possible to understand the Threefold Blessing as the Pentecostal hope in the Korean context?
- How is the Threefold Blessing related to, understood in, and developed in the Korean context?
- How does the Threefold Blessing influence Korean Pentecostals?
- What are the theological differences and similarities between Moltmann's theology of hope and the theology of the Threefold Blessing?
- To what extent is the Threefold Blessing still relevant?
- How can the Threefold Blessing be reinterpreted and recontextualized for the contemporary Korean context, especially in Pentecostalism?

One of the contributions of Korean Pentecostalism to Korean Christianity is its emphasis on the spiritual life of believers and the focus on the experience of the Spirit. Nevertheless, the emphasis on spiritual blessing has often been understood simply as salvation, healing, and financial prosperity, and thus has been criticized by mainstream Christianity as being influenced by Korean shamanism.

However, the Threefold Blessing is concerned with the practical life of Pentecostals, who understand the Kingdom of God not only in eschatological terms but as an existential matter. It will be evaluated from the perspective of contemporary Korean Pentecostals. Today, healing and prosperity need to be considered in a wider sense, beyond a focus on the individual. Healing needs to encompass not only the body but society as a whole. Prosperity also must extend to the whole community.

The book focuses on Korean Pentecostal churches affiliated with the Korean Assemblies of God and Christians in mainline Korean Churches who are influenced by Cho's theology. Previous studies have examined the relation between the Threefold Blessing and the church growth of the YFGC or the influences of shamanistic belief on the prosperity theology. Here, the Threefold Blessing will be understood in terms of a contextual hope in the Korean Pentecostal context.

Part Two

THE HISTORY OF KOREAN PENTECOSTALISM

Korean Pentecostalism and the Threefold Blessing developed in the setting of indigenous Korean religions, culture, traditions, and socio-political and economic circumstances. Pentecostal revivals emerged from Bible studies during the early 1900s, before the arrival of Western Pentecostal missionaries. Early Korean Pentecostals did not have theological or pneumatological perspectives from which to understand the manifestations of the Spirit. Nevertheless, Pentecostalism became successfully contextualized into the primal religiosity and socio-political context of Korea under Japanese occupation. Here is a brief history of Korean Christianity, the birth of Korean Pentecostalism, and the contextualization of Korean Pentecostalism under the Japanese rule.

CHAPTER 3
THE ARRIVAL OF CHRISTIANITY AS THE *SILHAK* LEGACY IN THE CHOSŎN DYNASTY

Before Christianity arrived, Korea was a hermit kingdom which isolated itself from the West. Buddhism and Confucianism were the traditional religions and ruling dispensations for about a thousand years: Buddhism led the Koryeo Dynasty (918-1392); Confucianism emerged during the Chosŏn Dynasty (1392-1897)[1] and undergirded the Greater Korean Empire (1897-1910).[2]

Buddhism lost its political influence during the Chosŏn Dynasty but remained a major religion due to its successful appropriation of Shamanism. Adopted by the Chosŏn Dynasty as the state philosophy, Confucianism became influential in every aspect of Korean life, including politics, economics, culture, family, and society.[3] It was both the most crucial persecutor of and the most significant contributor to the beginning of Korean Christianity.

It is worth noting that Christianity in Korea was begun by Korean indigenes, especially Confucian scholars, and self-propagated across the nation before Western missionaries arrived. Between the late seventeenth and early nineteenth centuries, the academic tendency of *Silhak* (Practical Thought) scholars seemed strange to traditional Confucianism. *Silhak* scholars rejected learning for learning's sake and pursued practical learning. They were interested in Western civilizations

---

[1] The Annals of the Chosŏn Dynasty is one of Korea's national treasures and is listed in UNESCO's Memory of the World registry of 1997. The Annals, consisting of 1,893 volumes, record national affairs and the activities of the country which were reported to the kings during the period 1392-1910. As a national treasure, it was not opened to the public until 1995. On December 12, 2005, the official website of the Annals of the Chosŏn Dynasty was opened to the public. Its official website is http://sillok.history.go.kr/main/main.jsp. Our discussion of Korean historical events, including the persecutions and martyrdom of Christians, will be based on the Annals.

[2] During the Chosŏn Dynasty, Buddhism lost its political function. Since 1392, it has sustained its religious function. Confucianism is much less influential in modern Korean society but is still deeply rooted in Korean ethics.

[3] Pow Key Sohn, Chol Choon Kim, and Yi Sup Hong, *The History of Korea* (Seoul: Korean National Commission for UNESCO, 1982), 129-132.

and tried to adopt new methodologies for their studies.[4] They also began to research Christianity from an academic standpoint.

Yi Sugwang (1563-1627) was the pioneer of *Silhak*. As an official of the Chosŏn Dynasty, he had opportunities to visit China three times.[5] Whilst in China, Yi studied basic Catholicism through the Catholic pamphlet, *Tianzhu shiyi* (The True Teaching of the Lord of Heaven) written by Matteo Ricci.[6] As an encyclopaedist, he had interests in various fields such as astronomy, geography, history, institutions, customs, religions, and culture. In 1614, based on his considerable learning, he wrote *Chibong yusŏl*.[7] In the book, he introduced Roman Catholicism and its doctrines for the first time. He mentioned some of the essential truths of Christianity such as the nature of God the Creator and the doctrine of the immortality of the soul. Furthermore, he criticized the idea of transmigration of the soul in Buddhism and even introduced the concept of the papacy.[8]

After Yi Sugwang, many *Silhak* scholars became interested in Christianity as well as in Western science and civilization. Initially, they approached Christianity with academic rather than religious curiosity. Later, they began to have an interest in the Christian faith. In 1610, Huh Goon (1569-1618) went to China and brought twelve Catholic prayer pamphlets back to Korea. He studied Christianity and the Christian faith sincerely and converted to Christianity.[9]

Yi Ik (1681-1763) mentioned that Christianity had concepts not existing in Confucianism: immutable truth and the true truth that mature men and scholars needed to follow. The Lord of Heaven in Christianity was similar to *Tao* (the great ultimate in Confucianism).[10] In his book *Sŏngho sasŏl*, he described the virgin birth of Jesus, his public life,

---

[4]Everett N. Hunt Jr., *Protestant Pioneers in Korea* (Maryknoll, NY: Orbis Books, 1980), 5.
[5]Michael C. Kalton, "An Introduction of Silhak," *Korea Journal* (May 1975): 31.
[6]Robert E. Buswell Jr. and Timothy S. Lee, eds., *Christianity in Korea* (Honolulu: University of Hawaii Press, 2006), 9.
[7]Kalton, "An Introduction of *Silhak*," 31.
[8]Gyeong Bae Min, *Hankook Gidokgyo Gyohoi Sa* [the History of Korean Christianity] (Seoul: Yeonsei Chulpansa, 1993), 51.
[9]*Kidokshinmoon* [Christian News Paper], March 17, 2009, available from http://www.kidok.com/news/articleView.html?idxno=58701, accessed July 6, 2010.
[10]Gyeong Bae Min, *Hankook Gidokgyo Gyohoi Sa*, 52.

crucifixion, and resurrection. However, he also approached Christianity scientifically and did not personally adopt the Christian faith.[11] During the eighteenth century, through the influence of Yi Ik, many Korean Neo-Confucian scholars became interested in Christianity. Among them was Hong Yoo Han, who became a Christian and observed the Sabbath from around 1770. In order to pursue an ascetic life, he spent the rest of his life on a mountain for the sake of his faith.[12]

In the winter of 1783, Sŭng Hun Yi visited China with his father, who was a member of the annual legations to China. In Beijing, he converted to Christianity and was publically baptised by Louis de Grammont in February 1784.[13] De Grammont gave him the baptismal name Peter with the hope that Yi would be the first stone of the Korean Church.[14] In the spring of 1784, when Sŭng Hun Yi returned to Korea, he brought religious books, tracts, images, and crucifixes with him, but the Bible was not given to him.[15] Soon after Peter Yi returned to his homeland, he baptized his friend Tŏk-Cho Yi and gave him the baptismal name of John.[16] Within five years of Yi's return, as a result of his enthusiastic evangelism, approximately four thousand Koreans converted to Christianity.[17]

As long as Christianity was accepted as a Western philosophy rather than a religion, there were no serious conflicts. Eventually, Christianity came into collision with Confucianism because early Korean believers denied practices such as ancestor worship, which combines filial piety with Korean shamanism. Confucianists believed fortune and misfortune were dependent on how they served their ancestors. Ancestor worship was not optional but an essential prerequisite for Koreans, so it was the greatest obstacle to evangelism.

---

[11]Ibid.
[12]Ibid., 54.
[13]Min, *Hankook Gidokgyo Gyohoi Sa* [the History of Korean Christianity], 56-57.
[14]George L. Paik, *The History of Protestant Missions in Korea 1832-1910* (Seoul: Yonsei University Press, 1980), 32.
[15]Arthur Judson Brown, *The Mastery of the Far East: The Story of Korea's Transformation and Japan's Rise to Supremacy in the Orient* (New York: Charles Scribner's Sons, 1919), 487-88.
[16]Harry A. Rhodes, ed., *History of the Korea Mission Presbyterian Church U.S.A.*, vol. 1, *1884-1934* (Seoul: The Presbyterian Church of Korea Department of Education, 1984), 59. See also, Paik, *The History of Protestant Missions*, 32.
[17]The Edinburgh Review, "Corea," *The Edinburgh Review* 136 (October 1872): 304.

The Chosŏn government regarded the refusal of ancestor worship by Christians as rebellion against traditional religion, the state, and the social system based on Confucianism. During the Chosŏn Dynasty, there were five nationwide persecutions of Christians: Shin-hae (1791), Shin-yoo (1801), Ki-hae (1839), Byoung-oh (1846) and Byoung-in (1866). Most early leaders of Korean Christianity were Christian Confucian scholars who had been influenced by *Silhak* scholars. They were martyred or exiled to *Heuksan, Jeju,* and other islands. The first persecution occurred because of religious reasons related to Confucian ancestor worship. (The others were related to two religious and political matters: *Che-Sa*, the Confucian ancestral worship, and the matter of opening a port.)

In 1742, Franciscan and Dominican missions in China had sent a petition to the Vatican in Rome with regard to Confucian ancestor worship. Pope Benedict XIV defined Confucian ancestor worship as a religious and superstitious practice which could not be accepted by the Roman Catholic Church.[18] Regrettably, this decision brought terrible persecutions to Chinese and Korean Christians. Thomas Kim Pum Wu, the first Korean victim, was arrested and tortured because he burned his ancestor tablets. He was exiled to an isolated island and died there of injuries caused by torture.[19] Yun Chi Choong and Kwan Sang Yeon also refused to practice the ancestral rite and burned their ancestor tablets.[20] They were accused and killed on November 8, 1791, in the first (Shin-hae) persecution.[21]

Political and diplomatic matters with Western powers added to later persecutions. The Western powers pressured the Chosŏn Dynasty to adopt an open-door trade policy for international trade, but the Chosŏn Dynasty resisted with a policy of seclusion. Christianity symbolized the Western powers, so persecutions occurred not only because of religious matters but also for political reasons. Conservative Korean Confucians sought to eliminate political adversaries who were favourably disposed

---

[18]Myung Hyuk Kim, "Ancestor Worship: From the Perspective of Korean Church History," *Ancestor Worship and Christianity in Korea*, ed. Jung Young Lee (New York: Edwin Mellen Press, 1988), 23.
[19]Paik, *The History of Protestant Missions*, 32.
[20]Min, *Hankook Gidokgyo Gyohoi Sa* [the History of Korean Christianity], 62.
[21]*Chosŏn WangJo ShilLok* [The Annals of the Chosŏn Dynasty], King Jŏng-Cho Year 15 (1791), November 8.

to Western civilization and Christianity. The hope of change by *Silhak* scholars was frustrated by the power of these conservatives, who had a vested interest in the country. The Chosŏn Dynasty reestablished a closed-door policy in the mid-nineteenth century.

In 1801, the Shin-yoo persecution broke out in response to a letter written by Hwang Sayŏng regarding a diplomatic and political issue. Hwang was arrested in Jaechŏn in Choong-Chŏng province.[22] The letter to a bishop in China reported the horrors of Christian persecutions in Korea. In the letter, he requested that Western Powers send two hundreds warships and 50,000-60,000 soldiers to Korea to press the Chosŏn Dynasty to allow Christianity.[23] In the eyes of the Chosŏn government, this letter presented a severe threat to the structure and survival of the nation. Hence, the government concluded that Christianity was dangerous to "the moral fabric of society by its refusal to perform the *che-sa* rites and raised the question of the political subordination of the nation."[24] Hwang was put to death by dismemberment on November 5, 1801, and all of his family members were exiled to different islands.[25] During the Shin-yoo persecution, about three hundred Christians were executed.[26]

In the Byoung-oh persecution of 1846, seventy-five Korean Christians and three European missionaries were killed.[27] After the Byoung-oh persecution ended, Christianity suffered severe suppression. Christianity, however, was not destroyed but rather spread rapidly. By 1866, there were 25,000 Christians in Korea. At least 8,000 Korean believers and seven priests, including two Western bishops, were martyred in the Byoung-in persecution that year.[28]

The fears of the Chosŏn government regarding Christianity can be analyzed in relation to three elements: first, "the subversion of traditional social mores," second, "the loss of national sovereignty," and third, "the

---

[22]*Chosŏn WangJo ShilLok* [The Annals of the Chosŏn Dynasty], King Soon-Jo Year 1 (1801), October 3.
[23]Ibid., 5.
[24]Buswell and Lee, *Christianity in Korea*, 10.
[25]Min, *Hankook Gidokgyo Gyohoi Sa* [the History of Korean Christianity], 70.
[26]Ibid.
[27]Samuel Hugh Moffett, *A History of Christianity in Asia*, vol. 2, *1500 to 1900* (Maryknoll, NY: Orbis Books, 2005), 315.
[28]Stephen Neill, *A History of Christian Missions* (Middlesex, England: Penguin Books Ltd., 1964), 415.

significant extent to which the church had taken root."[29] The Western powers politicized the martyrdom of their missionaries and dispatched forces to Korea with the justification of protecting their people. The main purpose of this military action, however, was to coerce the Chosŏn Dynasty into opening a port for foreign trade. Eventually, the Chosŏn government ratified the Kanghwa Treaty with Japan on February 27th, 1876 (King Ko-Jong year 13, February 3rd of the lunar calendar).[30] With this agreement, the Chosŏn government guaranteed the security of foreigners in Korea and the nationwide persecution for Christianity ended.

---

[29]Buswell and Lee, *Christianity in Korea*, 11.
[30]*Chosŏn WangJo ShilLok* [The Annals of the Chosŏn Dynasty], King Ko-Jong Year 13 (1876), February 3.

CHAPTER 4
CHRISTIANITY BECOMES ROOTED IN KOREA

From the early seventeenth century, Confucian *Silhak* scholars had hoped to reform the country with practical science and the promotion of Western civilization. Their curiosity about Western civilization led to their interest in Christianity. While traveling in China, they formed relationships with Western missionaries. They brought Christianity to Korea upon their return and translated the Bible into Korean.

Because Christianity arrived through Korean Confucian scholars before Western missionaries came, there were no existing teachers for the earliest Christians. Instead, believers became absorbed in Bible study and adopted a literal approach to interpreting the Bible. This is one reason that both Korean Christianity and Pentecostalism are conservative and Bible-centered.

Korea opened her ports to trade in February 1879, through the Treaty of Kanghwa, and became subject to Japan. Under Japanese rule, two significant developments of Korean Christianity occurred: remarkable church growth and the emergence of Korean Pentecostalism. Many Koreans began to attend church. They were attracted by the Christian faith but also knew that the churches under Western missionaries had a degree of independence from Japanese rule: the Japanese government did not want to enter into a diplomatic row with other countries. The church became a shelter for Koreans wishing to find hope in their difficult circumstances. Korean believers became actively involved in prayer meetings and Bible studies. They prayed intensely for their country and to overcome their circumstances.

Like Korean Christianity, Pentecostalism began spontaneously in Korea before the arrival of Western missionaries. It formulated its own Pentecostal practices in Korean contexts under Japanese rule. Revivals that broke out in Wonsan (1903) and Pyongyang (1907) became the catalyst for the emergence of Pentecostalism. Korean Pentecostalism focused on repentance, Bible study, and the future hope of the Kingdom of God since they lacked hope in the present. Most messages from early Pentecostal preachers also focused on repentance for salvation and the Kingdom of God.

In 1950, five years after independence from Japan, the Korean War broke out. In the aftermath, Koreans found little hope in the traditional religions they had practiced. The Pentecostal Threefold Blessing emerged in this hopeless setting. When Cho began his ministry on the outskirts of Seoul, the poor and sick became his church members. The YFGC started with six members, including Cho, on May 15, 1958.[1] Within three decades, it became the largest church in the world with 700,000 registered members in 1990.[2]

The Threefold Blessing became the primary focus of Cho's message and the central theological tenet of Korean Pentecostalism. The poor and the sick—the ordinary people of Korea—became the protagonists of Pentecostalism. Its emphasis on the Threefold Blessing gave them hope. Through Cho's influence, most Pentecostal pastors also preached sermons based on the Threefold Blessing, which became the main theme of the Pentecostal message and the hope of Pentecostals.

The emergence of Cho's Threefold Blessing roughly coincided with the development of Jürgen Moltmann's theology of hope in Germany. Both developed in similar contexts: the ruins of post-World War II Germany and the post-Korean War context. Cho and Moltmann's personal hardships during wartime influenced their theologies.

Moltmann's theology of hope was introduced to Korean Christianity by Korean *Minjung* and liberal theologians. The socio-political elements of his theology were magnified, and conservative Korean Pentecostals initially considered it as a form of liberal theology. As a result, direct theological dialogue between the Threefold Blessing and Moltmann's theology of hope did not take place until the mid-1990s.

In September 1995, through the arrangement of one of Moltmann's pupils, Dr. Jong Wha Park, Moltmann met Cho at the YFGC. After this theological dialogue, Moltmann recognized Cho as a Christian theologian. Moltmann was amazed at the similarities in their personal biographies as well as the theological and historical affinities between Cho's theology and his own theology of hope.[3]

---

[1] Karen Hurston, *Growing the World's Largest Church* (Kaduna, Nigeria: Evangel Publishers Ltd., 1994), 22.
[2] Young Hoon Lee, "Dr. Yonggi Cho's Influence on the Korean Church in Relation to His Pneumatology" [in Korean], *Journal of Youngsan Theology* 7 (August 2004): 138-39.
[3] Moltmann, "The Blessing of Hope," 148.

In June 2004, Moltmann was one of the main speakers at the 2004 Young San International Theological Symposium. The theme of the symposium was "Dr. Yonggi Cho's Theology of Hope." Moltmann presented a seminar paper, "Der Segen der Hoffnung: Die Theologie der Hoffnung und das volle Evangelium des Lebens" [The Blessing of Hope: The Theology of Hope and the Full Gospel of Life]. The paper introduced the theological and historical similarities of the two theologies. The theological conversation between Moltmann and Cho, however, did not continue following the symposium.

CHAPTER 5
THE INFLUENCE OF EARLY PROTESTANT MISSIONARIES AND BIBLE TRANSLATIONS

Roman Catholicism had already experienced socio-political conflicts and persecutions by the government during the early years of Christianity in Korea. In contrast, Protestantism and Pentecostalism were able to consolidate without experiencing persecution by the Chosŏn government.

1. Early Western Missionaries

Protestant missions in Korea began with the arrival of Horace Newton Allen, a medical missionary, in 1884.[1] Allen was originally appointed to China and sent by the Presbyterian Board of Missions. However, he struggled to find a satisfactory field for work in China because of his personality and his inability to get along with others. Fred Harvey Harrington, Allen's biographer, describes Allen's character as "thin-skinned, short-tempered, and unforgiving" and defines him as a "touchy and crotchety man."[2] While in China, Allen heard that Korea greatly needed Western doctors because there were none. Dr. Henderson of Shanghai suggested Allen consider moving to Korea.[3] When Allen requested permission to go to Korea, the Presbyterian Board of Missions hesitated before agreeing. The board judged that there was as yet no missionary work for him in Korea. After persuading the Presbyterian board that his move to Korea would be a great opportunity, he arrived in Korea on September 20, 1884.[4]

---

[1] Hunt, *Protestant Pioneers in Korea*, 17.
[2] Fred Harvey Harrington, *God Mammon, and the Japanese: Dr. Horace N. Allen and Korea—American Relations, 1884-1905* (Madison: University of Wisconsin Press, 1966), 6; Hunt, *Protestant Pioneers in Korea*, 16.
[3] O. R. Avison, "In Memoriam: Dr. Horace N. Allen," *Korea Mission Field* (May 1933): 103.
[4] Hunt, *Protestant Pioneers in Korea*, 16.

Although he arrived without an official status,[5] as a physician Allen had many opportunities to meet and build relationships with native officials as well as upper-class Koreans.[6] Three months after his arrival, on December 4, 1884 (October 17th of the lunar calendar, King Ko-Jong year 21), a coup d'état by a group of progressive scholars and officials who wanted to reform the nation, called *Gabshin Jŏngbyeon*, broke out against conservative factions with political powers in the Chosŏn government.[7] Many soldiers and two politicians were seriously wounded, including Yŏng Ik Min, a nephew of the queen and the most important man next to the king in the Chosŏn cabinet. A former ambassador to the United States,[8] he had just returned from the States after the ratification of the Korean-American treaty.[9] He was severely wounded by an assassin's sword.[10] None of the fourteen herbal doctors in the Royal Court could save his life.[11]

Mr. Scudder, Secretary to the U.S. Legation, came to Allen's house with a note from Mr. Paul G. von Moellendorff, a former secretary of diplomacy in the Chosŏn government. In the note, von Moellendorff asks Allen to come immediately and treat Yŏng Ik Min, who had life-threatening wounds.[12] Allen went to Min as he hovered between life and death, and spent a whole night performing a surgical operation on him.[13] Within three months of medical treatment, Allen was able to restore him to health.[14]

King Ko-Jong gave Allen the house of Hong Yong Sik, who was executed after the fall of *Gabshin Jŏngbyeon*, as a hospital building

---

[5]Ibid., 19.
[6]Ibid., 16.
[7]*Chosŏn WangJo ShilLok* [The Annals of the Chosŏn Dynasty], King Ko-Jong Year 21 (1884), October 17.
[8]Joseph H. Longford, *The Story of Korea* (London: T. Fisher Unwin, 1911), 321.
[9]Paik, *The History of Protestant Missions*, 102.
[10]Horace Newton Allen, *Things Korean: A Collection of Sketches and Anecdotes Missionary and Diplomatic* (New York: Fleming H. Revell Company, 1908), 70.
[11]Annette Hye Kyung Son, "Modernisation of the System of Traditional Korean Medicine (1876-1990)," *Health Policy* 44 (1998): 264.
[12]Horace Newton Allen, *Allen's Diary*, December 5, 1885 (Seoul: Dankook Daehakgyo Chulpansa, 2008), 407.
[13]Lee Sŏng Sam, "Gabshin Jŏngbyeon Gwa Kidokgyo [Gabshin Jŏngbyeon and Christianity]," *Kidokgyo Sasang* [Christianity Thoughts] (December 1973): 144.
[14]Allen, *Things Korean*, 70.

where Allen could practice modern Western medicine. For a cost of between six hundred and one thousand dollars, the house was remodeled into the first Western hospital in Korea. The king named the hospital *Kwang-Hye-Won* (Widespread Relief House), and it was later renamed *Je-Joong-Won* (House of Universal Helpfulness).[15] The hospital officially opened on April 10, 1885,[16] replacing two Korean traditional medical institutions, Hyeminso and Hwalinso.[17] The hospital was under Allen's supervision, whom the king had appointed as the court physician.[18] Allen had won the confidence of the Chosŏn government and paved the way for Protestant missions.[19]

2. Translating the Bible: The Use of *Hangŭl* and Missionary Efforts

There were three literary styles in Korea when Christianity arrived: first, *Hanmun*, Chinese characters mostly used by *Yangban*, the upper class; second, *Hangŭl* (Korean language), native characters used by *Joong-In* (the lower middle class) and the bureaucratic middle class; and third, *Kunhanmun*, the mixed script of Chinese and Korean.[20] Early Korean Christians were mostly literate and highly educated and included members of the aristocratic class.[21]

Most Korean Scriptures were printed in *Hangŭl* with some mixed scripts.[22] Using *Hangŭl* was highly significant for the contextualization

---

[15]Paik, *The History of Protestant Missions*, 106.
[16]Ibid.
[17]Son, "Modernisation of the System," 264.
[18]Robert E. Speer, *Presbyterian Foreign Mission: An Account of the Foreign Mission of the Presbyterian Church in the U. S. A.* (Philadelphia: Presbyterian Board of Publication and Sabbath School Work, 1901), 164.
[19]Paik, *The History of Protestant Missions*, 102.
[20]Thomas Herbert Darlow and Horace Frederich Moule, *Historical Catalogues of Printed Editions of the Holy Scriptures in the Library of the British and Foreign Bible Society Vol. II (cont.)*. (London: The Bible House Co., 1903), 885. *Han'gŭl* was invented by King Sejong at the end of 1443 or the beginning of 1444. Through the experiment of its practicality in publishing *Yongbi-ŏch'ŏn-ga*, *Han'gŭl* was officially introduced to the Korean people in 1446. However, it was not welcomed by the Korean *Yangban* upper class, who were proficient in Chinese literature until the early eighteenth century. See, Pratt and Rutt, *Korea*, 158.
[21]Buswell and Lee, *Christianity in Korea*, 10.
[22]Darlow and Moule, *Historical Catalogues*, 885.

of Christianity.[23] *Hangŭl*, the vernacular script of Korea, was not popularly used among the Korean upper class due to toadyism to China and their preference for the Chinese language. Yong Bock Kim says that translating the Bible into *Hangŭl* was "the injection of Christian language into the language of the common people in Korea."[24] Without it, Christianity could not have become quickly indigenized and propagated. Ordinary Korean people could easily read the Korean Bible and understand the gospel.

A second factor is significant: during the Chosŏn Dynasty, the education of women was mostly carried out at home and *Hangŭl* was the language of women. As Korean women could read the Korean Bible in *Hangŭl*, Christianity spread quickly among them.

The Lord's Prayer was the first Christian manuscript translated into *Hangŭl*. Karl Friedrich August Gützlaff, a German missionary to the Far East, came to Korea on 17th July, 1832. With the assistance of Koreans named Yang-chih and Teng-no, he inserted Korean phonetic alphabets under the Lord's Prayer which was written in Chinese. As a result, Koreans could read the Lord's Prayer in Korean pronunciation.[25] It was the first attempt of Western missionaries to translate Christian documents—including the Bible—into Korean language. Although this translation was defective, it was published as *Remarks on the Korean Language* and became a textbook for the Korean language.[26] It also was used as a reference to translate the Bible into the Korean language in 1880s.

Scottish Presbyterian missionaries John Ross and John McIntyre (Ross's brother-in-law) had ministered to Koreans in various regions of Manchuria since 1873. In 1876, McIntyre baptized his first Korean Protestant converts, Sung Ha Yi, Hong Chun Paik, and Sang Yun Sŭh of

---

[23]Donald N. Clark, "Christianity in Modern Korea," *Education About Asia* 11, no. 2 (Fall 2006): 38.

[24]Yong Bock Kim, "Korean Christianity as a Messianic Movement of the People," in *Minjung Theology: People as the Subjects of History*, ed. Yong Bock Kim (Singapore: The Commission on Theological Concerns of the Christian Conference of Asia, 1981), 79.

[25]Charles Gutzlaff, *Journal of Three Voyages Along the Coast of China in 1831, 1832, & 1833* (London: Thomas Ward and Co., 1840), 316-356; Deok Joo Rhie, *Chogi Hankook GidokgyoSa YeonGoo* [A Study on the Early Christian History in Korea] (Seoul: The Institute for Korean Church History, 1995), 327.

[26]Thomas Hobbs, "Pioneers," *The Korea Mission Field* 34, no. 5 (May 1938): 90.

Sorai. Sŭh received the gospel while he was under John McIntyre's care for a disease he picked up in Manchuria[27] and became the pioneer Protestant evangelist in Korea.[28]

In 1878, Ross made the long trip from Manchuria to the Korean Gate (probably the town of Wiju). Many Koreans stayed there temporarily while traveling between China and their homeland. Ross intended to acquire more knowledge about the Korean language. He met Sŭh there and hired him as his Korean language teacher. In 1882, under the supervision of Ross, Sŭh and two Korean assistants, Ung Chan Yi and Chin Kui Kim, completed the first Korean translation of Luke's Gospel.[29] They used the "Delegates' Version"[30] as the Chinese source text for the first Korean version.[31] The first translation work was imperfect, with many grammatical and spelling errors. Chinese idioms were often not translated. However, Koreans did not have a problem reading and understanding their first Bible.[32] Luke's Gospel was entitled *Jesu Sŏngkyo Lukabokum Jyunsŏ* (*The Book of Luke of Jesus Christ*). In March 1882, three thousand copies were published at Mukden in China.[33]

The same year, Ross translated and published the Gospel of John.[34] Ross then wrote a letter to R. Arthington about the cost of publication: £50 with an extra £10-12 for Sŭh.[35] In 1883, Ross translated Acts and

---

[27]Alex A. Pieters, "First Translations," *The Korea Mission Field* 34, no. 5 (May 1938): 91.

[28]Rhodes, *History of the Korea Mission*, 74.

[29]Ibid., 74.

[30]The Delegates' Version is one of the Chinese translations of the Bible. The earliest edition of the Delegates' Version was translated by Joshua Marshman, his collaborator Johannes Lassar, Marshman's unnamed Chinese assistant, and Marshman's son. In 1822, it was published at Serampore in India. The fourth revised edition is called the Delegates' Version. Its New Testament and Old Testament were published in 1852 and in 1854, respectively. See, Patrick Hanan, "The Bible as Chinese Literature: Medhurst, Wang Tao, and the Delegates' Version," *Harvard Journal of Asiatic Studies* 63, no. 1 (June 2003): 198-98.

[31]Pieters, "First Translations," 91.

[32]Ibid., 92-93.

[33]Darlow and Moule, *Historical Catalogues*, 886. See also footnote number 14 in Christine Sungjin Chang, "John Ross and Bible Women in the Early Protestant Mission of Northern Korea and Eastern China," *Rethinking Mission* (March 2008): 5.

[34]W. D. Reynolds, "Fifty Years of Bible Translation and Revision," *The Korea Mission Field* 31, 6 (June 1935): 116.

[35]*Editorial Correspondence of the British Foreign Bible Society* – Inward, Vol. 17, 76 f. Quoted in Christine Sungjin Chang, "John Ross and Bible Women," 5.

printed three thousand copies, along with three thousand copies of the revised Luke, in which he had removed the Chinese expressions and errors of the first version.[36] This publishing expense was refunded to Ross along with the previous expenditures of translation.[37]

In 1883, soon after the Scriptures were printed in *Hangŭl*, Sŭh left Manchuria for his homeland with the newly published Gospels.[38] At least 15,690 copies of the Ross Version of Luke's Gospel were circulated among the Korean people through colporteurs between 1883 and 1886.[39]

In 1883, Rev. Henry Loomis, an agent of the American Bible Society in Japan, asked Yi Soo Chon (Rijutei in Japanese), a converted Korean living in Japan, to translate the Japanese version of the Gospel of Mark into *Hangŭl*.[40] Three thousand Korean copies of Mark's Gospel were published by the American Bible Society in Yokohama, Japan.[41] Pioneer missionaries sent to Korea by U.S.A. Methodist and Presbyterian mission boards (including Appenzeller, a Methodist, and Underwood, a Presbyterian), arrived at Chemulpo on April 5, 1885. They brought bundles of Mark's Gospel translated into Korean.[42] They soon realized that Korean indigenes had obtained the Scripture written in their own language two years before they arrived.[43] By 1887, the entire New Testament was translated into Korean.[44] That year, R. Ross published the first Korean New Testament at the expense of the British and Foreign Bible Society (BFBS).[45] These translations resulted from the incredible cooperation between missionaries and national workers. Without Korean Confucian scholars who knew Chinese and Japanese, the Ross and

---

[36] Pieters, "First Translations," 92.

[37] Darlow and Moule, *Historical Catalogues*, 886.

[38] Ellasue Wagner, "Through the Hermit's Gate with Suh Sang Yun," *The Korea Mission Field* 34, no. 5 (May 1938): 94.

[39] Reynolds, "Fifty Years of Bible Translation and Revision," 116.

[40] Ibid.

[41] Pieters, "First Translations," 92.

[42] Reynolds, "Fifty Years of Bible Translation and Revision," 116.

[43] James Moulton Roe, *A History of the British and Foreign Bible Society 1905-1954* (London: The British and Foreign Bible Society, 1965), 151.

[44] Matthew's Gospel and Mark's Gospel were translated by J. Ross in 1884. In 1885, John's Gospel and Ephesians also were translated by J. Ross. See, Darlow and Moule, *Historical Catalogues*, 886-887.

[45] Ibid., 887.

Rijutei versions could not have been translated.[46] With the establishment of the Bible Committee in 1887, the Scriptures were no longer translated by individuals but by a board of translators.[47]

Both John Fox, treasurer of the American Bible Society, and J. H. Ritson, a superintendent in the translating and editorial department of the BFBS, came to Korea in 1907.[48] Ritson was deeply impressed by the revivals that had broken out.[49] After the conference with the Permanent Executive Bible Committee, Fox and Ritson authorized W. D. Reynolds and two Korean members of the board, Seung Tu Ye and Cheng Sam Kim, to translate the Old Testament into Korean. After the last verse was translated at 5 p.m. on April 2, 1910, Hugh Miller, an agent of the British and Foreign Bible Society, received a telegram saying, "Translation finished."[50] In 1911, the Old Testament was published and distributed to Koreans.[51] As many as eight thousand copies of the Old Testament were sold in the first year at a price of around of 1.00 yen (50 cents).[52] Early editions were printed on one side of the paper; later ones were printed on both sides.[53]

---

[46]Reynolds, "Fifty Years of Bible Translation and Revision," 116.
[47]Darlow and Moule, *Historical Catalogues*, 887-890.
[48]Henry Otis Dwight, ed., *The Blue Book of Missions for 1907* (New York and London: Funk & Wagnalls Co., 1907), 177-78.
[49]Roe, *A History of the British and Foreign Bible Society 1905-1954*, 148.
[50]Reynolds, "Fifty Years of Bible Translation and Revision," 118.
[51]H. G. Underwood, "Bible Translating," *The Korea Mission Field* 7, no. 10 (October 1911): 297.
[52]Gerald Bonwick, "The Year's Work of the British and Foreign Bible Society," *The Korea Mission Field* 8, no. 7 (July 1912): 212.
[53]Darlow and Moule, *Historical Catalogues*, 886.

CHAPTER 6
KOREAN REVIVALS AND THE BIRTH OF KOREAN PENTECOSTALISM

Two remarkable Pentecostal revivals occurred in the early twentieth century at Wonsan (1903) and Pyongyang (1907). The American Azusa Street Revival (1906) was characterized by the experience of speaking in tongues,[1] but Korean revivals were categorized by "emotional repentance with loud weeping and simultaneous praying."[2] Theologians continue to debate if the Korean revivals were Pentecostal movements because no one reported speaking in tongues at the beginning of the revivals. (In classical Pentecostalism, the tongues event was considered the predominant key for defining a Pentecostal movement.) However, Dayton says that glossolalia cannot define Pentecostal movements adequately because tongue-speaking also appeared in other religious groups such as the Shakers and Mormons in the nineteenth century.[3]

During the Korean revival movement, Korean Pentecostal leaders such as Seon Ju Gil, Ig Doo Kim, and Yong Do Lee commonly performed healings and miracles.[4] The revivals were accepted as Pentecostal by missionaries to Korea. At the Edinburgh Conference of 1910, the Pyongyang revival (1907) was declared a "genuine Pentecost."[5] According to Gale, during the Pyongyang revival, Chinese Christians came to Pyongyang to meet Gil and wanted to pray together: "They prayed, the Chinese in their unintelligible monosyllables, and the

---

[1] On April 18, 1906, the *Los Angeles Times* reported the event of the Azusa Street Revival right after the revival broke out with the headline "Weird Babel of Tongues." The writer reposted that "breathing strange utterances and mouthing a creed which it would seem no sane mortal could understand, the newest sect has started in Los Angeles." See Vinson Synan, *The Holiness-Pentecostal Tradition: Charismatic Movement in the Twentieth Century* (Grand Rapids, MI: William B. Eerdmans Publishing Co., 1997), 84.
[2] Anderson, *An Introduction to Pentecostalism*, 37.
[3] Donald W. Dayton, *Theological Roots of Pentecostalism* (Peabody, MA: Hendrickson Publishers, Inc., 1987), 15-16.
[4] Anderson, *An Introduction to Pentecostalism*, 136-137.
[5] World Missionary Conference (1910: Edinburgh), *Report of Commission 1: Carrying the Gospel to All the Non-Christian World* (Edinburgh: Olphant, Anderson & Ferrier, 1910), 77.

Koreans in their world-forgotten language of antiquity."[6] This may be considered as evidence of a tongue event during the Pyongyang revival movement, although speaking in tongues was not commonly practiced by early Korean Pentecostals.

1. The Wonsan Revival (1903)

Robert A. Hardie, a Canadian medical missionary, arrived in Korea in 1890. In August 1903, he led a group of Korean national believers and seven missionaries in a week of prayer meetings and Bible studies at Wonsan.[7] Reading Luke 11:13, he realized why his missionary work was not successful: he was depending on his own missionary skills instead of upon the Spirit. He felt "a deep conviction of sin and captivation by the holiness of God" and realized the power of the Holy Spirit upon him. He confessed "his own pride, hardness of heart, and lack of faith"[8] before the group of other missionaries and Korean believers. Furthermore, he humbly asked them to pray for him.[9] They were overwhelmed by Hardie's act and began to repent of their sins until they all received the baptism in the Spirit.[10]

The Wonsan revival marked the beginning of Korean Pentecostalism. Unlike the American revival, there was no report of tongues-speaking at Wonsan. There was public repentance instead. This public repentance became the standard charismatic phenomenon of the Korean Pentecostal movement and continued until the great Pyongyang revival (1907).[11] The story of the Wonsan revival soon spread over the

---

[6]James S. Gale, *Korea in Transition* (New York: Eaton and Mains, 1909), 216.

[7]As the city of Wonsan was one of the Canadian Mission territories, Hardie was able to lead the meeting of missionaries. See Roy E. Shearer, *Wildfire: Church Growth in Korea* (Grand Rapids, Michigan: William B. Eerdmans Publishing Co., 1966), 160-61.

[8]Young Hoon Lee, "Korean Pentecost: The Great Revival of 1907," *Asian Journal of Pentecostal Studies* 4, no. 1 (2001): 74.

[9]J. Edwin Orr, *Evangelical Awakenings in Eastern Asia* (Minnesota: Bethany Fellowship Inc., 1975), 26.

[10]Lillias H. Underwood, *Underwood of Korea* (New York: Fleming H. Revell Co., 1918), 224.

[11]Ibid.

nation.[12] Many similar conferences and spiritual crusades took place all over Korea.[13]

Many classical Pentecostal scholars regard either the Topeka revival or the Azusa Street revival as "the birth of Pentecostal movement."[14] Anderson argues that the American revivals are not the sole beginning of the Pentecostal movement because Pentecostal/Charismatic revivals occurred around the world at the end of the nineteenth and beginning of the twentieth century, many of them not connected to the American revivals.[15]

The Wonsan revival is significant in two ways for global Pentecostalism. First, it was the first Pentecostal event in Korea and generated a Pentecostal movement independent of American Pentecostalism. (Mary C. Rumsey, the first Pentecostal missionary from the Azusa Street revival, arrived in Korea in March 1928, via Japan.[16]) Second, the Wonsan revival was a spiritual event characterized by the public manifestation of repentance through the Spirit. Though there was no evidence of speaking in tongues, Koreans became overwhelmed by the Spirit and repented of their sins in public.

After Wonsan, Korean Christians spontaneously held many prayer meetings and Bible study classes to seek the baptism in the Spirit.[17] The Pentecostal movement broke down racism, clergy-lay dichotomy, denominationalism, and even gender inequalities, so there were also significant changes among the missionaries regarding ecumenical cooperation. They began to disentangle themselves from denominational boundaries.

---

[12]Ibid.

[13]Allen D. Clark, *A History of the Church in Korea* (Seoul: The Christian Literature Society of Korea, 1971), 159.

[14]J. R. Goff Jr., "Topeka Revival," in *The New International Dictionary of Pentecostal and Charismatic Movements*, ed. Stanley M. Burgess and Eduard M. Van der Maas (Grand Rapids, MI: Zondervan, 2002), 1147-1149. Goff insists that the Topeka revival marked "the birth of the Pentecostal movement."

[15]Anderson, *An Introduction to Pentecostalism*, 19-38. Because other Pentecostal revivals had already broken out, and Pentecostals experienced the manifestations of the Spirit in other parts of the world before the American revivals, the American revivals should rather be called "the beginning of American Pentecostalism" rather than "the birth of the Pentecostal movement." See Anderson, *An Introduction to Pentecostalism*, 23-24.

[16]Synan, *The Holiness-Pentecostal Tradition*, 140; Lee, *The Holy Spirit Movement in Korea*, 66.

[17]Lee, "Korean Pentecost," 75.

From the beginning of Protestantism in Korea, Presbyterianism and Methodism were the dominant forms of mainstream Christianity.[18] As circumstance dictated, they alternatively competed or cooperated with each other. They collaborated for the government hospital established by Allen until they started their own missions. Underwood described this cooperation as the spirit of harmony.[19]

In time, competition between the two denominations had escalated with the arrival of early missionaries, especially from the United States, who were influenced by the denominationalism of religious life in mid-nineteenth-century America.[20] For example, once a church was started, it clearly identified its denominational affiliation. The first Protestant church established by Underwood in September 1887 was named Saemunan Presbyterian Church.[21] One month later, the first Methodist church opened by Appenzeller in Seoul was named Jeongdong Methodist Church.[22] Before then, Northern Methodists and Presbyterians had worked together for years in North Pyengan province, Chulla province, Choong Chung province, Kyung Kui province, and some South Pyengan areas.[23] The Choong Chung province, the central area of the Korean peninsula, was occupied by the Southern Presbyterians, the Northern Methodists, and the Baptists.[24] With denominational distinctions, conflicts among mission groups were inevitable.

In 1893, the Northern Methodists and the Northern Presbyterians made a comity agreement to prevent friction and overlapping of mission territory. The substance of the agreement was that both missions could

---

[18] In the early years of Protestantism in Korea, there were four denominational groups: Anglican, Baptist, Methodist, and Presbyterian. Although these missions were started almost at the same time, the Anglicans and the Baptists did little, if any, cooperative work. See Paik, *The History of Protestant Missions*, 198-199.

[19] Underwood, "Division of the Field," 211.

[20] Richard J. Carwardine, *Evangelicals and Politics in Antebellum America* (New Haven and London: Yale University Press, 1993), 2-5.

[21] Shearer, *Wildfire*, 43.

[22] William Elliot Griffis, *A Modern Pioneer in Korea: The Life Story of Henry G. Appenzeller* (New York: Fleming H. Revell Co., 1912), 211.

[23] N. C. Whittemore, "Fifty Years of Comity and Co-operation in Korea: Comity in Division of Territory," *The Fiftieth Anniversary Celebration of the Korea Mission of the Presbyterian Church in the U. S. A. June 3-July 3, 1934*, ed. Harry A. Rhodes (Seoul: YMCA Press, 1934), 94-95.

[24] Paik, *The History of Protestant Missions*, 200-201.

coexist in a region having a population of five thousand but smaller districts should be given to the mission that came to the area first. Furthermore, without a letter of recommendation, no membership could be transferred from one denomination to another.[25] Due to excessive rivalry between denominations, the agreement was impracticable. Moreover, the Methodist Bishop R. S. Foster disapproved of the agreement when he came to Korea, so Methodist participation in the agreement was nullified.[26]

In 1905, after the Wonsan revival, four Presbyterian missions and two Methodist missions created a mission organization, *The General Council of Protestant Evangelical Missions in Korea*.[27] When they chose the name of the council, they decided to drop the terms *Jang Lo* (Presbyterian) and *Mi Gam Li* (American Methodist). The purpose of the council was to encourage cooperation between denominations in the mission field.[28]

The Wonsan revival had another significant impact, which changed the mission strategy in Korea. Before the revival, the churches had focused on visible results such as founding schools and hospitals. Afterwards, they became concerned about the spirituality of Korean Christians. They began to focus more on the spiritual life of Korean Christians. After the revival, the early Korean Pentecostals began to concentrate on three practices: fervent prayer, evangelism, and Bible study.[29]

2. The Pyongyang Revival (1907)

After the Wonsan revival, spiritual awakenings spread all over the nation. Bible study meetings became a regular feature. Korean churches held Bible study classes for a week or longer. Korean Christians set aside those days to study the Bible and to pray.[30]

---

[25]Ibid., 201.
[26]Ibid.
[27]Deok Joo Rhie, *Chogi Hankook GidokgyoSa YeonGoo* [A Study on the Early Christian History in Korea], 164.
[28]Hugh Miller, "The History of Co-operation and the Federal Council," *Korea Mission Field* (December 1934): 256.
[29]Taek Bu Jeon, *The Faith Mountains of Natives* (Seoul: Christian Literature Crusade, 1993), 132-205.
[30]William Newton Blair and Bruce F. Hunt, *The Korean Pentecost and the Sufferings Which Followed* (Edinburgh: The Banner of Truth Trust, 1977), 67.

Bible study was significant for two reasons. First, there were not many educated Christian teachers to teach the Bible. Korean Christians had to learn about the Christian faith by reading the Bible themselves. Second, Bible studies were influenced by the Confucian tradition of studying Confucian scriptures and discipline in daily life. The Jang Dae Hyun Church and the South Gate church in Pyongyang had remarkable meetings: seven hundred people converted to Christianity in two weeks in 1905.[31] In September 1906, Korean Christians and missionaries met for several evenings at the Jang Dae Hyun Church.

Dr. Howard Agnew Johnson, a visiting missionary, came to the church on his way to China. He introduced the awakenings happening in India (1905-07)[32] and in Wales (1904-05) to the whole congregation of the church, including missionaries, while he preached.[33] When Korean Christians and missionaries heard about the blessings in Wales and in India, they desired to be filled by the Spirit and experience the manifestations of the Spirit.[34] Johnson encouraged the church to bring a Pentecostal revival to Korea as it happened in Wales and India. Seon Ju Gil (1869-1935), the elder of the lay assistants in the central church, was the only one to raise his hand. Gil began to have a prayer meeting every day at 4 a.m. with another elder named Park.

This early prayer meeting became a tradition of Korean Christianity.[35] Two months after it started, a large group of six to seven hundred people joined in the prayer meetings and prayed for a new revival in Korea.[36] Although the revivals of India and Wales were not directly connected with the Korean revivals, they provided a stimulus for the Pyongyang revival. The Jang Dae Hyun Church decided to have a regular Bible study during the first two weeks of January each year. Normally, eight hundred to one thousand people walked between 10 to

---

[31] Orr, *Evangelical Awakenings in Eastern Asia*, 27.
[32] At Pandita Ramabai's (1858-1922) Muki Mission in Pune, young women were baptized by the Holy Spirit and experienced spiritual manifestations including speaking in tongues in the period 1905-07. See Anderson, *An Introduction to Pentecostalism*, 124.
[33] The Welsh revival broke out under Evan Roberts who, at that time, was twenty-six years old. Through him, over thirty thousand people converted to Christianity, and twenty thousand became new church members. See Synan, *The Holiness-Pentecostal Tradition*, 86.
[34] Blair and Hunt, *The Korean Pentecost*, 68.
[35] Kim, *History and Theology of Korean Pentecostalism*, 38.
[36] Ibid.

100 miles to participate. Various Korean teachers and missionaries taught the Bible for three hours in each session.[37]

On January 6, 1907, about 1,500 people gathered for evening meetings. As the capacity of the church building was too small to fit everyone, the meeting was rearranged for men only. The women met in four different places.[38] Korean pastors and missionaries led the meetings. Everyone sought "the Spirit's presence and the necessity of love and righteousness."[39] The church was crowded, and prayers seemed to be answered. However, William Newton Blair, one of the eyewitnesses of the Pyongyang revival, reported that something was hindering the work; he felt the devil was present.[40] Graham Lee also wrote, "The meeting seemed dead and God's Spirit seemed to have departed from us."[41]

The following Monday night, January 14, 1907, the Holy Spirit began to minister powerfully to the congregation. According to Blair, he could feel that the church was filled with the presence of God when he entered it.[42] After a short sermon by William B. Hunt, the meeting was led by Graham Lee.[43] Lee asked the whole audience to pray together. Then everyone began to pray out loud. Blair describes this audible prayer in the following terms: "The prayer sounded to me like the falling of many waters, an ocean of prayer beating against God's throne. It was not many, but one, born of one Spirit, lifted to one Father above."[44] McCune, another participant, wrote that "although there were so many voices, there was no confusion at all. It was all a subdued, perfect harmony… and there was perfect concentration in the prayer of each one."[45]

After the prayer, Lee asked the congregation to confess their sins. Everyone cried out loudly, "*Abouji*" (Father, in Korean) and began to confess their sins. Immediately, the audience was filled by the Holy

---

[37] Blair and Hunt, *The Korean Pentecost*, 67-68.
[38] G. Lee, "How the Spirit Came to Pyengyang," *Korea Mission Field* (December 1907), 33.
[39] Blair and Hunt, *The Korean Pentecost*, 69.
[40] Ibid., 69-70.
[41] Lee, "How the Spirit Came to Pyengyang," 33.
[42] Blair and Hunt, *The Korean Pentecost*, 71.
[43] Clark, *A History of the Church in Korea*, 161; G. S. McCune, "The Holy Spirit in Pyeng Yang," *Korea Mission Field* (January 1907), 1; Lee, *The Holy Spirit Movement in Korea*, 27.
[44] Blair and Hunt, *The Korean Pentecost*, 71.
[45] McCune, "The Holy Spirit in Pyeng Yang," 1.

Spirit.⁴⁶ Blair described the presence of the Spirit: "It seemed as if the roof was lifted from the building and the Spirit of God came down from heaven in a mighty avalanche of power upon us."⁴⁷ People repented of adultery, murder, drunkenness, thieving, lying, robbery, envying, hatred, spite, and more.⁴⁸ Some beat their hands and foreheads against the floor in an agony of repentance.⁴⁹ This spiritual phenomenon continued until two in the morning.⁵⁰

The Pyongyang revival was significant for three reasons. First, the ecumenical movement accelerated and extended itself, bridging denominationalism, gender inequality, and generational divisions. (During the early Pentecostal movement in Korea, there was no distinction among Presbyterians and Methodists, missionaries and Korean church leaders, men and women, or boys and girls.⁵¹) Similar outpourings of the Spirit occurred in young people's meetings.⁵²

Second, the Pyongyang revival was the most influential Pentecostal revival in the history of Korean Christianity. About one thousand people gathered every day for two weeks, and the Spirit movement quickly spread all over the nation.

Third, the revival was the turning point from mission to church in Korean Christianity. During the Pyongyang revival, missionaries mainly led Bible studies while Korean church leaders led prayer meetings.⁵³ Before, the major task of those leaders had been assisting missionaries by interpreting their sermons during the services. The leadership and financial support of missionaries had led the Korean church and Korean

---

⁴⁶Lee, "How the Spirit Came to Pyengyang," 34.
⁴⁷Blair and Hunt, *The Korean Pentecost*, 73.
⁴⁸W. M. Baird, "The Spirit Among PyengYang Students," *Korea Mission Field* (May 1907), 65.
⁴⁹Orr, *Evangelical Awakenings in Eastern Asia*, 28.
⁵⁰Ibid.
⁵¹W. B. Hunt, "Impressions of an Eye Witness," *Korea Mission Field* (December 1907), 38.
⁵²Lee, "How the Spirit Came to Pyengyang," 36; Lee, *The Holy Spirit Movement in Korea*, 29.
⁵³Ki Young Hong, "Tochakhwa Ghajungeseo Barabon 1907 Pyongyang Dae Booheungwoondong [The Great Revival of 1907 in Indigenization]," *Seongyo wha Shinhak* [Mission and Theology] vol.18 (2006), 11-12; Young Hee Park, "The Great Revival Movement of 1907 and its Historical Impact on Korean Church," presented to PCA (the Presbyterian Church in America) Korean-American English Ministry Pastor's Conference January 29, 2008, 11.

Christianity. Gradually, nationals began to take over church leadership. As the Korean church leaders matured, they started to conduct their own meetings and crusades, founding new churches.

In the Spring of 1907, soon after the Pyongyang revival, Seon Ju Gil led another revival in Seoul. Chan Sung Kim conducted the prayer meeting at Soong Duk Hak Gyo (Soong Duk School). About three hundred students repented of their sins at the meeting.[54]

The Pyongyang revivals also influenced a revival in Manchuria (1908) in China. Chinese believers in Mukden, Manchuria, heard about the Pyongyang revival. Two elders came to Korea to witness it for themselves. They met with Gil and other Korean leaders in Pyongyang in 1907.[55] Jonathan Goforth, a Canadian Presbyterian missionary to China, also came to Korea in the autumn of 1907.[56] He "carried the revival fire to China."[57]

In February 1908, a Pentecostal revival broke out in Manchuria. The Chinese revival was also a repentance movement. Eight to nine hundred people gathered daily and experienced the same Pentecostal phenomena that had occurred during the Korean revivals.[58] The spiritual manifestations in Manchuria included "public confessions of sin, extreme emotional and physical phenomena," followed by moral transformations.[59]

---

[54] Min, *Hankook Gidokgyo Gyohoi Sa* [the History of Korean Christianity], 268-269.
[55] Gale, *Korea in Transition*, 215-216.
[56] James Webster, *The Revival in Manchuria* (London: Morgan and Scott Ltd., 1910), 9-10.
[57] George T. B. Davis, *Korea for Christ* (New York: Fleming H. Revell Co., 1910), 41.
[58] Webster, *The Revival in Manchuria*, 9-25.
[59] Kenneth Scott Latourette, *A History of the Expansion of Christianity: The Great Century in Northern Africa and Asia*, vol. 4, *A.D. 1800-A. D. 1914* (London: Eyre and Spottiswoode Limited, 1944), 343-344.

CHAPTER 7
KOREAN PENTECOSTAL REVIVALS AND THE DEVELOPMENT OF KOREAN PENTECOSTALISM

It is significant in terms of global Pentecostalism that the spiritual manifestations of Pentecostal revivals in Asia during the early 1900s were different than those experienced at the Azusa Street revival. The assertion that the Pentecostal movement originated from the Azusa Street revival with an emphasis on speaking in tongues is unsustainable from the perspective of global Pentecostalism. Korean Pentecostal revivals planted deep seeds that continued to influence Pentecostalism in its own Korean context.

1. Analysis of the Korean Pentecostal Revivals

The Korean revivals were noteworthy for many reasons. First, they marked the beginning of Pentecostalism in Korea. Korean Christians experienced the baptism in the Spirit. The revivals directly influenced the explosive growth of Korean Christianity. The Pentecostal movement spread out across the nation after the revivals.

In contrast, Japanese Christianity and Pentecostalism have not grown as much as their Korean counterparts, even though Christianity came to Japan much earlier than to Korea. Missionaries to Korea initially stayed in Japan because missionary stations had not yet been established in Korea.[1] But there has been no nationwide spiritual revival in Japan. Korean Christians with Buddhist and Confucian backgrounds learned Christianity from missionaries, but they experienced a deepened Christian spirituality when the revivals broke out.

Second, the revivals marked the turning point from mission to church. From 1903 to 1910, following each revival, church growth was

---

[1] Since there was no Mission Board in Korea as yet, the early missionaries to Korea such as the Methodists Henry Appenzeller and his wife and the Presbyterian Horace G. Underwood left the States for Korea but had to go to Japan where they stayed for a while before they came to Korea in 1885. See Hunt, *Protestant Pioneers in Korea*, 22.

remarkable. In 1900, there were 20,914 Protestant Christians in Korea.[2] By 1905, the number of Protestant Christians had increased to 40,367, with 321 churches. In 1907, soon after the Pyongyang revival, there were 642 churches and 119,309 registered Christians and evangelists.[3] From 1906 to 1910, Korean Christianity produced 79,221 new converts.[4] By 1910, the number had increased to about 167,000.[5]

Due to the inability of the missionaries to cope with this rapid church growth, the leadership ability of Koreans grew. Early church leaders had relied on missionaries for financial and theological support, teaching, and instructions. In addition, they uncritically imitated the ways of the missionaries.[6] After the Pyongyang revival, Seon Ju Gil led his own crusades and Bible classes all over the country.[7] Nationals still needed support (especially for finances), but by 1907, 164 out of 642 churches were self-supporting.[8]

Until 1906, a missionary council in the Jang Dae Hyun Church made major decisions. After the revival in 1907, missionaries and Korean leaders established the Chosŏn Jasogyo Presbyterian Association to make joint decisions on behalf of the church.[9]

Third, the revivals acted as movements of spiritual renewal. In 1888, the Chosŏn government promulgated an edict proscribing the preaching of the gospel and the teaching of Christianity. This was a response to French Jesuits, who bought a site for their cathedral secretly in a location where people could look down upon the royal palace. This was considered disrespectable to the government.[10] Though this action did

---

[2]Kim, *History and Theology of Korean Pentecostalism*, 312.
[3]Min, *Hankook Gidokgyo Gyohoi Sa* [the History of Korean Christianity], 281.
[4]Gook Jae Shin Hak Yeon Goo Won [International Theology Institute], *Hananim euy Sunghoi GyoHoiSa* [The Church History of Assemblies of God] (Seoul: Seoul Mal Sseum Sa, 1998), 165.
[5]Kim, *History and Theology of Korean Pentecostalism*, 41.
[6]Rhie, *Chogi Hankook GidokgyoSa YeonGoo*, 170.
[7]Lee, *The Holy Spirit Movement in Korea*, 34.
[8]Horace G. Underwood, *The Call of Korea: Political-Social-Religious* (New York: Fleming H. Revell Co., 1908), 158.
[9]Gyoung Rho Yoon, "1900 Nyundae Chogi Janglogyohoieu Chili wha Chochanggi Gyoineu Sahoi Gyoungjaejeok Sunghyang [The socio-economic tendency of the early Korean Christians and the governance of the early Presbyterian church in 1900s]," *Hankook Gidokgyo wa Yeoksa* (January 1991): 85.
[10]Underwood, *Underwood of Korea*, 70.

not directly affect Protestant missionaries, Allen recalled all Protestant missionaries to Seoul. He asked the missionaries to focus only on medical and educational work rather than evangelism for a while.[11] Missionaries such as Underwood and Appenzeller were displeased with the recall, and evangelization became limited.[12] Missionaries focused on medical and educational work rather than on developing the spiritual life of believers.[13] The revivals helped missionaries and Korean leaders become more concerned about spirituality and about church growth.

Fourth, the revivals were ecumenical. Denominationalism and boundaries between missionaries and Korean Christians eroded. Missionaries confessed their mistakes and faults in front of Korean nationals and humbly asked for forgiveness. Koreans responded similarly to the missionaries. With reconciliation, they began to cooperate in ministry. Gender and generational divisions were broken down.

Before the revivals, Confucianism, the basic ideology of Korea, had restricted women's rights and social activities. Most women were unable to participate in public education and or express themselves publically.[14] In childhood, they followed their fathers. In marriage, they were subject to their husbands. In widowhood, they obeyed their elder sons.[15] During the revivals, restrictions for women, boys, and girls were erased. Since then, Christian women have participated fully in church ministries and activities.

Fifth, the revivals changed Korean ethics. During the Pyongyang revival, attendees at hour-long afternoon conferences discussed vital issues regarding church life and moral matters.[16] Through public repentance, Koreans confessed sins. They also confessed culturally-acceptable vices such as smoking tobacco, playing cards, drinking, and so on. They became conscious of sins not in a legal sense but in religious aspects. Christian ethics began to be contextualized into daily life and

---

[11] Min, *Hankook Gidokgyo Gyohoi Sa* [the History of Korean Christianity], 205.
[12] Underwood, *Underwood of Korea*, 70.
[13] Shearer, *Wildfire*, 56.
[14] Angus Hamilton, *Korea* (New York: Charles Scribner's Sons, 1904), 105-106.
[15] George Heber Jones, *Korea: The Land, People, and Customs* (New York: Eaton and Mains, 1907), 40.
[16] J. Z. Moore, "The Great Revival Year," *Korea Mission Field* (August 1907), 116.

transform community ethics as well. (Missionaries referred to this ethical change as "the new man experience.")[17]

Koreans in Pyongyang adopted Christian ethics as their moral standard. They visited neighbors from house to house to confess their sins and returned stolen articles and money to the owners. The entire city was stirred by this ethical change.[18] All believers were required to strictly keep the Ten Commandments. During sermons, Old Testament texts were used more often than those in the New Testament. Participation in church activities became more difficult for drinkers of alcohol, smokers, and those with concubines.[19]

Sixth, the revivals were a nationwide Pentecostal movement that focused on repentance. There were no reports of tongues speaking during the revivals.

One negative consequence of the emphasis on repentance emerged as this repentance movement began to standardize revival crusades and meetings: missionaries and local ministers focused on confession of sins rather than spiritual gifts. Missionaries influenced by the North American holiness movement of the 1860s and the revivals of D. L. Moody (1837-1899) made up about eighty percent of all missionaries who arrived in Korea before 1893.[20] Korean Presbyterians followed the thinking of Martin Luther (1483-1546) and John Calvin (1509-64) concerning spiritual gifts and miracles. According to Anderson, Luther believed that "tongues were given as a sign to the Jews and had ceased, and that Christians no longer needed miracles."[21] Calvin taught that "speaking in tongues facilitated the preaching of the gospel in foreign language, but God had removed it from the church and miracles had long

---

[17]W. G. Cram, "Revival Fires," *Korea Mission Field* (December 1905), 33.

[18]Blair and Hunt, *The Korean Pentecost*, 75.

[19]Harold S. Hong, "General Picture of the Korean Church, Yesterday and Today," in *Korea Struggles for Christ*, ed. Harold S. Hong, Won Yong Ji, and Chung Choon Kim (Seoul: Christian Literature Society of Korea, 1966), 15.

[20]Kim, *History and Theology of Korean Pentecostalism*, 35. According to Kim, North Americans Methodists and Presbyterians occupied about seventy percent of the mission territory across the country. Presbyterianism had become the largest Christian denomination in Korea.

[21]Anderson, *An Introduction to Pentecostalism*, 23.

since ceased."²² For this reason, Presbyterianism did not initially welcome Pentecostalism in Korea.

However, prayers for divine healing became common in the church soon after the revivals.²³ Spiritual gifts and the manifestations of the Spirit were practiced by early Pentecostal leaders such as Ig Doo Kim and Yong-Do Yi.²⁴ Two decades later, the arrival of Mary C. Rumsey in March 1928 established a direct connection between the Azusa Street revival and Korean Pentecostalism. Koreans began to understand the perspectives of American Pentecostals about the manifestations of the Spirit.

Seventh, the revivals brought hope to Korea and brought explosive growth to the church. Since the late nineteenth century, Korea was confronted with political uncertainty due to Western aspirations and Japanese imperialism. In 1895, Japanese mobs murdered the queen of Korea in her bedroom.²⁵ The king feared he would be the next victim.²⁶ Politically, Korea was in an extremely precarious state. Confucianism, the basis of the socio-political structure of Korea, forfeited its functions.²⁷ Koreans had found no hope for eternal life in their traditional religions of Buddhism, Confucianism, and shamanism.²⁸

Through the revivals, people in religio-political difficulties found hope and converted. They gained an eschatological hope in the Kingdom of God, and Korean Christianity grew explosively. The church became "the most influential single organization in Korea."²⁹ C. E. Sharp maintains that the Koreans converted to Christianity for three main reasons: the need for economic and political security, a desire for high civilization and culture, and their interest in Christian spirituality.³⁰

---

²²Ibid.; See also Dayton, *Theological Roots of Pentecostalism*, 116-117.

²³Davis, *Korea for Christ*, 17.

²⁴Gook Jae Shin Hak Yeon Goo Won [International Theology Institute], *Hananim euy Sunghoi GyoHoiSa* [Church History of Assemblies of God], 170-177.

²⁵L. H. Underwood, *Fifteen Years among the Top-Knots or Life in Korea* (New York: American Tract Society, 1904), 149; Underwood, *Underwood of Korea*, 147.

²⁶Kim, *History and Theology of Korean Pentecostalism*, 37.

²⁷Blair and Hunt, *The Korean Pentecost*, 22.

²⁸Buddhism is based on transmigration. Confucianism is closer to a philosophy than a religion. Shamanism emphasizes this-worldly secular blessings.

²⁹Orr, *Evangelical Awakenings in Eastern Asia*, 33.

³⁰C. E. Sharp, "Motives for Seeking Christ," *Korea Mission Field* (August 1906): 182-83.

Under the protection of Western missionaries, the church became a shelter for many who felt hopeless. Those interested in Western civilization used the church to learn Western culture. Others were genuinely interested in knowing more about the Christian faith. Eighth, Pentecostal practices emerged during the revivals. For about ten years before he converted to Christianity, Seon Ju Gil was a Taoist, practicing ascetic exercises such as fasting, meditation, and prayer. Gil started one of the important Korean Pentecostal practices, the daily dawn prayer. His influence was remarkable, especially after the Pyongyang revival. He travelled all over the country, preaching more than 20,000 times to about 3.8 million people. He baptized more than 3,000 people and planted more than sixty churches.[31] Many church leaders and members followed his spiritual practices. Ig Jin Kim insists that Gil used "his Taoistic discipline to express his Christian faith. In one way or another, Taoist spirit influenced Christianity." [32] Though Gil's previous Taoistic disciplines may have influenced his decision to begin the dawn prayer, the dawn prayer as a religious practice corresponded to the pattern of Christ's prayers in the Gospels (Mark 1:35).[33] It was also a broader Korean religious practice, followed by Buddhist monks, Shamanists, and other Korean religious groups for generations.

The Christian dawn prayer does not prove that Korean Christianity was influenced by Taoism. The phenomenon of audible prayer, which occurred during the revivals, is also a unique religious practice of Korean Christians that triggered the Pyongyang revival. Simultaneous audible prayer is still prevalent in Pentecostal and Charismatic churches today. Overnight prayer, dawn prayer, and earnest Bible study have become the traditional religious practice of Korean Pentecostals since the revivals.[34]

---

[31] Jin Gyung Gil, *Sun-joo Gil* [in Korean] (Seoul: Jongno, 1980), 326.
[32] Kim, *History and Theology of Korean Pentecostalism*, 39.
[33] "Now in the morning, having risen a long while before daylight, He went out and departed to a solitary place; and there He prayed" (Mark 1:35, NKJV).
[34] Anderson, *An Introduction to Pentecostalism*, 37.

2. The Contextualization of Korean Pentecostalism under Japanese Rule

The Chosŏn Dynasty ended in October 1897, and the name of the country was changed to Dae Han Jae Gook (Dae Han Empire). With the Korea-Japan Annexation Treaty forced on the government on August 22, 1910, the Dae Han Empire ended and became a Japanese colony.

Korean social, political, economical, cultural, and religious circumstances changed as a result of the treaty. Korean Christianity as well as Korean Pentecostalism entered a new phase. At the beginning of Japanese rule, the Japanese authorities did not persecute Korean Christians, even though Prince Marquis Hirobumi Ito, the administrator and Japanese Resident-General in Korea, was assassinated by Chung Kun An, a young Korean Catholic, in Harbin on October 20, 1909. Durham White Stevens, an adviser to the Department of Foreign Affairs in Ito's administration, was also killed by Chang In Hwan, a Protestant Christian, on March 23, 1908.[35]

In 1909 and 1910, a second nationwide revival occurred in Song-Do, known as the Million Souls movement. In July 1909, a group of Methodist missionaries decided to spend an entire week in Bible study and prayer because they felt that the spiritual passion of the church had declined. On the fourth day, the prayer meeting continued until midnight. Among them, F. K. Gamble, C. F. Reid, and M. B. Stokes decided to pray overnight. Around 4 a.m., they were filled with the Spirit.[36]

Soon after this event, ten missionaries, including these three and five Korean church leaders, met together for a week of prayer at a temple in the mountains.[37] In the afternoon on the same day, the Spirit came upon them and their hearts were filled with praise and joy.[38] After the week's meetings, Stokes came back to his church and made an impassioned plea to the congregation that he would make 50,000 converts within a year. His eagerness for the lost inspired them to actively participate in evangelism with him.[39]

---

[35]Paik, *The History of Protestant Missions*, 361.
[36]Davis, *Korea for Christ*, 6-7; Rhodes, 285; Lee, *The Holy Spirit Movement in Korea*, 38-39.
[37]Rhodes, 285.
[38]Davis, *Korea for Christ*, 7.
[39]Lee, *The Holy Spirit Movement in Korea*, 39.

On October 9, 1909, C. F. Reid, the chairman of the General Council of Evangelical Missions, coined the slogan, "A Million Souls for Christ," which was adopted by the council.[40] Though the Million Souls movement was started by Methodist missionaries, it expanded and spread across Korea as a non-denominational movement. About a thousand people promised to spend over 22,000 days in personal evangelization in Pyongyang.[41] Korean believers purchased 700,000 copies of the Gospel of Mark. Across the nation, Christians spent at least 100,000 days in evangelization. They visited nearly every home, shared the gospel with non-believers, and gave out millions of tracts.[42] There were less than 200,000 Christians in Korea at that time. The movement ended by 1910 without achieving its goal. (It would have been almost impossible to increase the number of Christians up to five times in a year.)

The effort lost its momentum due to the impact of the Korea-Japan Annexation Treaty. Although there was no direct persecution against the Million Souls movement by the Japanese government, it had ended by the time Japanese rule began. Koreans, church congregations, and national church leaders were shocked and enveloped in deep sadness because of this unexpected political event. There were no nationwide spiritual revivals or movements during the Japanese rule.

As church members, leaders, and students became "channels to spread [the independence] movement,"[43] the Japanese government began to persecute Christians. Pentecostalism had to address two issues: its continuous growth and its response to current socio-political matters. It was difficult to unite churches even for religious purposes, let alone for political concerns, because the Japanese government did not allow large gatherings. Consequently, the Pentecostal movement began to be led not through the cooperation of churches, but by individual evangelists.[44] The responsibilities of the church in relation to socio-political issues were growing under Japanese rule. However,

---

[40]Ibid., 7.
[41]Shearer, *Wildfire*, 57.
[42]Korea Mission Field, "The Million Souls Movement and Its Results," *Korea Mission Field* (January 1911), 5.
[43]Lee, *The Holy Spirit Movement in Korea*, 33.
[44]Gook Jae Shin Hak Yeon Goo Won [International Theology Institute], *Hananim euy Sunghoi GyoHoiSa* [Church History of Assemblies of God], 170.

Pentecostals were reluctant to be involved in secular matters since they preferred to focus on spiritual concerns.

CHAPTER 8
EARLY PENTECOSTALS AND THE QUICKENING OF PENTECOSTAL HOPE

Three prominent Korean Pentecostal evangelists, Seon Ju Gil, Ig Doo Kim, and Yong Do Yi, strongly influenced the church and Pentecostalism during Japanese rule. Their message of eternal hope and the coming Kingdom of God provided stability and focus for believers who were reeling under foreign occupation. The evangelists contributed individually to the development of the Pentecostal movement under Japanese rule. They brought new hope to Koreans who were in deep sorrow and shock after the loss of national sovereignty to the Japanese.

1. Seon Ju Gil (1869-1935) and Hope for Eternal Life

Seon Ju Gil's eschatological emphasis awakened Christians to the hope of eternal life and the future coming of the Kingdom of God.[1] He was reputed to have read the Old Testament thirty times, the New Testament 100 and the Book of Revelation 10,000 times.[2]

Gil's conservative and fundamentalist faith gave him a strong foundation in fundamental Christian beliefs such as Christ's virgin birth and deity, the infallibility and inerrancy of the Bible, the substitutional Atonement, the literal and physical resurrection of Christ, and the Second Advent. He applied these beliefs to his evangelization.[3] Young Hoon Lee says,

> The effect of his [Gil's] eschatology was to give people the power to overcome persecution and oppression with the spirit of martyrdom, for faith in the second coming would give them real hope and courage. Indeed the Korean church could

---

[1] Lee, *The Holy Spirit Movement in Korea*, 41. Lee says the major emphases of his evangelism were "eschatological faith and the imminent return of Jesus Christ."

[2] Gook Jae Shin Hak Yeon Goo Won [International Theology Institute], *Hananim euy Sunghoi GyoHoiSa* [Church History of Assemblies of God], 171.

[3] Lee, *The Holy Spirit Movement in Korea*, 34-39.

overcome the persecutions of Japanese rulers by their faith and hope for the second coming.[4]

Eschatological hope was very new to Koreans who had grown up with the ideas, thoughts, and spiritualities of Buddhism, Confucianism, and Shamanism. They were accustomed to Buddhist reincarnation and the shamanic spiritual world. Confucianism focused on the ethical life of individuals more than religious life, so its spirituality was not influential.

Gil overemphasized the imminent second coming of Christ, even predicting that it would take place either in 1974 or in 2002.[5] Due to his excessive focus on eschatology, he and his followers assumed the attitude of onlookers for present problems. Because of their indifference to socio-political matters, early Pentecostals became more concerned about God's future Kingdom rather than current issues. This eschatological hope of early Pentecostals for the future Kingdom continues today.

2. Ig Doo Kim (1894-1950) and Divine Healing

According to Samuel Hugh Moffett, one of the reasons behind Korea's remarkable church growth during the early twentieth century was "the earnest and faithful work of the Korean lay evangelists."[6] Ig Doo Kim, a former schoolteacher in the city of Chairyung, was one of them.[7] His Pentecostal practice differed from Gil's. Kim's ministry focused on divine healing and miraculous signs, while Gil's major focus was on salvation and the eschatological hope of eternal life.

Kim was called the "Billy Sunday of Korea," and his healing ministry was labeled the "Kim Ig Doo Revival."[8] He prayed for the sick and the demon-possessed in evangelistic meetings, which were regularly attended by 6,000 to 7,000 people.[9] After the Korean Independent Movement in 1919, attendance at his healing revivals increased to

---

[4]Ibid., 38.
[5]Ibid.
[6]Moffett, *A History of Christianity in Asia*, 539.
[7]Rhodes, *History of the Korea Mission*, 288.
[8]Ibid.
[9]Ibid., 289.

10,000.[10] His healing ministry caused a sensation: Koreans had never previously experienced divine healing. They were accustomed to shamanistic performances by necromancers on behalf of the sick or demon-possessed. They believed that the shamanistic cure was dependent on the quantity and quality of the sacrificial offering for the shamanistic ritual, regardless of faith or an earnest wish for healing.[11]

Although Korea was a Confucian country, shamanism was the most popular religion practiced among ordinary people at that time. Shamans performed rites to exorcise evil spirits on behalf of the sick and victims of disaster.[12] Koreans commonly sought shamans when they had problems in their lives, including physical matters. Against this religious background, Koreans experienced the power of the Spirit through Kim's healing ministry and were overwhelmed.

Kim's ministry was remarkable in early Pentecostalism. He preached about 28,000 times and led 776 revival meetings. Through his ministry, about ten thousand claimed they had received healing, 288,000 Koreans converted to Christianity, and two hundred laymen became ministers. One hundred fifty new churches were built and 140 churches enlarged. Kim also contributed to education by establishing 120 preschools and extending one hundred existing schools.[13]

Nevertheless, church leaders affiliated with the Presbyterian denomination did not accept Kim's healing ministry.[14] In 1921, the Kyoung Nam [the South Eastern province of Korea] Presbyterian Council decided not to perform prayer for divine healing during revival meetings. In 1923, the Hwang Hae [the West Midland province of Korea] Presbyterian Council asked the Korean Presbyterian Council to remove the clause, "the spiritual power for sign and wonders has ceased," in the

---

[10] Allan Anderson, *Spreading Fires: The Missionary Nature of Early Pentecostalism* (London: SCM Press, 2007), 141.

[11] Jee Byung Gu, *Shamanism Gwha Hankook GyoHoi* [Shamanism and Korean Church], (Seoul: Sae Han Publishing House, 1996), 23.

[12] Jones, *Korea*, 52-53.

[13] Moon Tak Oh, "The Impact of Korea Revival Movement on Church Growth of Korean Evangelical Christianity in 1903-1963," (PhD diss., Southwestern Baptist Theological Seminary, 2000), 126-127; Sean C. Kim, "Reenchanted: Divine Healing in Korean Protestantism," in *Global Pentecostal and Charismatic Healing* ed. Candy Gunther Brown (Oxford: Oxford University Press, 2011), 273.

[14] Harry A. Rhodes, "Some Results of the Kim Ik Tu Revival Meeting," *Korea Mission Field* (June 1921): 114.

Korean Presbyterian Constitution (Politics: Chapter 3, Clause 1). Their request was denied.[15] In 1926, Kim had to resign as pastor of his church (Seoul Nammoon Bark Gyohoi) due to his emphasis on the manifestations of the Spirit.[16] The divine healing movement was attenuated until the late 1950s, when Cho's healing ministry started with the theology of the Threefold Blessing.[17]

Kim's contributions to early Pentecostalism were significant in three ways. First, his healing crusade acted as a power encounter and demonstrated the visible victory over the indigenized shamanistic spirituality of Koreans who had not experienced the spiritual power of Christianity. Second, he gave Christians an expectancy to receive spiritual gifts and experience the manifestations of the Spirit. Third, he convinced Koreans that God could intervene not only in the spiritual dimension but also in the material problems of everyday life.

3. Yong Do Lee (1901-1933) and the Baptism in the Spirit

While Yong Do Lee was a seminary student, he suffered from severe tuberculosis. In 1925, his doctor told him that he had only a few months to live. A seminary friend prepared a place for him to recuperate in a village.

One day, he was invited to lead an evening service. During the service, he claims that he experienced divine healing for himself with other manifestations of the Spirit, including speaking in tongues and "a mysterious experience of a joyous living in dying."[18] Following his recovery, he became a revivalist and began to preach the gospel all over the country.

Lee's own experience of suffering from tuberculosis and his subsequent healing became the theological foundation for his ministry.

---

[15] Myung Soo Park, *Hankook Gyohoi Booheung Woondong Yeongoo* [A Study on the evival Movement in Korea Church], (Seoul: Hankook Gidokgyo Ryeksa Yeongooso, 2007), 90-93.

[16] Ibid., 92.

[17] Ibid., 93.

[18] Yoo, *Korean Pentecostalism*, 110; Yeol Soo Eim, "South Korea," *The New International Dictionary of Pentecostal and Charismatic Movements*, ed. Stanley M. Burgess and Eduard M. Van der Maas, 240.

Through his physical suffering, he began to deeply meditate upon the suffering of Christ. Lee identified the passion of Christ with the suffering of Christians under persecution as well as that of Koreans under Japanese rule.[19]

The slogan of Lee's spiritual movement was "Jesus-centred enthusiasm and prayer."[20] He emphasized "eschatological faith, faith in divine healing, and faith in mystical union with Christ."[21] He believed that Christians could be physically united with Christ in the love of God, and he called this physical union "vascular union."[22]

His dualistic theology was reflected in his belief that religious, spiritual, and immaterial things were good while material and worldly things were bad.[23] He believed that the physical body and the human spirit were "mutually independent and in conflict" with each other.[24] As the term "dying daily" in Christ became the motto of his life,[25] he sold his house to support seminary students financially. He often returned home without his coat after giving it to a beggar on the street.[26]

His dualistic view was influenced by three factors. The first was *Cheong-Bin- Sa-Sang* (the idea of honourable poverty) within Confucianism. Korean Confucian scholars and *Yangban* (the high class) considered honorable poverty as the sublime value of life. The leaders of society practiced honorable poverty in their lives. A second factor was the influence of the Holiness movement through the missionaries. Lee sincerely wanted to live a Christ-like holy life. Third, due to his imminent eschatology, he avoided all worldly desires and was opposed to the pursuit of wealth. This perspective on material prosperity, which mixed imminent eschatology and *Cheong-Bin- Sa-Sang*, prevailed among most Christians, including early Pentecostals.

---

[19]Yoo, *Korean Pentecostalism*, 110.
[20]Young Hoon Lee, "The Korean Holy Spirit Movement in Relation to Pentecostalism," in *Asian and Pentecostal: The Charismatic Face of Christianity in Asia*, ed. Allan Anderson and Edmond Tang (Oxford: Regnum Books International, 2005), 513.
[21]Lee, *The Holy Spirit Movement in Korea*, 41-42.
[22]Min, *Hankook Gidokgyo Gyohoi Sa* [the History of Korean Christianity], 437.
[23]Hollenweger, *Pentecostalism*, 101.
[24]Yoo, *Korean Pentecostalism*, 112.
[25]Ibid., 110.
[26]Hollenweger, *Pentecostalism*, 101.

After the Korean War, Pentecostal preachers began to focus on this-worldly blessings from God through the Threefold Blessing. Mainstream Korean Christianity regarded Pentecostalism as heretical or shamanistic because of its emphasis on earthly blessings, although most Koreans were struggling with extreme poverty at that time.

Despite Lee's negative perspective on material blessings and his mysterious view of the relationship between God and human beings, his role in giving Korean believers hope through the work of the Spirit cannot be overlooked. His services were always accompanied by visible manifestations of the Holy Spirit such as speaking in tongues, divine healings, and other supernatural signs.[27] His revival movement was one expression of the Pentecostal/Charismatic movement in Korea. Yet because of some of his unorthodox views, Korean Presbyterians declared him a heretic in September 1933,[28] as did the Methodists later the same year.[29] Hollenweger insists that Yong Do Lee's "influence on Korean spirituality should not be underestimated."[30]

The early Pentecostal leaders were accused of being heretics for two main reasons. First, Korean Christians did not understand Spirit manifestations at that time. Second, there was no one teaching Korean Christians about Pentecostalism and the spiritual gifts until Pentecostal missionaries arrived, about two decades after the Korean revivals broke out. At the time, Protestant missionaries in Korea were generally opposed to both Pentecostalism and the spiritual gifts.

---

[27]Gook Jae Shin Hak Yeon Goo Won [International Theology Institute], *Hananim euy Sunghoi GyoHoiSa* [Church History of Assemblies of God], 174; Eim, "South Korea," 240.
[28]Min, *Hankook Gidokgyo Gyohoi Sa* [the History of Korean Christianity], 438.
[29]Anderson, *An Introduction to Pentecostalism*, 137.
[30]Hollenweger, *Pentecostalism*, 102.

CHAPTER 9
THE ESTABLISHMENT OF KOREAN PENTECOSTALISM

The Pentecostal experience and message were part of the early twentieth-century revivals in Korea. Mainstream denominations frowned upon Pentecostalism and discouraged it. However, the arrival of North American Pentecostal missionaries provided new information and affirmation for existing Pentecostals and spurred new interest.

1. The Arrival of Pentecostal Missionaries

About twenty years after the Korean revivals, Pentecostal missionaries began to arrive in Korea. The first was Mary C. Rumsey, a former Methodist. She is recognized as the first Pentecostal missionary to Korea because she was the first one who experienced the Azusa Street revival (April 1906).[1] She was not sent by the Apostolic Faith Mission but came to the country as an independent missionary.[2] She received the calling to go to Korea when she was baptized in the Spirit at the Azusa Street revival but was unable to leave immediately due to lack of funds.[3]

Eighteen years later, she fulfilled her calling to Korea with the personal financial support of Denverd, a member of her Methodist church.[4] She landed in Japan before coming to Korea, as other missionaries did. She moved to Korea in March, 1928.[5]

American Pentecostals T. M. and Gladys Parson came to Korea as independent missionaries in 1930. Mrs. Parson requested Pentecostal churches in the States to send more missionaries to Korea. In 1933, two British Pentecostals, E. H. Meredith and L. Vessey, responded to her

---

[1]Gook Jae Shin Hak Yeon Goo Won [International Theology Institute], *Hananim euy Sunghoi GyoHoiSa* [Church History of Assemblies of God], 197.
[2]Anderson, *Spreading Fires*, 141.
[3]Synan, *The Holiness-Pentecostal Tradition*, 140; Kim, *History and Theology of Korean Pentecostalism*, 57; Gook Jae Shin Hak Yeon Goo Won [International Theology Institute], *Hananim euy Sunghoi GyoHoiSa*, 197.
[4]Kim, *History and Theology of Korean Pentecostalism*, 58.
[5]Lee, *The Holy Spirit Movement in Korea*, 66.

request and came as independent missionaries.⁶ (Mrs. Parson seems to have met them during a visit to England.⁷)

Following the arrival of Pentecostal missionaries, Pentecostalism entered a new phase. Pentecostal missionaries began to teach Pentecostal principles to Korean believers. They encouraged them to be baptized in the Spirit and to receive spiritual gifts. In her preaching, Rumsey taught the importance of spiritual gifts for the Pentecostal faith, speaking in tongues, praying for the sick, and receiving the baptism in the Spirit.⁸

Pentecostal churches and denominations began to be established in Korea. After the Korean revivals, churches—mostly affiliated with Presbyterian and Methodist denominations—sprouted and grew up rapidly. Most of these churches taught the beliefs of Presbyterianism or Methodism. Pentecostal missionaries began to cultivate Korean Pentecostal church leaders. Together with them, they started Pentecostal churches.

2. Korean Pentecostal Churches and Leaders

In 1931, Rumsey visited the office of the Salvation Army in Seoul. She met Hong Huh (1907-1991) where he was working as a secretary.⁹ She asked him to help her missionary work since he spoke English well.¹⁰ Soon after, he joined Rumsey's mission as her interpreter and was baptized in the Spirit through her.¹¹ In 1957, he became the first Korean superintendent of the Assemblies of God in Korea.¹²

In April 1932, Rumsey and Huh successfully planted the first Pentecostal church, Seo Bing Go Church, in Seoul.¹³ There was no senior pastor at the church since there was neither a Pentecostal ordained pastor nor anyone who had finished studies in a Pentecostal seminary. Rumsey

---

⁶Gook Jae Shin Hak Yeon Goo Won [International Theology Institute], *Hananim euy Sunghoi GyoHoiSa* [Church History of Assemblies of God], 198-99.
⁷Kim, *History and Theology of Korean Pentecostalism*, 61.
⁸Eim, "South Korea," 243.
⁹Ibid.
¹⁰Kim, *History and Theology of Korean Pentecostalism*, 58.
¹¹Ibid.
¹²Anderson, *Spreading Fires*, 141.
¹³Gook Jae Shin Hak Yeon Goo Won [International Theology Institute], *Hananim euy Sunghoi GyoHoiSa* [Church History of Assemblies of God], 203.

asked John Juergensen, the president of the Japan Bible School in Nagoya, to send one of the students, Sung San Park (1908-1956), to Korea.[14] Rumsey had met Park in Japan before she came to Korea.[15] Soon after graduation, Park returned to Korea and became the pastor of the Seoul church in 1932.[16]

In 1933, the second Pentecostal church, Soo Chang Dong Church, was opened by the Parsons, Mrs. Elfreda Offstead, and Boo Keun Bae (1906-1970). Bae had also graduated from the Japan Bible School and had been baptized in the Spirit through Juergensen while studying there. He returned to Korea eager to evangelize his country.[17] The Parsons and Offstead paid all the expenses of the church while Bae focused on evangelism. He visited people from house to house, preached the gospel on the street, and led revival meetings.[18]

That year, these two Pentecostal churches formed the Chosen Pentecostal Church, the first Korean Pentecostal denomination. The Chosen Pentecostal Church became the Korean Assemblies of God in 1955.[19] After organizing the denomination, Park, Huh, and Bae were credentialed on October 5, 1938, as the first ordained Pentecostal pastors.[20]

Tens of thousands people gathered for Pentecostal revival meetings conducted by revivalists like Yong Do Lee and Ig Doo Kim, but when the Pentecostal churches were founded, Korean Christians did not attend them. Compared to other churches, the Pentecostal churches grew very slowly until 1937, and then began to decline in membership starting in 1938 until after the Korean War.

---

[14]Ibid., 199.
[15]Lee, *The Holy Spirit Movement in Korea*, 68.
[16]Kim, *History and Theology of Korean Pentecostalism*, 63.
[17]Ibid., 65-66, 68.
[18]Gook Jae Shin Hak Yeon Goo Won [International Theology Institute], *Hananim euy Sunghoi GyoHoiSa* [Church History of Assemblies of God], 203.
[19]Kim, *History and Theology of Korean Pentecostalism*, 66.
[20]Lee, *The Holy Spirit Movement in Korea*, 68.

Table 1
The Statistics of Pentecostal Churches and Membership in Korea during 1934-1941[21]

Year	Churches	Ministers	Members
1934	2	7	99
1935	3	8	113
1936	3	9	130
1937	6	10	173
1938	6	11	129
1939	6	11	99
1940	5	4	80
1941	4	4	80

Some Pentecostal scholars have suggested two reasons for this slow growth: first, religious persecution by the Japanese colonial authorities, and second, the return of Pentecostal missionaries to their home countries due to Japanese persecution.[22]

These problems were by no means unique to Pentecostal churches. The worse the Pacific War became for Japan, the harsher was the Japanese persecution of Christians. The Japanese government forced all Korean Christians and missionaries to practice Shinto shrine worship. Anyone who declined was persecuted. This resulted in the imprisonment of Koreans and the expulsion of missionaries. The Japanese government intended to deport American missionaries not only for religious reasons but also for political reasons in preparation for the Pacific War against the United States.

During that time, there were more specific reasons for the lack of Pentecostal church growth. First, Pentecostals did not give hope to Koreans who were struggling with current socio-political difficulties under Japanese colonial rule. Church leaders and missionaries focused on spiritual gifts such as speaking in tongues, divine healing, and

---

[21] Gook Jae Shin Hak Yeon Goo Won [International Theology Institute], *Hananim euy Sunghoi GyoHoiSa* [Church History of Assemblies of God], 204; Lee, *The Holy Spirit Movement in Korea*, 69.

[22] Kim, *History and Theology of Korean Pentecostalism*, 72.

empowerment by the Spirit rather than being concerned about the current struggles of ordinary people.²³

Many church leaders were imprisoned for their involvement in the independence movement. Among thirty-three signatories of the Declaration of Independence on March 1ˢᵗ, 1919, sixteen were Christian leaders. After the event, 3,804 Presbyterian laymen and 134 pastors and elders were arrested. Furthermore, 202 other Christian leaders were imprisoned, forty-one were shot to death, and six were beaten to death. Twelve churches were also closed down by the Japanese government.²⁴ Thus, other denominational church leaders shared the sufferings which ordinary people were experiencing.

Second, as a result, the Pentecostals did not gain the favor of Koreans. As noted, those who experienced the manifestations of the Spirit during Yong Do Lee and Ig Doo Kim's revival meetings did not want to attend the Pentecostal churches.

Third, Pentecostal churches were labeled as heretical by other denominations. From the beginning, Protestantism in Korea expanded based on denominationalism and denominational rivalry. As a late starter, Pentecostalism was constrained by other denominations. Pentecostal churches were confronted with heresy disputes. They were unprepared for theological disputes and unable to refute the claims by other Korean churches that they were heretical.²⁵

3. Internal conflicts during Japanese rule

In its early days, Pentecostalism had to pass through conflicts and theological controversies with other denominations. Two major factors caused friction between Pentecostals and other denominations. First, the most significant theological dispute was over the gift of tongues as the initial evidence of the baptism in the Spirit. Pentecostal missionaries had been strongly influenced by leaders in America. Since 1901, that doctrine had been taught publicly by Charles Fox Parham as "the only

---

²³Lee, *The Holy Spirit Movement in Korea*, 68.
²⁴ Min, *Hankook Gidokgyo Gyohoi Sa* [the History of Korean Christianity], 345.
²⁵ Gook Jae Shin Hak Yeon Goo Won [International Theology Institute], *Hananim euy Sunghoi GyoHoiSa* [Church History of Assemblies of God], 199.

evidence of having received the baptism of the Holy Ghost."[26] This idea was passed to Parham's followers. In a sermon to a Californian congregation, based on Acts 2:4, William J. Seymour (1870-1922) preached that those who could not speak in tongues were not baptized in the Spirit.[27] The doctrine of tongues was already widely accepted by classical American Pentecostals as "the initial physical evidence" of Spirit baptism.[28] Influenced by American Pentecostal missionaries, Korean Pentecostal leaders also began to teach speaking in tongues as the initial evidence.In the 1930s, however, Presbyterian seminary students at the Theological Seminary in Pyongyang were studying pneumatology from *Pneumatology: The Work of the Holy Spirit in Salvation*, a textbook written by Yu Ming Chia (also known by his Korean name Ok Myung Ga).[29] The text mentioned speaking in tongues as the initial evidence of the Spirit baptism to criticize Pentecostalism:

> There is an assembly of Christians who say that speaking in tongues is the evidence of the baptism in the Spirit. As Paul the apostle mentioned, there are many other evidences of the Spiritual baptism: the word of wisdom is given to one through the Spirit, to another the gift of healings, to another the working of miracles, and to another the heart of love. Therefore, speaking in tongues is certainly not the only evidence of the Spiritual baptism.[30]

Seminarians who became future Presbyterian theologians and pastors learned about pneumatology through Chia's book and became opposed to Pentecostal teaching about tongues-speaking. Mainstream

---

[26]Synan, *The Holiness-Pentecostal Tradition*, 89.
[27]Lee, *The Holy Spirit Movement in Korea*, 66.
[28]Synan, *The Holiness-Pentecostal Tradition*, 165.
[29]Yu-ming Chia was a Chinese theologian who taught Theology at Nanking Theological Seminary in China. He originally wrote the book in Chinese. Later, Chai Myen Jung translated it into Korean under the oversight of William Davis Reynolds. The Korean translation was used at the Theological Seminary in Pyongyang. See Ok-myung Ga, *Pneumatology*, trans. Jae-yung Jung (Pyungyang: Pyungyang Presbyterian Bible School, 1931).
[30]Ok Myung Ga, *Pneumatology*, trans. Jae-yung Jung (Pyungyang: Pyungyang Presbyterian Bible School, 1931), 103 (translation mine).

churches proclaimed that Pentecostals were heretics and called them the "tongues faction."[31] Presbyterians adhered to Calvin's view that speaking in tongues had ceased after the first century AD, and tongues-speaking in modern times did not correspond with the phenomenon of the Bible.[32] Pentecostal churches were not welcomed by the mainstream of Korean Christianity for a long time.

The second factor behind the conflicts was allegations by Methodists and Presbyterians that Pentecostal practices were the products of shamanistic enthusiasms, which were indigenized into Christianity. This accusation, repeated over several decades, made Pentecostals defensive about the theological controversy over shamanistic elements in Korean Pentecostalism.

In October 1945, the Prayer Mountain Movement was started by the Methodist Elder Woon Mong Ra.[33] Traditionally, shamans and necromancers went to mountains to be possessed by shaman spirits. As most Buddhist temples were in the mountains, Buddhists also went to mountains to pray for their needs. When he was twenty-six years old, Ra went to Yongmun Mountain to pray and to meditate on the Bible. While he was there, he was baptized in the Spirit. He continued to go to the mountain regularly and held a revival meeting with other Christians there.

In 1947, thousands gathered for a revival meeting to celebrate the seventh anniversary of the visitation of the Spirit to the mountain. By 1945, there were just two prayer mountains. Thereafter, the number of prayer mountains increased rapidly. There were 207 prayer mountains in 1975, 239 in 1978, 462 in 1988, and 500 in 1994.[34] Speaking in

---

[31]Gook Jae Shin Hak Yeon Goo Won [International Theology Institute], *Hananim euy Sunghoi GyoHoiSa* [Church History of Assemblies of God], 199.

[32] Robert Glenn Gromacki, *The Modern Tongues Movement* (Philadelphia, PA: Presbyterian and Reformed Publishing Co., 1972), 140-141, 163-164. St. John Chrysostom believed that "tongues had died out and were no longer needed to establish Christianity." Based on the statement of Chrysostom, George W. Dollar, Dallas Theological Seminary, concludes that "the gift of tongues was neither widespread nor the normal Christian experience in the period A.D. 100 to 400" and also insists that "tongue speaking had no part in the Reformation, unless among heretical spiritualists." See E. Glenn Hinson, "The Significance of Glossolalia in the History of Christianity," in *Speaking in Tongues: A Guide to Research on Glossolalia*, ed. Watson E. Mills (Grand Rapids, MI: William B. Eerdmans Publishing Co., 1986), 183.

[33]Eim, "South Korea," 243.

[34]Ibid., 241-243.

tongues, divine healing, and other manifestations of the Spirit were common there. Although Ra's Prayer Mountain Movement and other ministries greatly influenced the Korean church, he was declared a heretic along with Yong Do Lee by the Methodists and Presbyterians.[35] Praying on a mountain was a common practice of shamanism that successfully transferred to Pentecostalism.

4. Persecution during Japanese Rule

Since religious freedom was guaranteed in the Japanese constitution, the Japanese government did not compel Christians to practice Shinto shrine worship at the beginning of Japanese colonial rule.[36] After invading Manchuria in 1931, the Japanese built Shinto shrines all over Korea and forced Koreans to worship Japanese emperors. Shrines were intended as a place to worship Japanese ancestors, the god who they believed founded Japan, and the spirits of great warriors and heroes of Japanese history. Later, the Japanese began to worship their emperor as a living god.

Shinto shrine worship became a religious rite not only to worship Japanese gods but to show loyalty and devotion towards Japan.[37] The Japanese had two purposes behind their insistence on Shinto shrine worship. One was "to destroy the spirit of Korea and make the Koreans a subject of the Japanese emperor."[38] The other was to persecute Korean Christians.

In November 1935, G. S. McCune, the principal of Pyongyang Soong Shil School, and V. L. Snook, the principal of Soong Ui Women's High School, were compelled to worship at the shrine as school representatives. They refused the request because of their Christian faith. The Japanese government gave them sixty days, warning that it would close the schools and deport them to the United States

---

[35]Anderson, *An Introduction to Pentecostalism*, 137.
[36]Blair and Hunt, *The Korean Pentecost*, 94.
[37]Byoung Ho Zoh, *Democratization and Evangelization: A History of the Christian Student Movements in Korea, 1884-1990* (Seoul: Tanggulshi Publishing House, 2004), 53.
[38]Lee, *The Holy Spirit Movement in Korea*, 41.

unless they complied. They continued to refuse, were discharged from their positions, and then were deported.[39]

On June 24, 1941, the Japanese organized the *Ilbon GidokGyoDan* (Japanese Christian Church) to control Christian denominations.[40] From 1942, Korean churches were no longer allowed to use their denominational names, but forced to use the name, *Gyo Dan*. Korean Christians who refused to join the organization were placed under house-arrest or imprisoned. Many Korean Christians went underground.[41]

Conservative Presbyterians who never attended shrines (fewer than ten percent of all Presbyterians) and denominations that emphasized the Second Advent of Christ were severely persecuted. About two thousand lay people, as well as three hundred pastors and church leaders, were imprisoned and tortured. More than fifty Christians were martyred. Even after their release from prison, many people suffered or died because of torture, illness, and malnutrition experienced in prison.[42]

On February 10, 1937, Rumsey was deported, followed by Vessey and Meredith on December 20, 1940.[43] The absence of the missionaries affected the Pentecostal churches, especially with regard to their finances. This restricted their activities.

In 1943, the Japanese Governor-General of Korea prohibited all church meetings except Sunday worship services. With the Korean liberation on August 15, 1945, the severe religious persecutions of Korean Christianity by the Japanese government ended.

On June 25, 1950, five years after independence, the Korean War broke out. During this tumultuous period, Korean Christianity struggled to survive. After the war, Pentecostalism and Pentecostal churches moved into a new phase that brought new hope to Koreans through the Threefold Blessing.

---

[39]Min, *Hankook Gidokgyo Gyohoi Sa* [the History of Korean Christianity], 480-481.
[40]Ibid., 486-487.
[41]Clark, *A History of the Church in Korea*, 231.
[42]Blair and Hunt, *The Korean Pentecost*, 130; Kim, *History and Theology of Korean Pentecostalism*, 74-75; Min, *Hankook Gidokgyo Gyohoi Sa* [the History of Korean Christianity], 486-487; Clark, *A History of the Church in Korea*, 202.
[43]Gook Jae Shin Hak Yeon Goo Won [International Theology Institute], *Hananim euy Sunghoi GyoHoiSa* [Church History of Assemblies of God], 207.

Part THREE

THE CONTEXTUALIZATION OF PENTECOSTALISM IN KOREA

With the effective contextualization of Pentecostalism into the Korean context, Pentecostalism grew rapidly in Korea, both numerically and spiritually. In order to understand Korean Pentecostalism, it is necessary to reflect upon Pentecostal ideas about God and the people of God, as well as the cultural, socio-political, and economic contexts of Korea.

Korean Pentecostals refer to God as *Hananim*. But is *Hananim* the same as the Hebrew God? In the universal sense, the answer would be "yes," but this must be qualified from a contextual perspective. For example, the God of Korean Pentecostals is not understood to be in a covenantal relationship with the Korean nation in the way that the Hebrew God was in a covenantal relationship with Israel. To Koreans, God is neither the God of war nor the punisher of lawbreakers, but rather the good God who blesses his people.

After the Korean War, most Koreans suffered severe poverty and sickness. Pentecostalism brought Koreans hope through the Threefold Blessing. The sick and the poor became the people of Korean Pentecostalism. The theology of the Threefold Blessing developed and became deeply rooted in Korea's socio-political, cultural, economic, and religious contexts. We next discuss the contextualization of Korean Pentecostalism and the Threefold Blessing.

CHAPTER 10
HANANIM, THE NAME OF GOD FOR KOREAN CHRISTIANS

Traditionally, Koreans believed in a god in the sky who controlled all of nature. The sky was simultaneously a fearful object and the source of blessings. From an anthropological perspective, worshipping the sky god is a common characteristic in different cultures. For instance, *Amateras* is the Japanese heavenly goddess, and *Sangje* is the Chinese heavenly host.[1] The name of the god of the sky in Korean Shamanism is *Hanŭlnim* or *Haneunim* (hereafter, *Haneunim*). *Hananim*, the name for God adopted by Korean Christians was derived from Shamanism's name for the sky god.

There are many similarities between the sky god in Shamanism and the Christian God. This raises some questions. First, who was *Haneunim* to Koreans before the arrival of Christianity? Second, how was *Haneunim* appropriated as God by Christians? Third, is the name *Haneunim* sufficient to be used as the name for God by Christians? Finally, who is *Hananim* for Korean Pentecostals?

1. Who is *Hananim*?

Worshipping *Haneunim* needs to be understood from a cultural anthropological perspective. The word *Hanŭlnim* is a compound of

---

[1] In Taoism, *Sangje* (in Chinese *T'ien shih*) is the ruler of Heaven and has similar divine characteristics to the Jade Emperor of the Chinese and the Sun goddess of the Japanese. All creatures, including humans and even the realm of hell, are under his power. However, he ranks below the Three Pure Ones: i) The Great Purity (Taiqing) – the Universal Lord of the Primordial Beginning; ii) the Supreme Pure One (Lingbao) – the Universal Lord of Numinous Treasure who produced Yin and Yang; and iii) the Celestial Worthies (Tianzun) – the most personified manifestations of Tao and Virtues. The Japanese Sun goddess *Amaterasu*, one of the principal Shinto deities (*kami*), is the ruler of the Higher Celestial Plain. Also, in sending her grandson named Jimmu, she is directly linked in lineage to the Imperial Household of Japan and the Emperor, who are considered descendants of the *kami* themselves. See Bulcsu Siklos, "Philosophical and Religious Taoism," in *The Religions of Asia*, ed. Friedhelm Hardy (London: Routledge, 1990), 14-19; Stephen F. Teiser, "Religion of China in Practice," in *Asian Religions in Practice*, ed. Donald S. Lopez Jr. (Princeton, NJ: Princeton University Press, 1999), 92-97; Joseph M. Kitagawa, *Religion in Japanese History* (New York: Columbia University Press, 1966), 7-8.

Hanŭl, meaning "sky" or "heaven," and the honorific suffix *nim*. Due to palatalization, *Hanŭlnim* is usually pronounced *Haneunim*. Historically, the worship of *Haneunim* is taken from the Dangun myth.[2] Dangun, the founding father of the Korean nation, performed a sacrificial rite for *Haneunim* on the high altar in Kangwha.[3] Heaven became the object of worship to the ancient Koreans because their economic activities such as sowing and harvesting were dependent on the sky. They also feared natural phenomena such as lightning, thunder, and other natural disasters. The more they feared nature, the more they came to worship the sky.

Traditionally, Koreans worshipped a supreme god in heaven. The ancient Koreans believed that *Haneunim* controlled nature, including the blessings and calamities of human life. Most rituals were performed for *Haneunim*, according to the agricultural cycle.[4]

Although there were other names for nature gods in Shamanism, ancient Koreans believed in a hierarchical structure in the spiritual world where all other nature gods and spiritual beings were controlled by the supreme god. In other words, there was a monotheistic element within Shamanism. This concept of hierarchic polytheism contributed to the contextualization of Christian angelology in the Korean context.

It is important to examine how the name of a shamanistic god, *Haneunim*, became the name adopted by Protestants for God, *Hananim*.

---

[2]The summary of the Dangun myth is that Hwanin or Hawaneen, the grandfather of Dangun, had a son named Hwanung who had a desire to live on the earth. Hwanin gave Hwanung the power to rule over the earth and allowed him to descend onto Baekdu Mountain, the highest mountain in Korea, along with 3,000 spiritual beings who controlled the rain, the clouds, the wind and other natural phenomena. A tiger and a bear prayed to Hwanung in order to become human. As Hwanung heard their prayers, he decided to give them a chance to become human beings. In order to test them, Hwanung gave them 20 cloves of garlic and a bundle of mugwort to eat, and let them pray for 21 days to become human beings. Soon, the tiger gave up but the bear persisted and became a woman. However, the bear-woman was alone and lonely. She prayed to Hwanung for a child under 신단수(神檀樹), the divine tree. Hwanung heard her prayer and took her as his wife. She gave a birth to Dangun, and he became the founder and first king of Korea, according to the Dangun myth. Dangun has both deity and humanity, and powers to control all nature. See Zong In Sob, *Folk Tales from Korea* (Seoul: Hollym Cor., 1970), 3-4; Jung Young Lee, "Concerning the Origin and Formation of Korean Shamanism," *Numen* 20 (August 1973): 149-150.

[3]David Kwang Sun Suh, *The Korean Minjung in Christ* (Hong Kong: The Christian Conference of Asia, 1991), 112-113.

[4]James Huntley Grayson, *Korea: A Religious History* (New York: Routledge Curzon, 2002), 19.

Linguistically, *Hananim* means "one supreme being," rather than "a heavenly god." Early Korean Christians often substituted *Haneunim* with *Sangje* (Jade emperor), *Chonju* (the lord of heaven), or *Hananim*.⁵ The term *Sangje* was not accepted as the name of God by the Vatican because the deity of *Sangje* was not considered sufficient to represent the character of Jehovah. Korean Catholics preferred the term *Sangju* (the ruler of heaven) or *Chonju*. In 1789, *Chonju* was used by Chong Yak Chon in his book, *Ship Kyemyong Ka* (Song of the Ten Commandments), as the Korean name of God.⁶ *Chonju* was accepted and used by Catholics and Anglicans in the formative era of Korean Christianity.

Both *Haneunim* and *Hananim* mean the sky god, but there is a small difference in their interpretation. *Haneunim* means the Lord of Heaven while *Hananim* is more accurately translated as one god. *Haneunim* is more popular among both Roman Catholics and Protestants influenced by progressive theology: they believe that *Haneunim* has been used as the name of Korea's god throughout Korean history and is sufficient to represent the God of Christians. Homer B. Hulbert, an American missionary linguist, simply translated *Haneunim* as the "Lord of Heaven."⁷

Protestants prefer using *Hananim* because of the monotheistic characteristic of the name.⁸ *Hananim* means "one supreme being" and its divine nature and character are similar to the Hebrew God of the Old Testament.⁹ Andrew E. Kim insists that "the power of *Hananim* is considered absolute: he is almighty, omnipotent, and omniscient."¹⁰ Until missionaries pointed it out, Koreans neither recognized the monotheism associated with the name nor comprehended the theological

---

⁵Charles Dallet, *Histoire de l'église de Corée* (Paris: Victor Palme, 1874), trans. Eung Ryel An and Suk Woo Choi, *Hankook CheonJu GyoHoisa* [The history of Korean Catholicism] vol. 1 (Seoul: Hankook GyoHoiSa YeonGooSo, 2000), 210.

⁶Don Baker, "*Hananim, Hanunim, Hanullim,* and *Hannolim*: the Construction of Terminology for Korean Monotheism," *The Review of Korean Studies* 5, no. 1: 116-17.

⁷Homer B. Hulbert, *The Passing of Korea* (New York: Doubleday, Page & Company, 1906), 404.

⁸Baker, "*Hananim, Hanunim, Hanullim,* and *Hannolim*," 119.

⁹Andrew E. Kim, "Korean Religious Culture and its Affinity to Christianity: The Rise of Protestant Christianity in South Korea," *Sociology of Religion* 61, no. 2 (2000): 123.

¹⁰Ibid., 121.

distinction between the deities of *Haneunim* and *Hananim*.[11] When Gale published the first Korean-English dictionary in 1897, he translated *Hananim* as "the King of Heaven" rather than "the One Supreme Being" without making a distinction between *Haneunim* and *Hananim*, because Koreans often used *Hananim* and *Haneunim* interchangeably.[12]

Early missionaries were deeply concerned about whether the names of these heathen deities should be applied to the Christian God and whether this might be considered a blasphemous act against the name of God. They found that when they explained the character of God by using the name *Hananim*, Koreans were able to understand more easily.[13]

Underwood concluded that not using the term *Hananim* for the name of God was an error because it not only clearly described the only and great One, but it was also the name of an indigenous god who had been worshipped by Koreans for generations, just as the Jews worshipped the God of the Old Testament.[14] Gale was amazed that Koreans had an indigenous god with similar characteristics to the Christian God. He wrote, "The Korean talks of God. He is *Hananim* the one Great One."[15] Afterward, *Hananim* became accepted as the name of God in the Korean language by most Presbyterian and Methodist missionaries.[16]

In September 1939, the Korean Presbyterian Council decided to use *Hananim* as the official name of God in all its publications.[17] In terms of contextualization, using *Hananim* as the Korean name for God was significant. Using *Hananim* meant that God was no longer a foreign deity imported from the West to Korea. Koreans were able to recognize God as the one who has been part of their lives throughout history. It also helped Koreans understand the monotheistic nature of God within their polytheistic religious traditions.

---

[11] Baker, "*Hananim, Hanunim, Hanullim,* and *Hannolim,*" 115.
[12] James S. Gale, *A Korean-English Dictionary* (Yokohama: Kelly & Walsh Ltd., 1897), 118.
[13] Underwood, *Fifteen Years*, 104.
[14] Baker, "*Hananim, Hanunim, Hanullim,* and *Hannolim,*" 120.
[15] Gale, *Korea in Transition*, 78.
[16] Underwood, *Fifteen Years*, 105.
[17] This decision was made during the 28th general meeting of the Korean Presbyterian Council (September 8-15, 1939), available from http://www.kmpnh.com /chonghye26-30.htm, accessed November 17, 2012.

2. *Joeushin Hananim* (Good God): the God of Korean Pentecostals

As noted, Pentecostal preachers focused on repentance during the Korean revivals. They most often used passages from the Old Testament in their sermons. They asked Korean Christians to strictly adhere to the Ten Commandments and focused on sin, the judgment of God, and the need for repentance in order to obtain eternal life. Due to their eschatological emphasis, God became the righteous God who will punish Koreans unless they repent of their sins. *Hananim* was contextualized as the fearsome God.

The eschatological view of early Pentecostals was dualistic, focusing on either redemption or judgment. Due to their imminent eschatology, early Pentecostals regarded *Hananim* as a fearsome God who dispenses judgment. They conceived of hope for the life to come, not for divine blessings in this life. Salvation was not extended to other dimensions such as redemption from poverty, political oppression, or sickness.

The end of the Korean War brought a prominent shift in the Pentecostal understanding of God. They added an adjective in front of *Hananim* and began to refer to God as *Joeushin Hananim* instead of *Hananim*. *Joeushin* means good. Thus, *Joeushin Hananim* means the good God. Korean Pentecostals attempted to change the character of *Hananim* from the fearsome God to the good God.

The use of *Joeushin Hananim* reflects a three-part transition in the Pentecostal understanding. First, God is perceived not as a fearsome God but as one who wants to give unlimited blessings to His people. For early Pentecostals, the fearsome God was not the giver of blessings but rather the God who punishes sin and would take away their belongings if they did not keep His commandments. Natural disasters, misfortunes, and diseases were God's punishments for their sins or unfaithful acts. This belief stemmed from the combination of a shamanic understanding about God and a misunderstanding of the God of the Old Testament by Pentecostal preachers.

In contrast, the later use of *Joeushin Hananim* reflects Pentecostals' discovery of the good God, who willingly takes care of their difficulties and dispenses blessings. Harvey Cox says that the "Pentecostals' God is more lover than judge, more concerned with human affection than with commanding obedience."[18]

Second, the use of the name was an indication of the change in the attitude of Korean Pentecostals towards prosperity. The use of the name *Joeushin Hananim* reflects their belief in the generosity of God, and also their expectation of receiving blessings from God in this earthly life.

Korean Christians believed that good Christians should not be prosperous because of three historical influences. The first was the influence of indigenous religion. Their bias against the "good life" was based on the ascetic lifestyle of Buddhist monks. They believed that "if one desires spiritual comfort, one has to suffer in the flesh."[19]

The second influence was cultural. Honorable poverty was accepted as the highest value in Korean Confucian society. It was almost impossible to become rich. Korean society was dominated by poverty, except for those who obtained wealth through corrupt means. Traditionally, Confucian scholars pursued the life of honorable poverty rather than a life of prosperity. Similarly, among early Pentecostals, Yong Do Lee practiced honorable poverty until he died.

The third factor was the impact of missionaries who were influenced by the North American holiness movement. Although their teachings were not directly opposed to prosperity, they did not focus on this-world prosperity. They believed material things had little value and would eventually pass away. Thus, they had little interest in temporal matters; they focused on eternal life. With these influences, Christians, including early Pentecostals, believed that material prosperity should not be pursued.

For contemporary Korean Pentecostals, *Joeushin Hananim* is not the God who rebukes and punishes people but the one who dispenses blessings to His people. [20] Pentecostals cognitively altered their understanding of God as they changed their conceptions about material blessings, the earthly life in God, and divine intervention in human life. They do not dualistically separate earthly and eternal life. In terms of

---

[18] Cox, *Fire from Heaven*, 201.
[19] Yoo, *Korean Pentecostalism*, 113.
[20] Gook Jae Shin Hak Yeon Goo Won [International Theological Institute], *Yoido SoonBokEum Gyo Hoi Ui Shin Ang Gwah Shin Hak* II [The Theology and Faith of Yoido Full Gospel Church] (Seoul: Seoul Seo Jeok, 1993), 98-99.

blessing, the earthly life is regarded as the precursor of eternal life. Well-being on earth is as important as eternal life for the soul.[21] One of their prominent prayers is to receive material blessings along with salvation and physical health.[22]

For early Korean Pentecostals, diseases and poverty were generally accepted as one's destiny, regardless of salvation. It did not matter how difficult one's life was as long as one could obtain eternal life. They were even willing to sacrifice their earthly life for the sake of eternal life. However, contemporary Korean Pentecostals regard diseases and poverty as caused by the devil, sin, and the curse.[23] They do not simply accept poverty and diseases as difficulties in life. Both the cause and the solution of poverty and diseases are spiritual.

The solution to these problems is associated with Christ's atonement. Christ was crucified on the cross not only to save souls, but also to break the curses of poverty and disease. They base their expectations on scriptures such as 2 Corinthians 8:9; Isaiah 53: 4-5; 1 Peter 2:24; Matthew 8:16-17; and Mark 16:17. Through the death and resurrection of Christ, they are set free from demonic curses. They have acquired the right to prosperity and well-being.[24] Their major hope no longer rests solely on a future eternal life but extends to blessings in this life. Their ultimate hope for eternal life has not changed, but they focus on living the good life in Christ on earth after receiving spiritual salvation.

Early Korean Pentecostals professed that God was concerned about their souls. Yet modern Korean Pentecostals believe that *Joeushin Hananim* is the God who intervenes in the difficulties of their lives. He is not only the judge on the throne who they will see at the Final Judgment; he is their Provider (*Jehova-jireh* – Exodus 13:13-14) and their Healer (*Jehova-raphah* – Psalm 103:1-3; Exodus 15:26) who will meet their daily needs.[25] God is not the Supreme One who not only reigns

---

[21]Kim, *History and Theology of Korean Pentecostalism*, 204-209.
[22]Yonggi Cho, *Salvation, Health and Prosperity* (Altamonte Springs, FL: Creation House, 1987), 11.
[23]Yonggi Cho, *Oh Jung Bok Eum Kwa Sam Jung Chuk Bok* [Fivefold Gospel and Threefold Blessing] (Seoul: Seoul Mal Sseum Sa, 2002), 145.
[24]Yonggi Cho, *Soon Bok Eum Ui Jin Ri* [The Truth of Full Gospel] *I* (Seoul: Young San Chul Pan Sa, 1979), 166-74; Yonggi Cho, *Oh Jung Bok Eum Kwa Sam Jung Chuk Bok*, 173-192.
[25]Cho, *Soon Bok Eum Ui Jin Ri* [The Truth of Full Gospel] I, 72-3.

over the eternal life after death but the One who reigns over the earthly life and cares for us on the earth.

This idea of a good God raises the existential question of why such a God ignores the sufferings of his people. Hope for the Kingdom in the "here and now" is also interwoven with contemporary matters and faith that the good God will intervene. Another question is how the good God can intervene in the suffering of his people. The Threefold Blessing is based on this expectation that the unmerited goodness of God will fulfill the needs of Koreans for both eternal and earthly life. God's goodness provides earthly blessings, but also offers salvation to those who are under eternal condemnation.[26] Pentecostals are convinced that the good God will intervene in their hardships by dispensing blessings such as prosperity for those suffering poverty and healing for those experiencing sickness.

Thus, the Korean Pentecostal understanding of God as *Joeushin Hananim* forms the basis for the hope contained in the Threefold Blessing. Rodrigo Tano says that the "message of the Threefold Blessing and the Fivefold Gospel is nothing less than an exposition and practical application of the Bible truth that God is good and His goodness meets the needs of human beings and fulfills their aspiration for the good, successful and abundant life." [27] Bae agrees that the theological foundation of Cho's Threefold Blessing is based on the theology of a good God, and "hope is a promise of blessing from a good God."[28] In his sermons, Cho often quotes Hebrews 13:8: "Jesus Christ is the same yesterday and today and forever" to emphasize that the "good God is not only the God of yesterday but also the God of now and here" who wants to bless his people.[29]

---

[26] L. Berkhof, *Systematic Theology* (London: The Banner of Truth Trust, First Edition, 1958; Reprinted 1960; 1963), 71.

[27] Rodrigo D. Tano, "Dr. Yonggi Cho's Theology of a Good God," in *Dr. Yonggi Cho's Ministry and Theology I*, ed. Young San Theological Institute (Gunpo: Hansei University Logos, 2008), 24.

[28] Hyeon Sung Bae, "Understanding Youngsan's Theological Horizon and Hope," in *2004 Young San International Theological Symposium*, ed. Hansei University Press (Gunpo: Hansei University Press, 2002), 211, 214.

[29] Lee, "Influence of Dr. Cho's God is so good-faith in the Korean Churches," 72.

CHAPTER 11
MINJUNG AND *HAN*: THE PEOPLE OF GOD IN SUFFERING

From the 1970s onward, the Pentecostal revival spread nationwide and developed into an interdenominational Holy Spirit movement.[1] Two important events were the Billy Graham Crusade held in 1973 and EXPLO '74 (August 13-18, 1974). EXPLO '74 was a mammoth training conference aimed at training 300,000 Christians. On the first night, 1.3 million people gathered in Yoido Plaza in front of the YFGC, and seventy percent of participants received salvation by faith.[2] In 1974, there were about three million Christians in Korea; four years later the Christian population had reached up to seven million. Statistically, in 1978, six new churches were started every day.[3] This remarkable church growth raises several questions. First, why did people come to church? Second, what type of people came to church? Third, why were they enthusiastic about Pentecostalism?

To answer these questions, it is necessary to understand the meaning of both *Minjung* (the mass of people)[4] and the *Han*[5] of *Minjung* (the perceived suffering of the people). *Minjung* refers to the group of people in Korea who have experienced substantial *Han* over generations. Regarding the relationship between *Minjung* and *Han*, David Kwang

---

[1] Lee, *The Holy Spirit Movement in Korea*, 83-85.
[2] Joon Gon Kim, "Korea's Total Evangelization Movement," in *Korean Church Growth Explosion: Centennial of the Protestant Church (1884-1984)*, ed. Ro Bong Rin and Marlin L. Nelson (Seoul: Word of Life Press and Asia Theological Association, 1983), 26-28.
[3] Lee, *The Holy Spirit Movement in Korea*, 84.
[4] *Minjung* combines two Chinese characters which are *Min* and *Jung*. *Min* means "people" and *Jung* can be translated as "the mass" in English. So the literal meaning of *Minjung* is "the mass of the people." However, *Minjung* has been used not just a massive group of people but as a socio-political terminology. In Korean Christian theology, *Minjung* is also considered as a group of people who need theological and pastoral intentions because they are politically oppressed, despised culturally, sociologically marginalized, and economically exploited.
[5] *Han* is a feeling of unsolved resentment accumulated for various reasons such as sexual, racial, social and political inequality and injustices, severe poverty, sufferings from diseases, and so on over a long time.

Sun Suh states that "the *Minjung* live with *han*, they accumulate *han*, and they die with *han*."⁶

Without dealing with *Minjung* and the issue of *Han*, no religious or social movement can be successful in Korea. To receive the support of the Korean people, Pentecostals needed to understand *Minjung* and the *Han* of *Minjung*. To contextualize, Pentecostalism had to appeal to the *Minjung* and address issues related to their experience of *Han*. *Minjung* Theology developed as a theological movement and became the dominant contextual theology of Korea because it was deeply rooted in matters related to *Minjung* and their *Han*. One of reasons that Korean Pentecostalism has its own religious characters and different ways of expressions from other Pentecostalisms in the world is that it is also profoundly interrelated with the nationalistic emotion, *Minjung* and their *Han*. It is one of factors how Threefold Blessing could be effectively contextualized into the Korean context.

1. *Minjung*: ὄχλος (*ochlos*) and λαός (laos)

Minjung literally means "the mass of people" or "the masses" or "a group of ordinary people."⁷ However, it has deeper meanings. It has commonly been used by Korean socialists, nationalists, and even liberal theologians and progressive Christians. *Minjung* theologians do not want to translate *Minjung* as "a group of ordinary people" for three reasons. First, the word "mass of people" is inadequate for their theological intentions. Their concern is not the whole people of Korea but a certain group of people who have been marginalized socially, politically, and economically. The second reason is the political implication of the word. As the term "the people" became part of the vocabulary of communists, nationalists, and socialists, the word itself came to have political implications.

---

⁶David Kwang Sun Suh, "Liberating Spirituality in the Korean *Minjung* Tradition: Shamanism and *Minjung* Liberation," in *Asian Christian Spirituality: Reclaiming Traditions*, ed. Virginia Fabella, Peter K. H. Lee and David Kwang Sun Suh (Maryknoll, NY: Orbis Books, 1992), 33.

⁷David Kwan Sun Suh, "A Biographical Sketch of an Asian Theological Consultation," in *Minjung Theology: People as the Subjects of History*, ed. Yong Bock Kim, 17.

During the Cold War era, *Minjung* theologians intentionally avoided using the term "the people" for reasons of political security. Instead, they decided to use "the people of God" as the translation of *Minjung*.[8] However, "the people of God" does not mean "the children of God" used in the general sense in Christianity. To *Minjung* theologians, "the people of God" refers to those who have suffered for a long time under difficult conditions of poverty, political oppression, violations of human rights, and injustice. Ahn Byung Mu (1922-1996), the founder of *Minjung* theology, distinguishes the Greek term οχλος (*ochlos*) from λαός (*laos*) as follows:

The term *ochlos* is used more often than *laos*. It [*ochlos*] occurs 174 times while the term *laos* occurs 141 times [in the New Testament] . . . quite often *laos* and *ochlos* are used inter-changeably and carry the same meaning as *ochlos* in Mark. . . . Luke, however, seems to prefer the term *laos* for Israelites, though understood on the same lines as *ochlos* in Mark. . . . the *laos* is in a situation of confrontation with those in power. This is similar to the use of *ochlos* in Mark. However, sometimes, Luke takes the *laos* and the ruling class together. . . . Besides this use of *laos* in Luke, other uses of this word in the New Testament are by and large in quotations from or allusions to the Old Testament and in the language of the rulers. References to Israel as the people of God also have *laos*.[9]

According to Ahn, Mark uses the term *laos* only twice in Mark 7:6 and 14:2 to quote scriptures from the Old Testament. Apart from these two verses, Mark intentionally uses the word *ochlos* to describe a group of people 36 times.[10] Ahn insists that Jesus of Galilee can only be found with the *ochlos*. At the same time, *ochlos* cannot be considered apart from Jesus in the four Gospels, especially in the synoptics. The *ochlos* of Jesus were the tax collectors and sinners (Mark 2:16), the flock of sheep without a shepherd (Mark 6:34), and the multitude in the wilderness without food whom Jesus fed (Mark 6:35-44).[11] Therefore,

---

[8]Ibid., 17.

[9]Byeong Mu Ahn, "Jesus and the *Minjung* in the Gospel of Mark," in *Minjung Theology: People as the Subjects of History*, ed. Yong Bock Kim, 148.

[10]Comparing with the other synoptic Gospels, *ochlos* is used 51 times and *laos* 13 times in the book of Matthew; in Luke's Gospel, *laos* is used 35 times and *ochlos* 40 times. Ahn insists that both Matthew and Luke were influenced by Mark. See Byeong Mu Ahn, *Galilea ui Yesoo* [Jesus of Galilee] (Seoul: Hankook Sinhak Yeongooso, 2008), 137.

[11]Ahn, *Galilea ui Yesoo* [Jesus of Galilee], 136-143.

Ahn recognizes *Minjung*, the people of Korea, as *ochlos* who were living under dictatorship and suffering from poverty.[12] To him, *Minjung* is not the people who became the children of God following repentance in the general Christian sense, but the people marginalized from socio-economic and political affairs.[13] Thus, factory workers working like a machine in underprivileged conditions for low wages, the urban poor, and women experiencing sexual segregation over a long period of time in Confucian society became the *Minjung*, ὄχλος (*ochlos*), of *Minjung* Theology. In this sense, socially and economically stable persons interested in Christianity and ordinary people without any interest in socio-political matters could not be the *Minjung* of *Minjung* Theology.

This raises a number of questions. Did Jesus bless and welcome only the economically poor or those marginalized socially and politically? Did he discriminate against the rich and those in positions of authority? Who were the *Minjung* of Jesus? They were the people who surrounded him at the Sea of Galilee, those he healed, the ones he fed with the five loaves and two fishes (Matthew 14:13-21; Mark 6:30-44; Luke 9:10-17; John 6:1-14), and those who cried out "Hosanna! Blessed is He who comes in the name of the Lord" as he entered Jerusalem (Matthew 21:9; Mark. 11:9; Luke 19:38; John 12:13). They were the people who cried out, "Crucify Him!" (Matthew 27:23; Mark 15:11-13; Luke 23:21; John 19:15), for whom he was crucified.

But what about Jairus, a ruler of the synagogue who asked Jesus to heal his daughter (Matthew 9:18-26; Mark. 5:21-24; Luke 8:40-56)? What about the centurion who came to Jesus, asking him to heal his servant (Matthew 8:5-13; Luke 7:1-10; John 4:43-54)?

With its dualistic understanding of the relationship between the oppressed and the oppressor and the wronged and the wrongdoer, the oppressed and the wronged are considered the *Minjung* of *Minjung* Theology. However, the *Minjung* of Pentecostalism include not only the oppressed and the wronged but also the wrongdoer and the oppressor who seek salvation, such as Nicodemus, a ruler of Jews, who came to

---

[12]Ahn, "Jesus and the *Minjung* in the Gospel of Mark," 150.
[13]Byeong Mu Ahn, "*Minjock, Minjung, Gyohoi* [Nation, People, and Church]," in Hankook Gidockgyo Gyohoihyubuihoi, *Hankook Yoeksa Sokui Gidokgyo* [Christianity in Korean History] (Seoul: Giminsa, 1985), 215.

Jesus at night (John 3:1-21). Se Yoon Kim argues that "Ahn's identification of the *ochlos* as the *Minjung* is quite arbitrary" because tax collectors who were the enemies of the *Minjung* were also welcomed to Christ. Jesus says that "whoever does the will of God is my brother, and sister and mother" (Mark 3:35).[14]

The *Minjung* with Jesus in Tiberias was a group who were seeking the Kingdom of God rather than political freedom. Jesus fed the hungry, healed the sick, and gave them hope for the Kingdom of God. Whereas the *Minjung* of *Minjung* Theology is οχλος (*ochlos*), for Jesus, the *Minjung* was closer to λαός (*laos*), the people of God, who were not only poor, sick, and neglected from a socio-political perspective, but also were longing for salvation.

In the post-Korean war context, the *Minjung* of Pentecostalism was not οχλος (*ochlos*) but rather λαός (*laos*)—ordinary Koreans struggling to obtain food for survival and suffering from the aftermath of the war. During the war, most people suffered the loss of loved ones and property. There was no hope for them.

During the transition period of rapid economic growth (1960s-1980s), Korean citizens were exploited by capitalists and suppressed by political dictatorship. Students, workers, intellectuals, journalists, and even pastors fought for human rights, freedom of speech, freedom of the press, and laborers' rights and interests. Many were arrested and tortured in prison. In these circumstances, *Minjung* theologians and churches recognized that their mission was to emancipate the people and Korean society from military dictatorship through Christ.[15]

The majority of Korean Christians remained politically acquiescent.[16] Pentecostals were also politically inactive. However, they offered Pentecostal hope to their *Minjung* with their theology of the Threefold Blessing, based on 3 John 2. The Threefold Blessing was effectively contextualized into Korean society because it provided the only real hope for the *Minjung*. Moltmann refers to the YFGC as a

---

[14]Se Yoon Kim, "Is *Minjung* Theology a Christian Theology?" *Calvin Theological Journal* 22, no. 2 (1987): 251-274.

[15]Seon Kwang Seo, *Hankook Gydokgyo Jeongchishinhak ui Jeon Gae* [the Development of Korean Christian Political Theology] (Seoul: Yewha Yeoja Dae Hak Chulpanboo, 1996), 81.

[16]Hwa Yung, *Mangoes or Bananas? The Quest for an Authentic Asian Christian Theology* (Oxford: Regnum, 1997), 180-181.

genuine *Minjung* church because seventy percent of church members are from the lower middle class.[17]

2. *Han* and Korean Pentecostalism

Han is both an individual and a collective emotion. *Han* can be understood as a person's feeling of suffering. Andrew Sung Park defines *Han* as "frustrated hope," "the collapsed feeling of pain," "letting go," "resentful bitterness," and "the wounded heart."[18] His definition of *Han* is inadequate to fully cover its meaning.

Han is produced in two ways. First, it forms from personal problems such as personal disease, poverty, and spiritual problems that cannot be solved over a long period of time. Second, it has external elements such as national poverty, social injustice, capitalist exploitation, and other socio-political matters. Accumulating *Han* is related to the recognition of one's inability to cope with continuous sufferings caused by these internal and external elements.

Hans are developed through human limitations in the face of socio-political ills and personal difficulties which people cannot overcome by themselves.[19] To understand *Han* from a Western perspective, imagine the bitterness of a bridegroom whose bride is violated by his lord due to the right of the first night (*Droit de seigneur*, in French).

Korean females suffered for generations from male chauvinism. Until at least the early twentieth century, the primary task of a wife was to give birth to a boy. If she failed to produce a son to continue the family line, she might be discarded by her husband or have to allow her husband to have a concubine or a surrogate mother. Her frustration becomes *Han*. Parents shedding bitter tears for children who are dying of disease or hunger will develop indelible *Han*.

---

[17]Mokhoi wha Sinhak, "Interview with Yonggi Cho (1 September 2009)," in *Mokhoi wha Sinhak* [Ministry and Theology] (October 2009), 28-35.

[18]Andrew Sung Park, *The Wounded Heart of God: The Asian Concept of Han and the Christian Doctrine of Sin* (Nashville: Abingdon Press, 1993), 15-20.

[19]Yvonne Young Ja Lee, "Religion, Culture of *Han* and *Hanpuri*, and Korean *Minjung* Women: An Interdisciplinary Post-colonial Religio-cultural Analysis of the Indigenous Encounter with the Colonial Religions in Korea," (PhD dissertation, The University of Denver, 1999), 42.

Minjung theologians believe that *Han* is formed mostly by unequal social structures or political oppression. Antagonism and inequality within society is the basis of *Han*: the opposition between the rich and the poor, the wrongdoer and the wronged, and the oppressor and the oppressed. They emphasize collective *Han* in unjust political or economic structures rather than individual *Han* in the lives of ordinary people. David Kwang Sun Suh states,

The feeling of *han*, however, is not just an individual feeling of repression. It is not just a sickness that can be cured by drugs or by psychotherapy. It is a collective feeling of the oppressed. This sickness of *han* can be cured only when the total structure of the oppressed society and culture is changed.[20]

There are two kinds of *Han*. In the inactive mode of *Han*, people usually accept unfortunate things that happen in their lives as their fate. When they experience misfortunes, they abandon themselves to despair and wish those occurrences to pass quickly. The active *Han* manifests in aggressive ways such as personal revenge against the oppressor and the wrongdoer. *Han* is also revealed in collective acts such as the Donghak Revolution in 1894 against the feudal system, the March First Movement in 1919 against Japanese imperialism, and the April 19th Revolution in 1960 against the autocratic reign of Syngman Rhee.

Minjung theologians regard *Han* as socio-political rather than personal and believe that it cannot be solved without a change in society and culture. In contrast, Korean Pentecostals are not primarily concerned with the *Han*s produced by economic and political conflicts within society. Pentecostalism is more concerned with individual *Han*. Not only the poor, the wronged, and the oppressed have *Han*, but also the rich, the wrongdoer, and the oppressor. Pentecostals do not believe that the *Han* of *Minjung* can be released through a social movement or a revolution. Instead, the *Han* of *Minjung* will only be resolved by blessings from God.[21]

The *Han* addressed by Pentecostals is diametrically opposed to the Threefold Blessing. Examples include the *Han* of the sick, like the *Han*

---

[20] Suh, *The Korean Minjung in Christ*, 50.
[21] Young Hoon Lee, "The Life and Ministry of David Yonggi Cho and the Yoido Full Gospel Church," in *David Yonggi Cho: A Close Look at His Theology and Ministry*, ed. Wonsuk Ma, William W. Menzies, and Hyeon Sung Bae (Baguio City, Philippines: APTS Press and Gunpo), 21.

of the woman with the twelve-year flow of blood, who spent all her property on physicians but was not cured (Matthew 9:18-26; Mark 5:21-43; Luke 8:40-48); the *Han* of mourners, like the *Han* of the widow who followed the crowd carrying the dead body of her only son (Luke 7:11-17); spiritual *Han*, like the *Han* of Zacchaeus, a chief tax collector, who was rich but still had unresolved spiritual issues (Luke 19:1-10); and the *Han* of Koreans struggling with absolute poverty after the Korean War.

The Threefold Blessing was important for ordinary Koreans regardless of socio-political class in the post-war context. Comparing his own life with that of Cho, Moltmann states that "Pastor Cho began his mission in the *Han* of the Korean people after the Korean War; I began my life in Christ in the *Han* of the Second World War and in the ruins of post-war Germany."[22] Young Hoon Lee says that "Cho, with his belief in a good and sovereign God, presented fresh hope to despairing people. He proclaimed God as the One who solves han *[sic]* in the present and declared a future life."[23]

Cho himself is also the subject of *Han*. He suffered from tuberculosis and extreme poverty for a long time. Cho found hope in the biblical text of 3 John 2, which enabled him to release the *Han*s of Koreans. He subsequently developed the theology of the Threefold Blessing based on this text. According to Dong Soo Kim, the message of the Threefold Blessings ("hopes" of Korean Pentecostalism) helped *Minjung* to escape from their *Han*s.[24] The Threefold Blessing was the theological and contextual hope for Koreans in the post-Korean War context.

3. The Weary and Burdened

After the Korean War, all infrastructures were destroyed and national functions were paralyzed. Korean society, culture, politics, and the economy collapsed. Most Koreans were overwhelmed by the heavy burdens of life. The poor became poorer. Unable to afford medical treatment for simple diseases, their physical conditions deteriorated.

---

[22] Moltmann, "The Blessing of Hope,"149.
[23] Lee, "The Life and Ministry of David Yonggi Cho," 21.
[24] Dong Soo Kim, "The Healing of *Han* in Korean Pentecostalism," *Journal of Pentecostal Theology* 15 (1999): 133.

Politically, after the coup d'état on May 16, 1961, the military government infringed on human rights and controlled freedom of speech.

Under these socio-economic and political circumstances, Koreans had no hope for the present or for the future. They could be considered among the weary and burdened as those in Matthew 11:28. Yet they found hope in the message of the Threefold Blessing and began to attend Pentecostal churches.

In 1952 after the Korean War, eight Pentecostal churches remained: Namboo church (Rev. Hong Huh) in Seoul, Soon Chun church (Evangelist Guei Im Park) in Jeon Nam province, Boollodong church (Evangelist Guei Im Park) in Kwang Joo, Busan church (Rev. Sugn San Park) in Busan, Mockpho church (Rev. Sung Hwan Kim) in Mock Pho, Jinweol church (Rev. Sung Duck Yoon) in Kwang Joo, Geujae church (Rev. Gil Yoon Kim) in Geoje Island, and Daegu church (Rev. Doo Yeon Kim) in Daegu.[25]

In 1958, Yonggi Cho and Jashil Choi (1915-1989), Cho's future mother-in-law, began a small tent meeting in Dae Jo Dong, a slum area of Seoul. The church building was made of used U.S. military tents, and the church consisted of five members: Cho, Choi and Choi's three children.[26] By 1993, this church, called the YFGC today, had become the largest Christian church in the world with 700,000 members and 700 full-time pastors.[27]

Like the YFGC, other Pentecostal churches also started on the outskirts of the city among the urban poor. Korean Pentecostalism began and developed among the poor and the sick, on the outskirts of the city. It flourished for two reasons. First, the central part of the city was already occupied by other denominations, including Presbyterians and Methodists. These denominations focused on medical and educational missions in the city, so their national expansion was largely based on their Christian schools and hospitals in urban areas. In contrast, Pentecostal ministries and messages, with their focus on healing and

---

[25]Gook Jae Shin Hak Yeon Goo Won [International Theological Institute], *Hananim euy Sunghoi GyoHoiSa* [Church History of Assemblies of God] (Seoul: Seoul Mal Sseum Sa, 1998), 214.

[26]Anderson, *An Introduction to Pentecostalism*, 137.

[27]Ibid., 138.

blessings, were more effective among the poor and the sick than among the rich or those with vested interests in Korean society.

In the early years, most Pentecostal church members were extremely poor.[28] Later, tens of thousand people came to the Pentecostal and charismatic churches regardless of their socio-political backgrounds. In 1969, there were 39,790 Korean Pentecostals. By 1982, this increased to 746,489. In terms of membership, Pentecostalism increased by 1,876 percent from 1969-1982. During this time, other denominations also grew significantly, but not as much as Pentecostalism.[29]

Table 2
The Rate of Korean Churches' Growth (1969 ~ 1982)[30]

Denominations	1969	1982	Growth Rate
Holiness Church	217,289	463,900	213 %
Salvation Army	40,604	90,700	223 %
Methodism	300,109	885,650	295 %
Presbyterianism	1,415,436	4,302,950	304 %
The Baptist	64,191	315,650	492 %
Pentecostalism (excluding YFGC)	30,790	491,100	1,595 %
YFGC alone	9,000	255,389	2,838 %

In 1999, of the fifteen largest mega-churches in Korea with more than 10,000 adult members, nine were Pentecostal or charismatic.[31] The

---

[28] Anderson, "The Contextual Pentecostal Theology of David Yonggi Cho," 115.

[29] Gook Jae Shin Hak Yeon Goo Won [International Theological Institute], *Yoido SoonBokEum Gyo Hoi Ui Shin Ang Gwah Shin Hak* [The Theology and Faith of Yoido Full Gospel Church] *II*, 110.

[30] There are computational errors on the rate of denominational churches' growth in the book, Gook Jae Shin Hak Yeon Goo Won [International Theological Institute], *Yoido SoonBokEum Gyo Hoi Ui Shin Ang Gwah Shin Hak* [The Theology and Faith of Yoido Full Gospel Church] *II*, 110. The rates of church growth must be corrected: 79% (Holiness Church) to 213%; 86% (Salvation Army) to 223%; 130% (Methodism) to 295%; 135% (Presbyterianism) to 304%; 240% (Baptists) to 492%; 742% (Pentecostalism) to 1,595%. The numbers were rounded off to one decimal place.

[31] Young Gi Hong, "The Backgrounds and Characteristics of the Charismatic Mega-Churches in Korea," *Asian Journal of Pentecostal Studies* 3, no. 1 (2004): 100-102.

explosive growth of the Korean Church was led by the Pentecostal/charismatic movement. In 1979, Yonggi Cho stated,

> Since 1970 I started praying, "Father, give us one thousand members per month." At first God gave 600, then He began to give more than 1,000 per month. Last year, we received more than 12,000 members in our church. I lifted my goal higher this year, and we are now going to have 15,000 additional members; next year I can easily ask for 20,000.[32]

What attracted this massive influx of people into the Pentecostal churches? The weary and burdened people of Korea discovered hope for the present and the future in Pentecostalism. Through the message of the Threefold Blessing, they found hope for eternal life, as well as for prosperity and healing in the present.

4. A Release from *Han* Through a Hunger for the Holy Spirit

Three remarkable crusades took place between 1973 and 1980. The first was the Billy Graham Crusade (May 30-June 3, 1973). During these five nights, millions of people gathered in the Yoido Plaza in Seoul.[33] The second was the weeklong EXPLO '74 (August 13-17, 1974), sponsored by Campus Crusade for Christ. About 1.3 million people attended the first night. The major purpose of EXPLO '74 was to train 300,000 Christians. As the result, 323,400 people from 78 countries were trained and sent onto the streets to share the gospel during the week of the crusade.[34] Among those trained, about 3,000 people returned to their home countries spiritually renewed.[35]

The third crusade, "Here's Life, Korea" (August 12-15, 1980), was organized by the World Evangelization Crusade. Over 90 percent of the 18,000 Korean churches were involved in the crusade, which was attended by a diverse crowd, including college and high school students,

---

[32] Paul Yonggi Cho, *The Fourth Dimension* (Plainfield, NJ: Logos International, 1979), 22.
[33] *Christianity Today*, "Epochal Event: What God Did in Korea," *Christianity Today*, June 22, 1973, "http://www.christianitytoday.com/ct/2006/februaryweb-only/108-53.0.html, accessed June 4, 2017.
[34] Kim, "Korea's Total Evangelization Movement," 26-27.
[35] Ibid.

children, doctors, women, teachers, and elders. Each day more than 2.5 million people gathered in Yoido Plaza to take part in rallies. Over 1.5 million people remained in the plaza from midnight to 4 a.m. to pray for national evangelization. During the crusade, about 1.8 million people were baptized in the Spirit and one million people accepted Jesus as Savior. About one million people pledged to be involved in world missions.[36]

Table 3
The Participants of '80 WEC-Here's Life[37]

Meeting	Attendance
Yoido rally	10,500,000
All night of prayer	5,200,000
Morning sessions	250,000
50 Church conferences	240,000
12 Major conferences	160,000
Total	16,350,000

Statistics Korea reported in 2005 that 24,970,766 Koreans out of 47,041,434 had some form of religion: 22.8 percent (10,856,370) were Buddhists, 18.3 percent (8,616,438) were Protestants, 10.9 percent (5,146,147) were Catholics, and 0.2 percent (104,575) were Confucianists.[38] Among Protestants, there were 2,393,749 Pentecostals, 2,020,598 Charismatics, and 3,165,652 Neocharismatics. In addition, there are more than 700,000 Catholic Pentecostals today.[39] Through these large inter-denominational and international crusades, many distinctions between denominations—apart from denominational doctrines—blurred in Korea. Most churches practice speaking in tongues, audible prayers during services, and other spiritual gifts in everyday Christian life.

Why did millions of Koreans throng to these crusades and what did they pray for? Joon Gon Kim points to political unease and social

---

[36]Cox, *Fire from Heaven*, 233.
[37]Kim, "Korea's Total Evangelization Movement," 29.
[38]Available from Statistics Korea, http://kosis.kr/gen_etl/start.jsp?orgId=101&tblId =DT_1IN0505&conn_path=I2&path=, accessed May 23, 2011.
[39]Eim, "South Korea," 239-46.

insecurity as one reason why massive numbers attended and participated in all-night prayers.[40] They wanted to release their life burdens and *Han*s through prayers. In their hopelessness, they wanted a means of release from their unbearable present life and a hope for the future, especially for eternal life in Christ. Also, through the fullness of the Spirit, they were able to release their *Han*s, anger, humiliations, and sorrows. Dong Soo Kim insists that Korean Christians could release their *Han*s through singing gospel songs, clapping their hands and praying in loud voices with tears, especially with speaking in tongues.[41]

From a psychological perspective, Cyril G. Williams says, "*Glossolalia* may be a release mechanism leading to a reorientation which could be of a permanent order. It is an energy discharge which can have therapeutic value as a reducer of tension and resolver of inner conflict."[42] David Kwang-sun Suh defines tongue-speaking as "the language of *Minjung*" and states that *Minjung* can feel the release of *Han* through speaking in tongues.[43] However, it is questionable whether *glossolalia* has this kind of function.

Apart from speaking in tongues, *Han* can be released through inner healing by the Spirit. *Han* is something like twisted strings which people cannot unravel by themselves.[44] To resolve *Han*, the ministry of the Spirit for inner healing is indispensable. Without inner healing, the oppressed cannot forgive what the oppressors did to them. They also cannot release their *Han* without forgiveness. Their *Han* will not be removed from their hearts unless they forgive their oppressors: the longer they take to forgive, the longer they will be attached to their *Han*. Through forgiveness and reconciliation, a new relationship between two opposing groups can be rebuilt.

However, forgiveness and reconciliation are not what Koreans are seeking. Their ultimate goal is to change their unhappy circumstances. Is it possible to release the *Han* of the poor without providing a solution to their poverty? Is it possible to take away the *Han* of the woman who

---

[40]Kim, "Korea's Total Evangelization Movement," 32.
[41]Kim, "The Healing of *Han* in Korean Pentecostalism," 137.
[42]Cyril G. Williams, *Tongues of the Spirit: A Study of Pentecostal Glossolalia and Related Phenomena* (Cardiff: University of Wales Press, 1981), 166.
[43]David Kwang Sun Suh, "The Korean Pentecostal Movement and its Theological Understanding (Korean)," in *A Study on Pentecostal Movement in Korea*, ed. W. Y. Kang (Seoul, Korea: Korea Christian Academy, 1981), 77.
[44]Kim, "The Healing of *Han* in Korean Pentecostalism," 127.

had a flow of blood for twelve years without providing healing? Even though reconciliation and forgiveness might have been achieved, if nothing has changed in their lives and there is no hope for the poor, the sick, and the oppressed, it will mean nothing to them.

People want to be healed, become prosperous, and find a hope that gives new motivation to sustain life for the future. Those who hear the Threefold Blessing firmly believe that the blessed messages will be actualized in their lives. Through the Spirit, they have hope for the present and the future in Christ. John Calvin says, "Hope is nothing else than the expectation of those things which faith has believed to have been truly promised by God" through the fullness of the Spirit.[45]

Jürgen Moltmann says, "Faith in Christ gives hope its assurance."[46] Through the infilling of the Holy Spirit, Koreans came to believe the Pentecostal hope. They prayed hard day and night in order to be free from their problems and struggles in life. There seemed to be nothing they could do to change the circumstances but to pray. The sick found that most hospitals were destroyed during the Korean War and doctors were scarce. The poor encountered ruined social and economic infrastructures and few job opportunities. They believed that nobody but God could help them. While they prayed, they were baptized in the Spirit.

After Korean indigenous religions collapsed, there was no religion that could comfort Koreans. With spiritual eagerness, tens of thousands of Koreans gathered in large crusades and experienced Spirit baptism. After being baptized in the Spirit, they returned to their own churches where they contributed to church growth.[47]

Pentecostals rediscovered God as *Joeushin Hananim* (the good God) with the hope that he will bless them in their hopeless situations. In *Joeushin Hananim*, they found not only eschatological hope for the future but also hope for the present life. With this new understanding of the nature of God, the message of the Threefold Blessing was contextualized into the impoverished life of Koreans after the Korean War. As a result, the sick, the poor, and those seeking spiritual blessings were attracted to Pentecostal churches in Korea. However, the *Minjung*

---

[45]John Calvin, *Institutes of the Christian Religion*, trans. Ford Lewis Battles (Grand Rapids, MI: Wm. B. Eerdmans Publishing Co., 1995), 65.
[46]Moltmann, *Theology of Hope*, 20.
[47]Kim, "Korea's Total Evangelization Movement," 28.

of Korean Pentecostalism whose *Hans* are taken away are neither the common people nor those who stand in opposition to the government. Rather, these *Minjung* have similar spiritual experiences and engage in similar spiritual practices in the Spirit, regardless of their social status, wealth, or reputation. Furthermore, they are those who have hope not only for eternal life but also for life in the present.

CHAPTER 12
THE INFLUENCE OF KOREAN SHAMANISM ON THE CONTEXTUALIZED HOPE OF THE THREEFOLD BLESSING

Pentecostalism and Pentecostals intentionally distance themselves from Shamanism. However, it is impossible to remove indigenized shamanic elements and influences entirely from Korean Pentecostalism and Pentecostal praxis. Shamanism never disappeared while Buddhism and Confucianism were becoming indigenized into the Korean context. It has contributed significantly to the indigenization of the higher religions into Korean contexts. One prominent reason that Korean Buddhism and Confucianism differ from other Asian countries is due to the influence of Korea's indigenous folk religion. If Shamanism can be understood as a vessel containing the religiosity of Koreans, there is no reason not to accept the shamanic influences on Pentecostalism. Just as Paul Tillich says that "religion is the substance of culture, culture is the form of religion,"[1] so Shamanism has become part of Korean culture. It is not surprising that Pentecostalism adopted certain positive elements of Shamanism.[2]

1. Korean Shamanism and Pentecostalism

Should we regard Pentecostalism as a folk religion with shamanic spirituality or as part of traditional culture? The conservative nature of Korean Pentecostals leads them to strongly deny that there are shamanic influences or elements in their Pentecostalism. This is not because they ignore the positive contributions of shamanic elements to church growth and its role in Korean culture, but because they do not want to syncretize shamanic spirituality with their Pentecostalism.[3] In other words, they accept the cultural and traditional aspects of shamanism but not its spirituality as a religion.

However, many Pentecostal/Charismatic scholars, including Hollenweger and Koreans such as Boo Woong Yoo, think that shamanic

---
[1] Paul Tillich, *Theology of Culture* (Oxford: Oxford University Press, 1964), 42.
[2] Lee, *The Holy Spirit Movement in Korea*, 13-14.
[3] Cox, *Fire from Heaven*, 240-241; Lee, *The Holy Spirit Movement in Korea*, 13-14.

influences have contributed to the extraordinary growth of Pentecostalism. Shamanism is not only a folk religion. Throughout history, Shamanism has been used to express joy, sorrows, desires, and even *Han*s. Shamanism existed before the higher religions came to Korea, providing a way for Koreans to express their religiosity. Over time, Shamanism became both the substance and the vessel for Korean folk culture. David Kwang-sun Suh calls Shamanism "the religious soil of Korea."[4]

Every religion undergoes the process of indigenization and contextualization in a new context when it is imported from its place of origin. Likewise, there are shamanistic elements in Korean Confucianism and Buddhism. Cox says that certain elements of pre-existing religion must be included and transformed in any growing religion where they remain as part of the cultural subconscious. These elements are absorbed into the higher religions, making the religions unique compared with their expressions in other nations. Korean Pentecostalism is one example of this.[5] Anderson affirms, "Pentecostal converts and local preachers began to relate their messages of the transforming power of the gospel to their own religious worlds, creating continuity between certain aspects of the old religions and the new form of Christianity."[6]

In the Korean context, it is necessary to approach Shamanism not from a religious perspective but from an anthropological perspective: it reflects the Korean psyche, tradition, culture, and religiosity throughout Korean history. Understanding the differences between Korean Pentecostalism and other expressions of global Pentecostalism is difficult without considering this anthropological perspective.

Shamanism contains elements of Korean primal religiosity from before Christianity. Undoubtedly, Pentecostalism could not have grown in such a short period of time without the successful contextualization of Pentecostalism into Korean contexts.

---

[4]David Kwang Sun Suh, "Liberation Spiritual in the Korean *Minjung* Tradition: Shamanism and *Minjung* Liberation," 31.
[5]Cox, *Fire from Heaven*, 218-219.
[6]Anderson, *Spreading Fires*, 238.

Pentecostals need to reconsider whether pre-existing religions only had a negative influence upon Christianity and also whether Shamanism exerted only negative influences upon Pentecostalism. Normally Korean Pentecostals are persuaded that there are no shamanistic influences on their Pentecostalism.[7] They are reluctant to mix shamanistic spirituality with Christian spirituality and the manifestation of the Holy Spirit. Harvey Cox points out that "a massive importation of shamanic practice into a Christian ritual"[8] has been denied by Pentecostals.

From its early days, Korean Christianity radically de-shamanized all shamanic element. As a result, Pentecostalism was not welcomed by Korean Christians due to the similarity between Pentecostal manifestations and those of Shamanism. Similarities exist between Pentecostal modes of prayer and shamanistic ecstasy, between Pentecostal healing and shamanistic healing, and between speaking in tongues and spirit possession.

It is important to regard Shamanism as a form of Korean primal religiosity rather than comparing it with the various ancient Canaanite religions in the Old Testament that opposed Judaism. Thus, the influences of Shamanism on Pentecostalism and the contributions of Shamanism to the growth of Pentecostalism need to be re-examined.

2. Practices of Pentecostalism and Shamanism

The practices of Korean Pentecostalism are unique compared to other expressions of global Pentecostalism. After observing passionate Pentecostal services at the YFGC, Cox insisted that Korean Pentecostals overlook "a massive importation of shamanic practice into a Christian ritual."[9] He also suggests that one reason for the extraordinary growth of Pentecostalism is the "ability to absorb huge chunks of indigenous Korean shamanism and demon possession into its worship."[10]

Cox does not realize that there is no collective demon possession phenomenon during shamanistic rites. During a shamanistic rite, only the

---

[7] Allan Anderson, "The Gospel and Culture in Pentecostal Mission in the Third World," represented at the 9th Conference of the European Pentecostal Charismatic Research Association, Missions Academy, University of Hamburg, Germany, July 1999, 4.
[8] Cox, *Fire from Heaven*, 226.
[9] Ibid., 222.
[10] Ibid., 226.

shaman who conducts the ritual can be possessed by a spirit and act as an intermediary between the spirit and the audience. Although a member of an audience can be possessed by a spirit instead of the shaman, the phenomenon of collective spirit possession does not happen during the ritual. Without a sufficient understanding of Korean Shamanism, Cox simply equates Korean shamanistic rituals with the collective enthusiasm of African Shamanism. In this sense, it is a theological misunderstanding to equate the manifestations of the Spirit with shamanic enthusiasm in Korean contexts. Identifying the manifestations of Pentecostalism with the shamanistic enthusiasm of Korean Shamanism would be like identifying the phenomenon of the Toronto blessing with Canadian Shamanism.[11] Nevertheless, there are shamanistic influences present in Pentecostal practices. These influences are evident in the prayers of Korean Pentecostals.

Compared with other expressions of Christianity, the most prominent feature of Korean Pentecostalism is its emphasis on prayer. Since the beginning of Pentecostalism in the early twentieth century, Pentecostals have concentrated on prayer. As noted earlier, the practice of daily dawn prayer was started by Seon Ju Gil and others during the Pentecostal revivals. The Prayer Mountain Movement, started in 1952 by Woon Mong La (also known as Elder Ra), greatly contributed to the rapid growth of Pentecostalism and has prevailed over the nation. In 1994, there were about 500 prayer mountains in Korea. Approximately twenty-six percent of Korean Christians visited prayer mountains in order to pray for problems related to their family, business, and personal struggles, as well as for spiritual experiences and divine healings.[12]

The enthusiastic, audible prayer of Korean Pentecostals is also unique. Regardless of denomination, audible prayer and overnight prayers are a common Christian practice. This kind of prayer shows

---

[11]The Toronto Blessing started in 1994 at the Toronto Airport Vineyard Church led by pastors John and Carol Arnott. They were inspired by Argentinean evangelist Caludio Freidzon, who was an AG evangelist. The Toronto Blessing was a sort of a charismatic movement until late 1994, but it has been denied by conservative Pentecostals because of unusual physical manifestations such as laughing, rolling over, making strange animal sounds and others. Nevertheless, about 250 to 300 people attend at weeknight meetings and about 500 are attending on weekends. See M. M. Poloma, "Toronto Blessing," in *The New International Dictionary of Pentecostal and Charismatic Movements*, ed. Stanley M. Burgess and Eduard M. Van der Maas, 1149-1152.

[12]Eim, "South Korea," 242-243.

undeniable shamanistic influences. Before Christianity arrived, the habit of prayer had been formed already through Shamanism. In shamanistic practice, Koreans pray early at dawn with a vessel of water drawn from a well as an offering that nobody has touched or drunk from. They pray for the success of their children, to have a good harvest, and for the health of their households. They also go to a mountain to pray for one hundred days.

Korean Pentecostals argue that there are no shamanistic influences or elements within Korean Pentecostalism because they fail to differentiate between shamanistic spirituality and shamanistic elements. Although the manifestation of divine healing is similar to demonic healing within Shamanism, the origins of the healing and the spirituality are different. Those who have experienced divine healing would never agree that their healing originated from demonic spirits or shamanistic spirituality.

Shamanism greatly contributed to the way Koreans appropriated Christianity as well as Pentecostalism in at least two aspects. First, Korean people were easily able to understand the sovereignty of God as a supreme being and the spiritual world of his subordinate spirits, devil, and angels: Shamanism had a similar worldview. Second, the aspirations within Shamanism for this-worldly material blessings helped to indigenize the theology of the Threefold Blessing for Christians.[13] Pentecostalism successfully adapted these indigenous shamanistic elements into the new movement and merged them into the life of the *Minjung*. Thus, it is important for Korean Pentecostals to reassess these shamanistic influences, not regarding them as part of a pagan heritage that should be excluded from their new faith, but as the praxis of their religiosity formulated through generations.

3. *Ki-Bock-Shin-Ang*
(Blessings through faith and religious practices)

In the early days of Korean Protestantism, believers did not focus on this-worldly blessings due to their imminent eschatology. They neglected to address practical matters of current concern to Koreans. After the Korean War, Pentecostalism began to respond to these

---

[13]Lee, *The Holy Spirit Movement in Korea*, 13-14.

concerns of ordinary people. Young Hoon Lee says that one of prominent influences of Shamanism on Pentecostalism is "its [shamanism's] emphasis on the present and material blessings."[14]

Through a shamanistic ritual called *Han-puri* (resolution of *Han*), Koreans tried to overcome their bitterness of life. Shamanism gave ordinary people temporary relief of sufferings during the performance of the ritual. Although most shamanistic rituals did not provide a permanent solution to their sufferings, Koreans clung to them for temporary relief.

Young Hoon Lee says, "Shamanism implicitly drove Korean Christians to focus on blessings."[15] Korean Shamanism focuses on secular hopes. Its fundamental purpose is to fulfill the earthly desires of its adherents. It is not concerned with ethical values or matters of eternal life. Shamanistic rituals are to fulfil hopes for material blessing, male children, wealth, health, fame, success, longevity, and so on. The recipients of shamanic rites are depending on supernatural powers from their ancestors, nature gods, or certain sacred objects.

The deep concern of Pentecostals for practical matters was one of reasons that Pentecostalism could be successful in Korea. Pentecostalism, with its emphasis on the divine blessings of health, wealth, and eternal salvation, has replaced the function of shamanistic rituals in relation to the sufferings of ordinary people within Christian faith. Heung Soo Kim, a theological professor at Mokwon University, insists that, due to the Korean War, survival became the primary basis of Koreans' action and cogitation. To satisfy this need for survival, Christianity emphasized the elements of blessings and prosperity in this world.[16] Cho distinguishes his theology of blessing from the shamanistic desire for blessings. He says that the Threefold Blessing will be dispensed by God when people believe in Jesus as their Savior, confess their sins, and have faith to seek first his kingdom and righteousness.[17]

The Threefold Blessing appealed to Koreans in three ways. First, the audience of Pentecostal messages were referred to not as sinners but as

---

[14]Ibid., 13.
[15]Ibid., 14.
[16]Heung Soo Kim, *Hankook Jeonjaeng gwha Gibokshinang Hwaksan Yeongoo* [a Research for the Korean War and the Expansion of the Health and Wealth Gospel] (Seoul: Hankook Gidokgyo Yeoksa Yeongooso, 1999), 199.
[17]Cho, *Oh Jung Bok Eum Kwa Sam Jung Chuk Bok* [Fivefold Gospel and Triple Blessings], 42.

heirs of God through Christ (Galatians 4:7). Second, it gave hope to those who were concerned about the future. Third, it corresponded to the needs of the times and indigenous shamanistic desires for wealth and health.

Although Korean Pentecostalism was able to successfully assimilate shamanistic elements, shamanistic influences have proved to be a double-edged sword. Most Christians say, "If you believe in Christ, you will be blessed" ("*Yeosoo Miteumyeon Chukbok Bateuseyo*") when they evangelize non-believers, instead of introducing Christ as the Savior. Certainly this can be construed as evidence of shamanic influences on Korean Christianity, but at the same time it reflects the inseparable relation between blessing and evangelism in Korean contexts. Regardless of theological controversies on it, many Koreans come to church in order to receive this-worldly blessings.[18] This materialistic belief is called *Ki-Bock-Shin-Ang*, which is rooted in Shamanism.[19]

For many, being blessed in Christ became equated with being rich, healthy, and successful in this life. This was reinforced by the example of Korean pastors. Leading a large church with a high salary and having a luxury car became the standard mark of a being successful pastor.[20] According to the Korea Gallup Poll, 39.2 percent out of 328 Korean Protestants and 12.1 percent out of 119 Roman Catholics answered positively to the inquiry: "Do you think a person who does an offering will be blessed more than the amount of offering he made?"[21] Regarding a relationship between offering and blessing, Korean Protestant responses demonstrate more evidence of shamanistic influences than Roman Catholic responses.

Pentecostal preachers often preach "Tithe, and the Lord will bless you."[22] They tend to misinterpret the relationship between offering and material blessing in terms of cause and effect. The Bible neither implies that material blessings are evil nor justifies the accumulation of wealth in the midst of poverty.[23] For instance, the wealth of a tax collector was

---

[18]Byung Gu Jee, *Shamanism gwa Hankook Gyohoi* [Shamanism and Korean Church] (Seoul: Sae Han Publishing House, 1996), 227.
[19]Sebastian C. H. Kim, "The Problem of Poverty in Post-War Korean Christianity: Kibock Sinang or *Minjung* Theology?" *Transformation* 24, no. 1 (January 2007): 43.
[20]Jee, *Shamanism gwa Hankook Gyohoi* [Shamanism and Korean Church], 227.
[21]Available from http://panel.gallup.co.kr/Gate/Panel/F025.aspx?seq=10919&Dae BunryuCd=02&BunryuGb=D&Bunryu=02&SearchGb=&SearchKey=&PageID=F055& date=Tue May 24 10:27:10 UTC+0100 2011, accessed June 8, 2011.
[22]Cox, *Fire from Heaven*, 231.
[23]D. L. Munby, *God and the Rich Society* (London: Oxford University Press, 1961), 54.

not acceptable in Jewish society but shameful to the ordinary people of Israel. Tax collectors accumulated wealth without consideration of the suffering of others and were reluctant to share their affluence (Matthew 9:10-13 and Luke 19:1-10).

The shamanistic desire for wealth is self-centered. The Pentecostal prayer for blessings is not necessarily intended as a shortcut to becoming rich, but it can be interpreted as self-serving. Pentecostals pray diligently to resolve their own problems and for personal blessings rather than for the benefit of their neighbors and the wider society.[24] Unless their focus on personal blessings is broadened to include neighbors and the wider society, their beliefs will be criticized as shamanic materialism. It will also be regarded as *Ki-Bock-Shin-Ang* if they do not emphasize the future aspects of the gospel as much as earthly blessings.

---

[24]Lee, *The Holy Spirit Movement in Korea*, 13.

CHAPTER 13
KOREAN PENTECOSTALISM AND THE STATE

There were no winners in the Korean War. According to the Ministry of Korean National Defence, 2,150,000 people (including about 900,000 soldiers) were killed, injured, or missing in combat. About ten million lost their homes, family members, and properties.[1] More died of cholera, frostbite, typhus, and other diseases due to the war.[2] After the war, Korea was in a state of chaos. Economically, Korea could not have survived without the assistance of foreign countries. Politically, the nation was extremely unstable.

Under the slogan 'Rebuilding the Nation,' a *coup d'état* took place under the leadership of Chung Hee Park on May 16, 1961. Park took control of the country, believing that political stability was necessary for the economic growth. The longer he could remain in power, the more the country would become stable politically and economically.[3] Through a constitutional amendment to the electoral system by *Yushin* (revitalizing) Reforms in 1972, he changed the presidential election system from direct voting to indirect election by the incumbent.[4] As the result, he was able to rule the country for 18 years until he was assassinated by Jae Goo Kim on October 26, 1979.[5] During his rule, Korea showed remarkable economic growth in a short period of time. The Korean GNP per capita increased "from $87 in 1961, to $532 in 1975, and to $1,735 in 1981."[6] However, Korea was overrun by severe riots and demonstrations. Many

---

[1] Ministry of National Defence, "The Korean War," *The Ministry of National Defence of Korea*, n.d., available from http://www.mnd.go.kr/mndPolicy/6war/0625war/0625war_3/index.jsp?topMenuNo=2&leftNum=27#, accessed June 15, 2011.
[2] Anthony Farrar-Hockley, "The China Factor in the Korean War," in *The Korean War in History*, ed. James Cotton and Ian Neary (Manchester: Manchester University Press, 1989), 9.
[3] Chung Hee Park, *Korea Reborn: A Model for Development* (New Jersey: Englewood Cliffs, 1979), 47.
[4] Donald Gregg, "Park Chung Hee," *Time*, August 23, 1999. http://www.time.com /time/world/article/0,8599,2054405,00.html, accessed June 15, 2011.
[5] The New Encyclopaedia Britannica, "Park Chung Hee," *The New Encyclopaedia Britannica* vol. 9 15th ed.
[6] Nahm, *Korea*, 486.

intellectuals, professors, students, Christian pastors, and theologians who opposed his dictatorship were imprisoned and even died under torture.

Korean mainline denominations and Pentecostal churches remained politically acquiescent. Pentecostalism aligned itself with the political authorities and grew without persecution.

1. *Kookga Jochan Gidohoi* (National Prayer Breakfast)

Ten days after the *coup*, the Christian community declared its support for the military administration. Most influential pastors, including Kyung Chik Han (1902-2000, the founder of Young Nak Presbyterian Church), Dae Sun Park, Joon Gon Kim (1925-2009, the founder of Korea Campus Crusade for Christ), Chun Han Lee, Sang Geun Lee, Yong Gi Cho, and other pastors gathered to pray for the success of Chung Hee Park and his military government.[7] In 1966, the most influential Protestant pastors started a prayer meeting for the president called *Daetongryoung Jaochan Gidohoi* (the Presidential Prayer Breakfast). Two years later, the prayer meeting was renamed *Kookga Jochan Gidohoi* (the National Prayer Breakfast).[8]

After Park's assassination, Korea plunged into political turmoil. On December 12, 1979, another military coup was led by Doo Hwan Chun. He disbanded parliament and quelled democratic demonstrations and assemblies by military force. In May 1980, a democratic movement was organized against his military administration called the Gwangju Democratization Movement. During this movement, 170 people (144 civilians, 22 soldiers, and 4 policemen) were killed, 380 wounded, and 1,740 arrested.[9]

---

[7]Man Yel Lee, *Hankook Gidokgyo wha Minjocktongil Woondong* [Korean Christianity and Reunification Movement] (Seoul: Hankook Gidokgyo Yeoksa Yeongooso, 2001), 287.

[8]Han Goo Mu, "Kookga Jochan Gidohoi Moouteul Namgyutna? [What did Kookga Jochan Gidohoi Leave Behind?]," *Gidockgyosasang* 48 (2004): 28.

[9]Bo Young Lee, "5.18 Minjuhwa Woondong Gaheaja wha Phyheajaye Daehan Hyungsabumjeok Byungga [The Criminal Evaluation of Those Responsible and Victim in the 5.18 Democratic Movement]," *Bubhakyeongoo* 27, no. 4 (1992): 284.

Korean Christianity remained supportive of the state, even under the dictatorship. On August 6, 1980, twenty-three influential pastors (including Kyung Chik Han, Yoon Shik Kim, Hyang Rok Cho, Jee Gil Kim, Jin Gyoung Kim, Chang In Kim, Bong Sung Lee, and Won Sang Lee) attended the *Kookga Jochan Gidohoi* at the Emerald Room in the Lotte Hotel in Seoul to pray for Doo Hwan Chun and his success.[10] In November 1972, some academic deans of seminaries (including Jong Sung Lee, Hui Bo Kim, Jung Jun Kim, Jong Nam Cho, Hyun Seol Hong) and forty well-known pastors (including Yong Gi Cho, Kyung Chik Han, Chang In Kim, Won Sang Jee, Yoon Chan Kim, and Ho Jun Yoo) officially announced their support for the *Yushin* Regime.[11]

Korean Pentecostals have been indifferent to political matters for four reasons. First, Pentecostals are very dynamic and active in Christian service but are traditional and conservative in their faith.[12] In accordance with Romans 13:1-2, they believe that they should obey all authorities since the authorities are ordained by God. Furthermore, to resist the authorities is to be against the ordinance of God. Second, they were historically unable to distinguish right from wrong in socio-political matters since the press was under military government control. Third, economic growth was more important than political issues to the ordinary people. Fourth, for the sake of stable church growth, Christianity, including Pentecostalism, cooperated with the military administration and tried to minimize political friction with the state. This enabled Korean Christianity and Pentecostalism to grow without undergoing persecution.

2. Economic Growth and Pentecostalism

Despite political chaos, the Korean economy continued to grow significantly. Chung Hee Park stated that his economic plans were based on *"the jaju spirit* [self-support spirit],"[13] and that "the *Saemaul* [new

---

[10] Lee, *Hankook Gidokgyo wha Minjocktongil Woondong* [Korean Christianity and Reunification Movement], 288.

[11] Lee, *Hankook Gidokgyo wha Minjocktongil Woondong* [Korean Christianity and Reunification Movement] (Seoul: Hankook Gidokgyo Yeoksa Yeongooso, 2001), 288.

[12] Kelly H. Chong, *Deliverance and Submission: Evangelical Women and the Negotiation of Patriarchy in South Korea* (Cambridge, MA: Harvard University Press, 2008), 26.

[13] Park, *Korea Reborn*, 57.

village]" movement had recovered the *jaju spirit*."¹⁴ In the proclamation of the Pentecostal message, especially its focus on divine blessings, economic growth was more important than political matters. Pentecostals made the mistake of ignoring the current socio-political matters with which ordinary people struggled. Therefore, the Threefold Blessing did not become contextualized into Korean socio-political life. In contrast, from the perspective of economics, the emphasis on financial blessing corresponded with the top priority given by Park's government to the task of overcoming national poverty.

After the Korean War, Korea needed economic assistance from foreign countries. Park wanted Korea to become independent economically. To bring about change in the whole nation, he believed that each village had to be changed. The *Saemaul* movement could not be successful without a change in the Korean mentality, so he focused on changing the mind of Koreans from a defeatist attitude to a more self-confident and positive frame of mind. Pentecostal messages were in concert with this key government focus. In the post-Korean War context, the "cannot-do spirit" prevailed across the country. One emphasis of Pentecostal messages was "changing the thinking attitude from a negative one to positive one."¹⁵ Cho emphasized the importance of a positive mindset, the "can-do spirit," the possibility of miracles to overcome human difficulties, and receiving blessings from God.¹⁶ In this sense, the Korean government and Pentecostalism were moving in the same direction. The Threefold Blessing closely linked the religious life of Koreans and a change in their economic circumstances, emphasizing hard work, saving money, and tithing.¹⁷ There was a direct correlation between the growth of Korean Pentecostalism and the economic growth of Korea (see Table 4). With Korea's economic growth, Pentecostals experienced answers to their prayers for financial blessings and prosperity. The Threefold Blessing was contextualized into the economic life of Koreans and responded to their urgent needs in the post-war context.

---

¹⁴Ibid., 78.
¹⁵Cho, *The Fourth Dimension*, 124; Kim, *History and Theology of Korean Pentecostalism*, 216.
¹⁶Ibid., 119-124.
¹⁷Cox, *Fire from Heaven*, 231.

Table 4
Growth of GNP per capita and Pentecostalism[18]

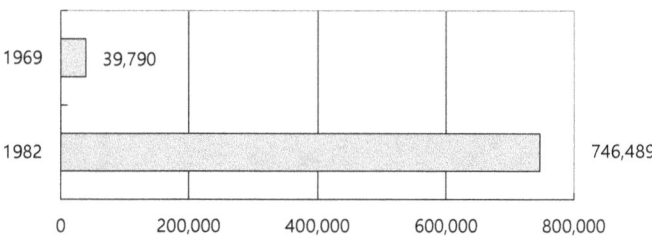

The Pentecostal understanding of salvation was restricted to the spiritual dimension. The Threefold Blessing was an effective response to the urgent needs of Koreans after the war. Although the Threefold Blessing is related to the daily life of Korean Pentecostal *Minjung*, Korean Pentecostals have been reluctant to engage in socio-political action. In fact, because it cooperated with the state, Pentecostalism was able to develop without undergoing persecution by Park's dictatorship. However, in neglecting their social and political responsibility and their attention to human rights and freedom of the press and speech, Pentecostals have not contextualized the Threefold Blessing into the socio-political life of Koreans.

---

[18]Nahm, *Korea*, 486.

Part FOUR

THE THREEFOLD BLESSING AND HOPE IN THE KOREAN CONTEXT

After the Korean War, most Koreans suffered absolute poverty and disease. The theology of the Threefold Blessing was developed by Yonggi Cho, based on the hardship of his personal life and his pastoral experiences amongst the urban poor, although the theology was not original to him.[1] The message of the Threefold Blessing effectively applied in the everyday lives of Koreans and became the main theme of Pentecostal messages in Korea. It gave Koreans hope to overcome hopeless circumstances. Moltmann's theology of hope was also developed in Germany after the Second World War. However, theological conversations between Moltmann and Korean Pentecostals did not occur until the 1990s. The Threefold Blessing used to be understood in terms of its contributions to pastoral care and church growth rather than as a contextual hope.

---

[1] See chapter 3, section 2.3.

CHAPTER 14
YONGGI CHO AND THE THREEFOLD BLESSING

Yonggi Cho's influence on global Christianity and Pentecostalism through the theology of the Threefold Blessing cannot be underestimated. The Threefold Blessing is deeply rooted in Cho's experiences in the Korean context of the mid-to-late twentieth century.

1. Yonggi Cho: a Brief Biography

On February 14, 1936, Yonggi Cho was born in Ulju County, Gyeongnam Province, in southern Korea.[1] He was the second child and eldest son among five brothers and four sisters.[2] Growing up in a typical Buddhist family, he often visited Buddhist temples with his parents. He suffered huge adversities: the oppression of Japanese imperialism, the Second World War, and the Korean War. The after-effects of the Korean War were extreme poverty and sickness. Cho plunged into the depths of despair psychologically, physically, and circumstantially. It seemed that there was no hope: he was always weak and often sick.

When he was about nine years old, he spent six months in bed due to lack of appetite and a high fever. On May 30, 1950, his father Doo-Chun Cho failed to win the congressional election despite selling all his property to finance his campaign. Cho's family then struggled with severe financial problems.[3] Although Cho was not a healthy teenager, he worked night shifts at a harbor to pay his middle school tuition. In 1952, he entered a technical high school to support his large family. He could normally only afford one meal a day and also worked on the street as a fruit seller. His physical condition and cough became worse.

In 1954, when he was eighteen, Cho fell in the street, vomiting blood. He had pulmonary tuberculosis and was told by his doctor that he could live no more than three months.[4] Although he prayed every day to

---

[1] Lee, *The Holy Spirit Movement in Korea*, 93.
[2] Nell L. Kennedy, *Dream Your Way to Success: The Story of Dr. Yonggi Cho and Korea* (Plainfield, NJ: 1980), 4.
[3] Lee, "The Life and Ministry of David Yonggi Cho," 4.
[4] Kim, *History and Theology of Korean Pentecostalism*, 120-121.

Buddha to be healed, his condition deteriorated. Eventually, he stopped praying to Buddha and started crying out *Hananim* instead. At the time, he regarded *Hananim* not as the Christian God but as the shamanistic supreme god in heaven. Nevertheless, he made a sincere promise to God that he would spend the rest of his life serving him if he healed him. Many years later, Cho realized that *Hananim* whom he entreated was the Christian God and he often said that this short prayer changed his life.[5]

A few days after his prayer, he got a visit from Jong Ae Kim, a Christian high school girl who was a friend of his sister, Hye Sook Cho.[6] Jong Ae was eighteen years old.[7] She became one of the significant women in his life, along with Ja Sil Choe (1915-1989),[8] his mother-in-law and the most influential partner in his ministry.

Despite Cho's resistance, Jong Ae Kim continued to visit him after school. Cho firmly told her that he did not want to change his religion since he wanted to die as a Buddhist.[9] She kept telling him about the life of Christ, the crucifixion, and the resurrection. Her zealous evangelism impressed him, and Cho converted to Christianity. He began to read the Bible she gave him and discovered that Jesus healed the sick and forgave sinners.[10] "Every morning I would pick up my Bible for breakfast and I would feast till dinner."[11]

One day, he sincerely prayed, "Jesus, you even healed lepers, can you heal my tuberculosis?"[12] At that moment, he experienced divine healing. Though he was cured from his fatal disease through divine healing, his family rejected him because of his conversion.[13] He had

---

[5]Cho, *The Fourth Dimension vol. II* (Plainfield, NJ: Bridge Publishing Inc., 1983), Preface, xiii.
[6]Hurston, *Growing the World's Largest Church*, 20.
[7]Kennedy, *Dream Your Way to Success*, 79.
[8]When she was a child, Ja Sil Choe heard the gospel for the first time at a tent revival. However, she did not convert to Christianity until her Buddhist husband left her with three children and the oldest child was on the brink of death. She almost committed suicide due to her hardship. At that time, she had another chance to hear the gospel and fully devoted herself to Christ. Soon after, she moved to Seoul with all her children and began to attend the school where she met Yonggi Cho. See Hurston, *Growing the World's Largest Church*, 21.
[9]Cho, *The Fourth Dimension vol. II*, Preface, xiv.
[10]Kim, *History and Theology of Korean Pentecostalism*, 122.
[11]Cho, *The Fourth Dimension vol. II*, Preface, xviii.
[12]Kim, *History and Theology of Korean Pentecostalism*, 123.
[13]Ibid.

promised to give his life to God if he was healed, but he became a medical trainee at a hospital since he wanted to become a doctor. During two years of medical training, he did not attend church.[14] Either he did not realize the implications of his prayer to devote the rest of his life to God, or he simply forgot after he received divine healing.

In the spring of 1955, Cho's painful cough returned. He began to attend the Full Gospel Mission led by Rev. L. P. Richard. His parents started attending the mission and converted to Christianity. Cho built friendships at the mission with Assemblies of God (AG) missionaries: he studied the Bible with Rev. Richard and met Kenneth Tice. Cho also began to interpret their sermons.[15] Reading the Bible with the AG missionaries, Cho understood divine healing more clearly and repented of his former unbelief.[16]

In September 1956, after being trained by the missionaries for about a year, he was sent to Seoul to become a seminarian at the *Sunbogeum* Theological Seminary. That winter, during the first year of seminary, he became ill with pneumonia. While he was confronted by death for several days, Ja-Sil Choe, an experienced nurse and his future mother-in-law, carefully nursed him. His classmates prayed for him. Several days later, he recovered his health.

Cho and Choe began to work together.[17] Cho's personal suffering from a fatal disease and experience of divine healing made him concentrate on divine healing in his ministry. During every service, he prays for the sick. His divine healing ministry is the most significant reason for the remarkable growth of the YFGC (even more so than *glossolalia*).[18] Many members of the YFGC are convinced that they have experienced healing after being prayed for by Cho.[19]

Cho's experiences of extreme poverty and suffering from disease stimulated his desire for physical and financial blessings and also became the soil for the development of the theology of the Threefold

---

[14]Ibid.
[15]Cho, *The Fourth Dimension vol. II*, Preface, xviii.
[16]Lee, *The Holy Spirit Movement in Korea*, 94.
[17]Kim, *History and Theology of Korean Pentecostalism*, 123-124; Lee, *The Holy Spirit Movement in Korea*, 94.
[18]Vinson Synan, "Roots of Yonggi Cho's Theology of Healing," in *Dr. Yonggi Cho's Ministry and Theology I*, ed. Young San Theological Institute, 284.
[19]Hurton, *Growing the World's Largest Church*, 170-171.

Blessing. He shared his hope for prosperity and health in God with his church members who were fish sellers, factory workers, and the urban poor. Looking back on the early days of the YFGC, Cho says that the church looked like a house of refuge. The church was filled with fishy odors and many poor children. Fish sellers came to church for Sunday services with their fish baskets and most poor people had many children.[20]

2. The Development of the Threefold Blessing

Cho developed his pastoral and theological theology, which he called the Threefold Blessing and the Fivefold Gospel. The Threefold Blessing was the core theological and pastoral doctrine of the YFGC from its tent church era. Cho started to teach the Fivefold Gospel from 1974.[21] The elements of Cho's Fivefold Gospel are salvation, baptism in the Spirit, diving healing, the second coming of Christ, and blessing. Cho subdivided "blessing" in the Fivefold Gospel into the Threefold Blessing of salvation from sin, prosperity, and health.

Cho's Fivefold Gospel was inherited from Classical Pentecostal teaching. The term "the Fivefold Gospel" was used by American Pentecostals during the Azusa Street Revival as well as early Holiness Pentecostal denominations like the Pentecostal Holiness Church, the Church of God in Christ, and the Church of God. Their Fivefold Gospel consists of Jesus as Savior, Sanctifier, Spirit Baptizer, Healer, and Coming King.[22] Until the late nineteenth century, it was debated whether the baptism in the Spirit was adequate to describe "the second blessing" of sanctification.[23] After the Finished Work movement of W. H. Durham

---

[20]Mokhoi wha Sinhak [Ministering and Theology], "Interview with Yonggi Cho (September 1, 2009)," 32.

[21]Hurston, *Growing the World's Largest Church*, 139-140.

[22]Synan, "Roots of Yonggi Cho's Theology of Healing," 264-265; Synan, *The Holiness-Pentecostal Tradition*, 140; Wonsuk Ma, "Dr. Yonggi Cho's Theology of Blessing: New Theological Basis and Directions," in *2003 Young San International Theological Symposium*, ed. Hansei University (Gunpo: Hansei University Press, 2003), 187-210.

[23]Donald W. Dayton, "The Good God and the Theology of Blessing in the Thought of David Yonggi Cho," in *Dr. Yonggi Cho's Ministry and Theology I*, ed. Young San Theological Institute, 44.

(1911),[24] "sanctification" was omitted from the Fivefold Gospel, and it became the Fourfold Gospel. The Finished Work theology was rejected and denounced as a threat to the existence of the Pentecostal movement by Parham, Seymour, and other Holiness Pentecostal leaders. The AG was organized by independent Pentecostals in 1914. They accepted Durham's teaching as their official statement of belief, which consisted of salvation, baptism in the Holy Spirit with speaking in tongues as the initial evidence, divine healing, and the pre-millennial return of Christ. Since then, the Fourfold Gospel has been accepted by most Pentecostal churches and leaders as well as the International Church of the Foursquare Gospel.[25]

After joining the AG, Cho had more fellowship with AG missionaries. Through their influence, he adopted the doctrines and beliefs of the AG. William W. Menzies insists that Cho borrowed the Fourfold Gospel for his Fivefold Gospel from "the American Evangelical Christianity, particularly the cardinal doctrines of the Assemblies of God."[26] From the beginning of the YFGC, Cho adopted this Fourfold Gospel as the official doctrine of his church and later developed his Fivefold Gospel by adding "blessing."[27]

Cho did not accept speaking in tongues as the initial evidence of Spirit baptism. Although he accepted the doctrine of the AG in the early years of his ministry, later he changed his perspective with regard to tongues-speaking by considering it as "one of the evidences of baptism

---

[24]By 1911, Durham had fashioned the finished work of Calvary theology. He insisted that sanctification could not be a second blessing or "crisis experience" because both sanctification and salvation were accomplished in the atonement on the Cross. See Vinson Synan, "The Finished Work Pentecostal Churches," in *The Century of the Holy Spirit: 100 Years of Pentecostal and Charismatic Renewal 1901-2001*, ed. Vinson Synan (Nashville: Thomas Nelson Publishers, 2001), 123-124; see also Allan Anderson, *An Introduction to Pentecostalism*, 45-47.

[25]Vinson Synan, "The Finished Work Pentecostal Churches," in *The Century of the Holy Spirit: 100 Years of Pentecostal and Charismatic Renewal 1901-2001*, ed. Vinson Synan, 124.

[26]William W. Menzies, "David Yonggi Cho's Theology of the Fullness of the Spirit: A Pentecostal Perspective," in *David Yonggi Cho: A Close Look at His Theology and Ministry*, ed. Wonsuk Ma, William W. Mezies, and Hyeon Sung Bae, 36; Thomson K. Mathew, "Oral Roberts and David Yonggi Cho: A Comparative Evaluation of Their Theologies of Healing," in *Dr. Yonggi Cho's Ministry and Theology I*, ed. Young San Theological Institute, 294.

[27]Wonsuk Ma, "Dr. Yonggi Cho's Theology of Blessing: New Theological Basis and Directions," in Hansein University, ed., 188-191.

in the Spirit."[28] In his book *The Nature of God*, Cho discusses the evidence of the Holy Spirit, but does not mention "tongues-speaking" as the initial evidence of the Spirit. Rather, he emphasizes the fruit of the Spirit as evidence of Spirit baptism.[29]

This change of Cho's perspective about speaking in tongues as initial evidence is related to his secession from the Korean Assemblies of God (KAG). Theological conflicts arose between Cho and other Korean classical Pentecostals who sincerely followed the classical beliefs and ideas of the AG.

Korean classical Pentecostals had power in the denomination and wanted to control Cho and the YFGC. They brought up five issues of disagreement, either as a pretext for dismissing Cho from the denomination or to pressure him into obeying the authority of the KAG. First, illegal ordination of pastors (some ordinations in the YFGC were conducted by the church, not by the KAG); second, Cho's healing ministry;[30] third, Cho's perspective regarding ancestor worship;[31] fourth, the mysterious event of a young female who resurrected from the dead; and fifth, the failure of the YFGC to pay the required denominational membership fee. According to the KAG's constitution, affiliated churches owed three percent of their income of the church every month to the KAG. The YFGC paid about $20,000-30,000 each month, which

---

[28]Cho, *Ohjungbokeum kwa Samjungchukbok* [The Fivefold Gospel and the Threefold Blessing], 100.

[29]Yonggi Cho, *The Nature of God* (Lake Mary, FL: Charisma House, 2001), 183-194.

[30]In 1960, due to Cho's healing ministry, Cho's pastoral license was revoked by the committee of the KAG at the instigation of Gyu Chang Jeong and Wan Sik Lee. His license was restored the next year as they left the denomination. See Kim, *History and Theology of Korean Pentecostalism*, 125.

[31]On November 30, 1979, during his sermon Cho said, "Ancestor worship is nothing but honouring one's parents. I do not understand why people say that it is idol worship. . . . It is quite all right to prepare food thinking of our deceased parents as if they were present, to erect a cross instead of an ancestral tablet, and to bow down . . . We honour our parents with bowing down. It is not an idol . . . Thus, to perform ancestral worship (*Che-sa*) is really a good thing." Myung Hyuk Kim, "Ancestor Worship: From the Perspective of Korean Church History," in *Ancestor Worship and Christianity in Korea*, ed. Jung Young Lee, 29. Afterward, the debate about whether Cho was a heretic became more severe and cynical.

was much less than three percent of the church's income.³² Furthermore, they issued a summons to Cho that unless he appeared at the planned committee meeting they would dismiss him from his position in the YFGC.

On October 13, 1981, Cho and the YFGC decided to secede from the KAG and became an independent church.³³ On December 7, the KAG divided into three groups: the *Chonghoe* [General Council] of the KAG with 237 churches, 306 pastors and about 70,000 members; *Banpo*, the anti-group of the KAG with 233 churches, 330 pastors and 38,000 members; and the YFGC as an independent church.

As the YFGC had 229 pastors and about 200,000 members, it was bigger than the other two new groups.³⁴ Cho no longer had to follow all the beliefs of the classical Pentecostals or to adhere to more contentious doctrines such as tongues-speaking as the initial evidence of Spirit baptism. Cho kept his relationship with American Pentecostals and developed his own theology, rooted in their theologies.

The Fivefold Gospel is the theoretical basis and the Threefold Blessing is the practical application of the Fivefold Gospel. The Fourfold and Fivefold Gospel of American classical Pentecostals and Cho's Fivefold Gospel are Christ-centered (see Table 5 below). Wonsuk Ma argues against the notion that, as Cho overemphasizes the work of the Spirit, he has minimized the saving work of Christ.³⁵

---

³²Kim, *History and Theology of Korean Pentecostalism*, 176-77; Gook Jae Shin Hak Yeon GooWon [International Theology Institute], *Hananim euy Sunghoi GyoHoiSa* [The Church History of Assemblies of God], 235-36.
³³Gook Jae Shin Hak Yeon Goo Won [International Theology Institute], *Hananim euy Sunghoi GyoHoiSa* [The Church History of Assemblies of God], 235; Kim, *History and Theology of Korean Pentecostalism: Sunbogeum*, 178.
³⁴Kim, *History and Theology of Korean Pentecostalism*, 178.
³⁵Ma, "Dr. Yonggi Cho's Theology of Blessing: New Theological Basis and Directions," 189-190.

Table 5
Comparison between the Four/Fivefold Gospel by Classical Pentecostals, the Four-Fold Gospel by A. B. Simpson and the Five Fold Gospel by Cho.[36]

The Fourfold Gospel by A.B. Simpson	**Jesus is** the Savior	the Healer	the Coming King	the Sanctifier	
Pentecostal Fourfold Gospel	the Savior	the Healer	the Coming King	the Baptizer in the Spirit	
Pentecostal Fivefold Gospel	the Savior	the Healer	the Coming King	the Baptizer in the Spirit	the Sanctifier
Cho's Fivefold Gospel	the Savior	the Healer	the Coming King	the Baptizer in the Spirit	the Blesser

Cho established the Fivefold Gospel and the Threefold Blessing as the creed of the YFGC from its beginning.[37] According to Vinson Synan, with the Threefold Blessing, the YFGC was the first church in the world to adopt "prosperity language as an official doctrine."[38] Synan evaluates Cho's theology as "a singularly Korean contribution to the world of Pentecostal theology."[39] Though Cho's theology is unique and creative, many significant teachers inspired him to develop his Threefold Blessing theology.

---

[36] A. B. Simpson published the book, *The Four-Fold Gospel* with four contents: 1. Christ our Saviour, 2. Christ our Sanctifier, 3. Christ our Healer, and 4. Christ our Coming Lord. See A. B. Simpson, *The Four-Fold Gospel* (New York: The Christian Alliance Publishing Co., 1925). Ma mistakenly addresses Simpson's Four-Fold Gospel as "Jesus as Saviour, Healer, Baptizer, and Coming King" on page 189. Other than that, Ma insightfully compares Cho's Fivefold theology with the Four and Five-fold Gospel of Classical Pentecostals on the same article on page 190. See Ma, "Dr. Yonggi Cho's Theology of Blessing: New Theological Basis and Directions," 189-190.

[37] Cho, *Ohjungbokeum kwa Samjungchukbok* [The Fivefold Gospel and the Threefold Blessing], Preface.

[38] Synan, "Roots of Yonggi Cho's Theology of Healing," 284.

[39] Ibid., 265-66.

3. Theological and Historical Influences on the Threefold Blessing

Pentecostals did not emphasize material blessings before the Second World War. After the war, the idea of the material blessing from God for believers emerged, and the prosperity gospel began to be promoted within the movement.[40] Cho's Threefold Blessing developed based on 3 John 2, but his theology was originally inspired by Oral Roberts, an American healing evangelist in the Pentecostal Holiness Church. In 1947, Roberts meditated on 3 John 2 and was deeply impressed.[41] His ministry was transformed and entered a new phase with an emphasis on divine healing and prosperity. In 1948, he published a book of sermons entitled *If You Need Healing Do These Things*. In the mid-1950s, he created the Blessing-Pact (later, Seed-Faith) to raise funds for his television ministry. In public, he promised a refund to those who contributed $100 to his mission but did not receive blessings from God within one year.[42] In 1955, he published another book emphasizing material welfare entitled *God's Formula for Success and Prosperity*.

When Cho opened his tent church (Daejo Dong Full Gospel Church in Daejo Dong)[43] in a slum area on the outskirts of Seoul, he was discouraged. The church was not growing quickly. In the late 1950s, Cho obtained Roberts' sermon books and tapes through American missionaries.[44] These books and sermons significantly influenced Cho. Like Roberts, 3 John 2 became the center of Cho's sermons and the foundation of his ministry.[45] Later, Cho and Roberts built a very close relationship: Roberts spoke of Cho as "my beloved friend and brother."[46]

---

[40]Simon Coleman, *The Globalisation of Charismatic Christianity: Spreading the Gospel of Prosperity* (Cambridge: Cambridge University Press, 2000), 41.

[41]Oral Roberts, *Expect a Miracle: My Life and Ministry* (Nashville: Thomas Nelson Publishers, 1995), 71-74.

[42]Coleman, *The Globalisation of Charismatic Christianity*, 41-42.

[43]Yonggi Cho, *Successful Home Cell Groups* (North Brunswick, NJ: Bridge-Logos, 1999), 1-3. As the name and the boundary of districts have been changed, the name of the place Cho started his tent church is often confused between two district names: Pulkwang Dong and Daejo Dong. In his book, *Salvation, Healing and Prosperity*, 11, Cho mentions that he started his church in Pulkwang Dong.

[44]Cho, *Salvation, Healing and Prosperity*, 8.

[45]Ibid., 11-12; see also Oral Roberts, *Expect a Miracle: My Life and Ministry* (Nashville: Thomas Nelson Publishers, 1995), 71-74.

[46]Roberts, *Expect a Miracle*, 142.

Although the influence of Roberts on the development of the prosperity gospel cannot be overlooked, Roberts actually placed more emphasis on his healing ministry than prosperity.[47] Early American Pentecostal evangelists such as Charles Parham and William J. Seymour were opposed to using medicines, preferring to rely on divine healing. In a 1906 issue of *Apostolic Faith* magazine, Seymour stated, "The doctor gives you poison and you die because you dishonour the atonement."[48] He believed that seeing doctors or taking Western medicine demonstrated a lack of faith in God.

However, Seymour's perspective was opposed by the Holiness Church. In 1920, both prayer for the sick and using Western medicine were accepted by the Congregational Holiness Church.[49] The debate over the relative merits of divine healing and Western medicine ended and Pentecostals began to practice both.[50] Theologically, the early American Pentecostals emphasized "divine healing as in the atonement."[51] Based on Isaiah 53:4-6, Roberts also believed that divine healing is related to the atonement.[52] Roberts suggests six steps toward healing:

1) Know that it is God's will to heal you and make you a whole person; 2) Remember that healing begins in the inner man; 3) Use a point of contact for the release of your faith; 4) Release

---

[47]In 1947, Roberts began a citywide healing ministry in Enid, Oklahoma. In the same year, his first book on healing, *If You Need Healing*, was published, and his healing messages were broadcast on the radio. Also the monthly magazine, *Healing Waters*, was started. In 1955, he initiated a weekly nationwide television program with which he could reach millions of people with his healing message. By the 1950s, more than 500 radio stations broadcasted his healing message, and he conducted more than 300 major crusades during the period 1947 to 1968. See G. Chappell, "Roberts, Granville Oral," in *The New International Dictionary of Pentecostal and Charismatic Movements*, ed. Stanley M. Burgess and Eduard M. Van der Maas, 1024-1025.

[48]William J. Seymour, "Salvation and Healing," *Apostolic Faith* (December 1906): 2.

[49]Vinson Synan, *The Old-Time Power: A History of the Pentecostal Holiness Church* (Franklin Springs, GA: Advocate Press, 1973), 166-171.

[50]Synan, "Roots of Yonggi Cho's Theology of Healing," 279.

[51]Ibid., 276.

[52]Oral Roberts, *Holy Bible: With My Personal Commentary* (Tulsa, OK: Oral Roberts Evangelistic Association, 1981), 64; Thomson K. Mathew, "Oral Roberts and David Yonggi Cho: A Comparative Evaluation of Their Theologies of Healing," 291.

your faith; 5) Close the case for victory; 6) Join yourself to companions of faith.[53]

Three prominent differences emerged between Roberts' and Cho's theologies of divine healing. First, Cho's theology of healing is anchored in Christ' redemption on the Cross.[54] Cho often states that healing is part of Christ's redemption, but he rarely uses the term "the atonement" in relation to divine healing.[55]

Second, Cho defines the three origins of disease as the devil, the sin of human beings, and the curse of God as the punishment for their sins.[56] Healing is not just a cure of physical difficulties but also includes deliverance from sin, evil spirits, and the curse of God. Jesus also connected divine healing to the forgiveness of sins when he healed the paralytic carried by other men (Matthew 9:2; Mark 2:5; and Luke 5:20). Cho believes that "the source of illness is Satan and the cause of illness is sin."[57] This belief in sin as the cause of illness implies the fall of humanity and individual sins. According to Cho, there were no diseases in the Garden of Eden; these came to human beings after the Fall.[58] For this reason, sin and disease are inseparably related to each other. Repentance is prominent in Cho's healing methodology.

Third, in comparison with Roberts' six, Cho offers five steps toward healing:

> 1) We must have hope of perfect health; 2) We must confess and be forgiven of our sins; 3) We must forgive others, even our enemies; 4) We must have faith; and 5) We must ask God to help us stay holy and sin free.[59]

Roberts was Cho's main mentor during the early period of his healing ministry. Cho tried to follow Roberts' approach to the healing

---

[53] Oral Roberts, *Better Health and Miracle Living* (United States: Oral Roberts Evangelistic Assn., Inc., 1976), 11-19.
[54] Yonggi Cho, *How Can I Be Healed?* (Seoul: Seoul Logos Co., Inc., 1999), 51.
[55] Cho, *Salvation, Health and Prosperity*, 126-131, 141.
[56] Cho, *Ohjungbokeum kwa Samjungchukbok* [The Fivefold Gospel and the Threefold Blessing], 145.
[57] Cho, *How Can I Be Healed?*, 29.
[58] Yonggi Cho, *Ohjungbokeum kwa Samjungchukbok* [The Fivefold Gospel and the Threefold Blessing] (Seoul: Seoul Malsseumsa, 2002), 14.
[59] Cho, *How Can I Be Healed?*, 52.

ministry. From the 1970s, Cho's ministry came under other influences such as the Word of Faith Movement (hereafter the Faith Movement). Essek William Kenyon (1867–1948) provided the theological basis for Faith Movement leaders like Kenneth Hagin, Kenneth Copeland, Fred Price, and Charles Capps. Kenyon also strongly influenced Kenneth Hagin (1917–2003), an influential American Pentecostal preacher and the father of the Faith Movement.[60]

Hagin and his followers distinguish between the Greek words *rhema* and *logos* in the New Testament. The *rhema* word is the word of God for specific situations and includes words of prophecy, interpreted messages in tongues, or God's answer to a prayer through the Spirit. The *logos* word, on the other hand, is the unchangeable, written word of God in the scripture.[61] Cho followed the *rhema-logos* teaching,[62] referring to the *logos* as "the general Word of God" and the *rhema* as "the revealed Word of God to an individual."[63] According to Faith movement followers, including Cho, the promises in the Scripture are personalized through verbal confession since the Lord is bound to what He says in the Bible.[64] They emphasize the importance of "positive confession as a literal bringing into existence" of healing for the body and even for financial prosperity.[65] Cho insists that the *logos* word becomes the *rhema* word through the Spirit, and miracles begin with the *rhema* word.[66]

Later, Cho also followed the prayer style of the American faith healer Kathryn Kuhlman (1907–1976). Kuhlman used "words of knowledge" to identify and call out the sick from the platform. Unlike Roberts, she prayed for the sick from the pulpit without laying hands on them. Using this method, Cho could minister to thousands of sick people from the pulpit during services, although he continued to lay hands on the sick individually after the service.[67]

---

[60]Synan, "Roots of Yonggi Cho's Theology of Healing," 281.
[61]Synan, *The Century of the Holy Spirit*, 357-359.
[62]Synan, "Roots of Yonggi Cho's Theology of Healing," 284.
[63]Cho, *Successful Home Cell Groups*, 9.
[64]Synan, "Roots of Yonggi Cho's Theology of Healing," 281.
[65]Synan, *The Century of the Holy Spirit*, 358.
[66]Synan, "Roots of Yonggi Cho's Theology of Healing," 284.
[67]Ibid.

CHAPTER 15
THE THREEFOLD BLESSING IN THE KOREAN CONTEXT

Koreans uniquely appropriated and contextualized the theology of the Threefold Blessing. Their post-war hardships made them receptive to the idea of God's blessings as an alleviation of current hardships as well as the promised of eternal life in the future. Third John 2 became the foundational text for the Threefold Blessing theology.

1. Interpretation of 3 John 2

Theologians paid little attention to the scripture text 3 John 2 before it was brought into relief by twentieth-century Pentecostals. The understanding of this passage by early church fathers was different from today's Pentecostals. Tertullian used the scripture to emphasize separation from the things that could be the cause of soul's corruption.[1] Augustine said that "the prosperity of the soul (3 Jn. 2) might be injuriously affected by the prosperity of the body"[2] and "the body's prosperity may testify to the soul's poverty or vice versa."[3] Unlike the dualistic and ascetic perspectives of the early church fathers, Bede the Venerable (673-735) paraphrased 3 John 2 to depict the Benedictine ideal of prosperity:

> I earnestly long for this, he says, from the Lord in my frequent prayers, that you bring to a good end what you are doing well, and as your soul, that is the inward intention of your mind, now does favorably, that is, makes progress in your works of almsgiving, since you are rich both in the goodness of a generous spirit and in resources of money, that you bestow

---

[1] Timothy David Barnes, *Tertullian: A Historical and Literary Study* (Oxford: Clarendon Press, 1971), 136.
[2] Heather L. Landrus, "Hearing 3 John 2 in the Voice of History," *Journal of Pentecostal Theology* 11, no. 1 (2002): 72.
[3] Ibid., 73.

these on the needy and so with the Lord's help always be able to lead a life full of virtues.[4]

According to Landrus, prosperity in the Benedictine ideal is "communal in nature and frees others from want, both spiritually and physically. Spiritual and financial riches are a blessing when they are poured forth to bless those who have need. For it is in giving to others that the soul makes progress."[5] In contrast to Bede, Ambrosius used the term "success" and "flourish" instead of "prosperity." He translated 3 John 2, "My dearest, I make speech from all that you walk successfully and flourish, thus as your soul successfully leads you."[6]

In 1854, Albert Barnes commented on 3 John 2, based on the KJV translation, "I wish *above all things* that thou mayest prosper and be in health, even as thy soul prospereth."[7] He insisted that the Greek περι παντων (*peri panton*) rendered as "above all things" should have been translated as "concerning, or in respect to all things" since the term "above all things" can be misunderstood to imply that John valued prosperity and health above salvation.

These early thinkers were concerned about defining what the scripture actually meant to the original readers and in its original context. In contrast, modern Pentecostals are more interested in interpreting it for today's Christians and making it relevant for contemporary society.

2. The Contextualized Theology of the Threefold Blessing

The Threefold Blessing is very relevant to the socio-economic life of Koreans as well as to the issue of salvation. It was successfully contextualized into the desperate situation after the Korean War.

---

[4] Bede the Venerable, *The Commentary on the Seven Catholic Epistles*, trans. David Hurst (Kalamazoo, MI: Cistercian Publications, 1985), 236.

[5] Landrus, "Hearing 3 John 2 in the Voice of History," 75.

[6] Ambrosius Catherinus, *In omnes diui Pauli Apostoli: et alias septem canonicas Epistolas*, trans. Vas Bakierowski (Parisiis: Apud Claudium Fremy, 1566), 596. Quoted in Landrus, "Hearing 3 John 2 in the Voice of History," 75.

[7] Albert Barnes, *Notes: Explanatory and Practical on the General Epistles of James, Peter, John and Jude* (New York: Harper & Brothers Publishers, 1875), 369.

Cho and his theology were criticized by mainstream Korean Christianity as being heretical. During the 68th Annual Convention of *Tong Hap* (the Korean Jesus Presbyterian Church) in 1983, they branded Cho a heretic because of his teachings and theology, in particular his focus on this-worldly salvation through the Threefold Blessing, which they regarded as a mixture of Shamanism, radical evangelism, and speaking in tongues. They also accused Cho of threatening the unity of Korean Christianity and churches by stealing other church members.[8] After over a decade of theological controversies, at the 79th Annual Convention in September, 1994, they concluded that Cho's church was not a cult. Their official statement agreed that "the sermons and theologies of Yonggi Cho coincide with the beliefs of the Apostolic Universal Church although there are dogmatic matters that still persist which we need to consider (translation mine)."[9]

Some Pentecostal and non-Pentecostal scholars relate Cho and his theology to Korean Shamanism. Harvey Cox argues that Cho's theology is syncretized with Shamanism.[10] Boo Woong Yoo identifies Cho's role in the worship service as "exactly like that of a shaman"[11] in the shamanic ritual. Walter J. Hollenweger, Yoo's doctoral supervisor, also states that Cho could be considered "a Pentecostal Shaman par excellence."[12] However, Charles H. Kraft points out that God's revelation comes through culture and considers God as "a perfect communicator,"[13] who communicates with humanity through culture. Kraft says that God takes "not only humanity and human weakness but also human culture into consideration."[14] Although the truth of the gospel is the same everywhere all the time, the reason each nation's

---

[8]Yeol Soo Eim, "The Influence of Dr. Cho's Goodness of God Theology upon His Ministry," in *Dr. Yonggi Cho's Ministry and Theology I*, ed. Young San Theological Institute, 84-5.

[9]Park, *Hankook Gyohoi Booheung Woondong Yeongoo* [A Study on the Revival Movement in Korea Church], 238.

[10]Cox, *Fire from Heaven*, 221-228.

[11]Boo Woong Yoo, "Response to Korean Shamanism by the Pentecostal Church," *International Review of Mission 75* (January 1986): 74.

[12]Hollenweger, *Pentecostalism*, 100. See footnote 2.

[13]Charles H. Kraft, *Christianity in Culture: A Study in Dynamic Biblical Theologizing in Cross-Cultural Perspective* (Maryknoll, NY: Orbis Books, 1979), 169, 257.

[14]Ibid., 169.

Christianity as well as Pentecostalism is unique and different from others is that the soils for the gospel—the social, cultural, and political contexts—are not the same.

Myung Soo Park argues that Korean Pentecostalism is more influenced by external factors like American Pentecostal/Charismatic movements than by Shamanism as the internal religio-cultural context of Korea:[15] the Pentecostal message of divine healing and prosperity was neither inspired by shamanic faith nor capitalistic desire, but rather originated with Oral Roberts. Hagin's Faith Movement influenced Cho's *logos* and *rhema* theology. Since the 1980s, Cho was deeply influenced by Robert Schuller's Possibility Thinking. His televangelism was also influenced by American Pentecostal/Charismatic televangelists.

In this sense, Cox's assertion that indigenous Shamanism and shamanic spirituality are key reasons for the extraordinary growth of Pentecostalism is not persuasive.[16] Rather than shamanic influences, two other factors may explain the extraordinary growth of Pentecostalism: first, the effective adaption of those approved and optimized methodologies for evangelism, and second, the successful contextualization of the gospel in the current socio-economic Korean context. According to Stephen B. Bevans, "Indigenization focused on the purely cultural dimension of human experience, while contextualization broadens the understanding of culture to include social, political, and economic questions."[17]

Unlike Cox, Yoo, Hollenweger, and others, Anderson understands Cho's theology from the perspectives of contextual theology. Anderson says that, through contextualization, theology becomes meaningful to ordinary people and more than written or academic theology: "the spiritual dimension" cannot be separated from "God's involvement in

---

[15]Myung Soo Park, "David Yonggi Cho and International Pentecostal/Charismatic Movements," in *Dr. Yonggi Cho's Ministry and Theology II*, ed. Young San Theological Institute (Gunpo: Hansei University Logos, 2008), 333.

[16]Cox, 222.

[17]Stephen B. Bevans, *Models of Contextual Theology* (Maryknoll, NY: Orbis Books, 1997), 22.

the whole life."[18] Anderson uses the term "theology in practice."[19] He insists that this sort of theology is found in Pentecostalism around the world; Cho's theology of the Threefold Blessing is one example.[20]

When Cho preached the gospel to those who were experiencing severe poverty, he faced the deep theological tensions between the theology he learned at the seminary and the reality of his ministry. He was taught about the God of the future at the seminary, but in his ministry, people looked for the God of the present who cared for them in their sufferings.[21]

Traditionally, Buddhists pursued the monastic life and Confucians valued honorable poverty rather than prosperity. Mainstream Christianity also ignored the reality of the life of Koreans such as poverty, disease, and socio-political struggles. Lesslie Newbigin says that in contextualization "the Gospel comes alive in particular contexts."[22] Bevans suggests that external factors such as historical events, political forces, cultural shifts, and intellectual currents "bring to light certain internal factors within Christian faith itself that point not only to the possibility but also to the necessity of doing theology in context."[23]

The main reason for the success of Pentecostalism in Korea was Pentecostal messages based on the Threefold Blessing, which addressed the needs of ordinary Korean people. One of Cho's major preaching philosophies is "find need and meet need."[24] His sermons directly deal with the current problems of Koreans[25] and provide them with hope in the form of prosperity for poverty, divine healing for diseases, and salvation for the Last Judgment.[26] As hope always begins in hopeless

---

[18] Allan Anderson, *Zion and Pentecost: The Spirituality and Experience of Pentecostal and Zionist/Apostolic Churches in South Africa* (Pretoria: University of South Africa Press, 2000), 3.

[19] Allan Anderson, *African Reformation: African Initiated Christianity in the 20th Century* (Trenton, NJ and Asmara, Eritrea: Africa World Press Inc., 2001), 217-243.

[20] Anderson, "The Contextual Pentecostal Theology of David Yonggi Cho," 109.

[21] Cho, *Salvation, Health and Prosperity*, 11.

[22] Lesslie Newbigin, *The Gospel in a Pluralist Society* (London: SPCK, 1989), 152-153.

[23] Bevans, *Models of Contextual Theology*, 5.

[24] Cho, *Church Growth vol. 3* (Seoul: Youngsan Press, 1983), 30; Yoo, "Response to Korean Shamanism by the Pentecostal Church," 73.

[25] Wonsuk Ma, "The Effect of Rev. Cho's Sermon Style for Church Growth on the Development of Theology," in *Charis and Charisma: David Yonggi Cho and the Growth of Yoido Full Gospel Church*, ed. Sung Hoon Myung and Young Gi Hong, 162.

[26] Cho, *Salvation, Health and Prosperity*, 11-12.

situations, the Threefold Blessing as hope was contextualized for Koreans experiencing hopeless situations. For example, God as Judge cannot be regarded as a source of hope for victims of poverty and illness because they already feel they are living under judgment. Likewise, pietism is not appealing to the extreme poor. Without Jesus as the Healer the gospel cannot be good news to the sick. The Threefold Blessing became a source of hope for the sick, the poor, and the lost.

3. Reconciliation and the Threefold Blessing

Two theological premises undergird the Threefold Blessing theology: the goodness of God and reconciliation with God. The goodness of God assumes that any bad thing cannot proceed from a good God; all that God creates must be good. Thus, poverty, diseases, and sin cannot be the will of God for Pentecostals. There was neither lack nor hardship in the Garden of Eden, but after the corruption of human beings, they could not eat without hard work. The ground produced thorns and thistles (Gen 3:17-19).

The corruption of humanity included both the separation of humankind from God and the withdrawal of blessings. Augustine states that good does not stand in opposition to evil. "Evil is nothing but the corruption of natural good,"[27] because, as evil does not exist of itself, it is just non-existence or the lack of existence of good.[28] Thus, the essence of evil can only be removed by the goodness of God.[29] In other words, suffering can be removed by the Threefold Blessing. Sam Hwan Kim says that the Threefold Blessing is "the removal of evil from one's life."[30] In regard to this ontological evil, Martin Luther says, "God arranged to take away through Christ whatever the devil brought in through Adam."[31] Korean Pentecostals are convinced that living under

---

[27] Augustine, "The Nature of the Good," in *Augustine: Earlier Writings*, trans. and ed. John H. S. Burleigh (London: SCM Press Ltd., 1953), 325.

[28] Ibid., 324-350.

[29] Sam Hwan Kim, "The Question of Good and Evil in Full Gospel Faith: A Study of the Theological Foundation for the Three-fold Blessing of Dr. Yonggi Cho," in *2002 Young San International Theological Symposium*, ed. Hansei University, 292.

[30] Ibid., 282.

[31] Martin Luther, *Lectures on Romans*, trans. Wilhelm Pauck (London: SCM Press Ltd., 1961), 179.

hardship is not the will of God[32] and the Threefold Blessing is the way to restore "the original state before the fall."[33] Christ was crucified under the ontological curse, and evil causes their present sufferings.

Cho distinguishes the Threefold Blessing from the blessings in Shamanism, which are not concerned about the source or the means of blessings. By the grace of God, the Threefold Blessing will be given to those who accept Christ as Savior through true repentance—to those who have the faith to seek first the Kingdom of God and His righteousness.[34] In Cho's understanding, blessings come after a person is reconciled with God. The Threefold Blessing begins with salvation, which is prior to financial blessing or physical health.

Traditionally, Koreans accepted physical and financial sufferings as their destinies. However, Pentecostals have come to believe that ontological evil can be removed by the blessing of God through Christ. Isaiah 53:5 and 2 Corinthians 8:9[35] are often used as supporting texts for 3 John 2. With these verses, Pentecostals assert the appropriateness of the Threefold Blessing. Based on these scriptures, they can be healed because Christ was whipped. They can be rich because he became poor.

The crucifixion is directly related to the Threefold Blessing. Indeed, the crucifixion was the means of redeeming the soul as well as removing the ontological evil and curse, the causes of hopelessness in the present life. There is no doubt that the agony of Christ was the will of God to bring about reconciliation with human beings. According to Luther, although God has to sentence all sinners to death, the God on the cross endured terrible pain in order "to heal our wounds, which were caused by God's wrath; this Lord suffers wounds, himself receiving his

---

[32]Eim, "The Influence of Dr. Cho's Goodness of God Theology upon His Ministry," 86.
[33]Ibid., 87.
[34]Cho, *Ohjungbokeum kwa Samjungchukbok* [The Fivefold Gospel and the Threefold Blessing], 42.
[35]"But He was wounded for our transgressions, He was bruised for our iniquities; The chastisement for our peace was upon Him, And by His stripes we are healed" (Isa 53:5, NKJV); "For you know the grace of our Lord Jesus Christ, that though He was rich, yet for your sakes He became poor, that your through His poverty might become rich" (2 Cor 8:9, NKJV).

wrath.... The death of Christ is the death of death."[36] Jesus on the cross is "God fighting with God at Golgotha (da streydet Gott mit Gott)."[37]

In his book *The Crucified God*, Moltmann says that the agony of Christ on the cross intervened in the suffering of human life and society.[38] "God experiences suffering, death and hell. This is the way he [God] experiences history."[39] As black slaves who were suffering under inhuman circumstances directly connected themselves to the passion of Christ, Pentecostals relate their sufferings to the affliction of Christ on the cross. To black slaves, the suffering and death of Christ were the symbol of their own agony, inhuman situations, sufferings, and even fate.[40] James H. Cone writes, "When black slaves suffered, God suffered."[41] He also writes, "The liberation of the oppressed is a part of the innermost nature of God . . . the blackness of God means that the essence of the nature of God is to be found in the concept of liberation."[42] Korean Pentecostals also directly relate their spiritual, physical, and financial difficulties to the suffering of Christ and the crucifixion. Unlike black theology and liberation theology, they seem indifferent to communal sufferings, injustice, unrighteousness, and inequality. They do not actively engage in social action or address issues related to communal hardship.

According to Pentecostals, before the fall of humankind, there was no harm, hurt, or destruction but only prosperity for all creatures. After the fall, the ecosystem was disrupted and society collapsed. The ground produced thorns. People killed each other. Thus, the suffering of Christ and his resurrection intend to bring about reconciliation with God and the restoration of divine blessing. Pentecostals do not believe that this reconciliation and restoration extends to the ecological or communal dimensions. They have great concern about individual healing and prosperity without caring about social inequality, injustice, or the

---

[36]Luther, *Lectures on Romans*, 179-180.
[37]Kazoh Kitamori, *Theology of the Pain of God* (London: SCM Press Ltd., 1966), 21. Quoting Martin Luther.
[38]Jürgen Moltmann, *The Crucified God*, trans. R. A. Wilson and John Bowden (London: SCM Press, 2001).
[39]Jürgen Moltmann, *The Church in the Power of the Spirit: A Contribution to Messianic Ecclesiology*, trans. Margaret Kohl (London: SCM Press, 1977), 64.
[40]Moltmann, *The Crucified God*, 44.
[41]James H. Cone, *The Spirituals and the Blues* (New York: Orbis Books, 1995), 62.
[42]James H. Cone, *A Black Theology of Liberation* (New York: Orbis Books, 1996), 64.

destruction of ecosystems caused by human greed. In other words, they are concerned with individual blessing rather than societal transformation.

Pentecostals are criticized for neglecting to address social inequalities and injustice. Therefore, Korean Pentecostals need to broaden the meaning of reconciliation and blessing to include the social and ecological dimensions.

4. Holistic Salvation

In the trichotomic view, human beings consist of three elements: spirit, body, and soul. Dualists such as the Gnostics understand that the body and the soul are separable, with the body inferior to the soul. In the Hebrew Scriptures, Jews neither understand humankind in terms of dichotomy nor trichotomy. They do not separate human beings into the body and the spirit: human nature is an integrated unity.[43] Karl Barth argues that human beings cannot be understood "as merely a soul, merely as body, or as a creature split up into a body and a soul as it were."[44] He disagrees with psychophysical parallelism because he understands that the body and the soul are inseparable: human beings can only be understood as a unity combining the body and the soul.[45]

Traditionally, mainstream Korean Christianity has emphasized spiritual salvation. An emphasis on hope for prosperity and blessing is due to shamanic or secular influences. However, Pentecostal worldviews are holistic and God-centered.[46] Jackie Johns says that for Pentecostals, "all things relate to God and God relates to all things."[47] Pentecostals neither polarize the body and the soul, nor demand the sacrifice of the body for the soul.

---

[43]Byung In Ko, "Recovery Based on Threefold Blessing," in *Dr. Yonggi Cho's Ministry and Theology I*, ed. Young San Theological Institute, 235-236.
[44]Otto Weber, *Karl Barth's Church Dogmatic: An Introductory Report on Volumes I: 1 to III:4*, trans. Arthur C. Cochrane (London: Lutterworth Press, 1953), 159.
[45]Ibid., 159.
[46]Cheryl Bridges Johns, "Healing and Deliverance: A Pentecostal Perspective," in *Pentecostal Movements as an Ecumenical Challenge*, ed. Jürgen Moltmann and Karl Josef Kuschel (London: SCM Press, 1996), 46.
[47]Jackie Johns, "Pentecostalism and the Postmodern Worldview," *Journal of Pentecostal Theology* 78 (1995): 88.

Cho also does not separate hope into two aspects: hope for eternal life and hope for blessings in this present life:

> I had such complicated feelings that I could hardly bear it. The people to whom I tried to preach the gospel were living in a spiritually barren state, facing a wall of despair, and were so destitute that they had difficulty finding enough food to eat. While preaching the Word to them and feeding them, I found myself involved in gross self-contradiction, for the God I had learned about at the seminary seemed to be merely the God of the future. I could not find the God of the present to show Him to people who were living in such question stirred in my heart. Introducing the God of the past could hardly make any impression on those people; on the other hand, the urgent situation of their present state kept the Christ of the future from being preached to them. So I cried out to God. I cried out not only for them, but I cried out for myself; "Oh, my Lord! Where is the God of the present? With what can I give hope and new life to these people who are in despair, starved and poorly clothed? Oh, Lord! Where are You at this hour-You who are God to them as well as to me?" I cried and prayed with tears day in and day out, earnestly seeking. After I spent much time in supplication, God finally spoke to my heart. His words, warm and full of hope, were a revelation to me. The word from God contained the truth of the Threefold blessings of salvation, health and prosperity written in 3 John 2.[48]

Cho does not restrict salvation to the spiritual dimension but extends it to include redemption from the hardships of life. Salvation must include saving "the whole person including spirit, body, and everything in life."[49] "God's desire for all of His people is good health."[50] Salvation not only redeems our souls from mortal death, but also frees us from

---

[48]Cho, *Salvation, Health and Prosperity*, 11.
[49]Ko, "Recovery Based on Threefold Blessing," 242.
[50]Mathew, "Oral Roberts and David Yonggi Cho," 299.

curses and blessings in life.⁵¹ The holistic salvation of the Threefold Blessing not only caters for spiritual blessing but includes physical health and financial prosperity and opposes the idea that Christians have to sacrifice earthly blessings for spiritual salvation.

Theologically, Cho's holistic soteriology relates to three calamities brought about by the fall of humanity: spiritual death, the curse of poverty and destitution, and the suffering caused by disease and physical death.⁵² Since the fall, humankind lives under the influence of a threefold corruption: spiritual (Gen 3:17-18), physical (Gen 3:19), and circumstantial death (Gen 3:17-18). ⁵³ The soul was corrupted, humankind became egoistic, and the body suffered from various diseases and sicknesses. The land began to produce thorns and thistles.⁵⁴ Thus, salvation and suffering of Christ must provide holistic deliverance: spiritual, physical, and circumstantial blessings, including financial prosperity through restoration of humanity's relationship with God in Christ.⁵⁵ Cho defines the three calamities as curses from God following the Fall and declares that "believers are already redeemed from the curses" through Christ.⁵⁶

Moltmann had a clear understanding of Cho's holistic soteriology: "Dr. Cho, splendidly, sees here a double meaning: (1) Christ shed his blood and died for our sins, in order to bring us the eternal salvation of fellowship with God; (2) Christ carried our sickness in order not only to redeem our souls, but so as to heal our bodies too from the curse of sickness and to bless us."⁵⁷ The Threefold Blessing addresses the question of why believers still have to endure devastating experiences despite all the curses having been removed for believers through the sufferings and death of Christ on the Cross. Because diseases and poverty are evil, and a curse, salvation includes healing and blessing.

---

⁵¹Cho, *Salvation, Health, and Prosperity*, 16; Mathew, "Oral Roberts and David Yonggi Cho," 299.

⁵²Yonggi Cho, "Three Calamities and Three Blessings" (Sunday sermon, November 9, 2003), available from http://www.fgtv.com/fgtv/F1/WF1_1.asp?shType=1&code =2003&mm=11, accessed on 12 April 2012.

⁵³Yonggi Cho, *The Story of Fivefold Gospel* (Seoul: Seoul Logos, 1998), 47.

⁵⁴Yonggi Cho, *Fivefold Gospel and Threefold Blessing* (Seoul: Seoul Logos, 1998), 132.

⁵⁵Pan Ho Kim, "Paul Tillich and Dr. Yonggi Cho: A Dialogue between Their Respective Theologies of Healing," in *Dr. Yonggi Cho's Ministry and Theology I*, Young San Theological Institute, 371.

⁵⁶Eim, "The Influence of Dr. Cho's Goodness of God heology upon His Ministry," 90.

⁵⁷Moltmann, "The Blessing of Hope," 153.

Physical health and prosperity are neither equal, nor prior to, spiritual salvation in the Threefold Blessing. The blessings of health and financial prosperity are not considered apart from spiritual salvation; physical health and material prosperity are not emphasized at the expense of spiritual health and prosperity. Salvation is not restricted to spiritual salvation, but health and prosperity follow from the salvation of the soul. For Cho, Christ's suffering is the basis of hope for healing and prosperity. The resurrection and the Second Advent provide the hope for eternal life. Jesus is the Redeemer, the Blesser, and the Healer in the Threefold Blessing.

It seems healing and prosperity are often emphasized by Pentecostals without emphasizing salvific hope. In contrast, Moltmann says eschatological hope is primary and essential for Christian faith.[58] Healing and prosperity without salvation are meaningless in Christian life. Moltmann's theology of hope can prevent this theological danger. Furthermore, eschatological hope can prevent the Threefold Blessing from becoming secularized or becoming Christian mammonism.

---

[58]Moltmann, *The Theology of Hope*, 16-18.

CHAPTER 16
THE HOPE OF THE THREEFOLD BLESSING

In situations of abundance in all aspects of life, hope will be not necessary. If someone has all they need in life but still desires to have more, this cannot be hope but reflects an attitude of greed. Lack normally is accompanied by suffering, and hope begins in such circumstances. When Christians suffer, they are forced to seek God to find hope to overcome their hardship. The basis for hope in hopeless situations is the promise of God.

1. Hope in Hopelessness

During the 1960s and 1970s, the theology of hope in Germany and the Threefold Blessing in Korea developed and contextualized in similar socio-political and economical contexts. Germany, a defeated nation following World War II, was similar to Korea after Japanese rule and the Korean War. The socio-economic and religio-cultural functions of both countries collapsed, and people suffered from the aftermath of the war. Both countries seemed without hope.

Moltmann notes that hope always emerges in situations of hopelessness. While Moltmann was interned as a prisoner of war (1945-1948), he experienced the realty of God. He experienced both "God as the power of hope" and "God's presence in suffering."[1] This became the foundation of his theology of hope, developed in the late 1960s and early 1970s.[2] "Hope's statements of promise must stand in contradiction to the reality which can at present be experienced."[3]

Christians experience the contradictions between the experiential life of suffering and the promise of God. Moltmann says that "hope must prove its power" in this contradiction.[4] Hope enables Christians to

---

[1] Richard Bauckham, *The Theology of Jürgen Moltmann* (London: T&T Clark Ltd., 1995), 1.
[2] Ibid.
[3] Moltmann, *The Theology of Hope*, 18.
[4] Ibid., 19.

endure suffering patiently until the promise of God becomes a reality. Hope is not merely an uncertain wait, but an intense, faith-based expectation that God will replace their sufferings with blessings. "Hope is nothing else than the expectation of those things which faith has believed to have been truly promised by God."[5]

Similarly, Cho says that without expecting God to remove their sufferings, people cannot escape from the tribulation and sufferings they are facing.[6] Cho emphasizes the importance of combining expectation with prayer: "When we want to receive something we must set a goal through prayer, and then have a burning desire and great expectation to achieve the goal" in God.[7]

Compared to Moltmann's hope theology, the hope of the Threefold Blessing is less well-developed theologically. If Moltmann's hope is based on the theology of resurrection of Christ and His second coming,[8] the hope of the Threefold Blessing has developed from one Biblical scripture: 3 John 2. Moltmann's hope has eschatological and soteriological perspectives, but the hope of the Threefold Blessing relates to Korean prosperity theology, which became deeply rooted after the Korean War.

The hope in the Threefold Blessing stood in stark contrast to the dire circumstances in the post-war context. Pentecostals expected God to bless them in their hopelessness. Along with spiritual salvation, they expected divine healing of their diseases and prosperity in their extreme poverty. The Threefold Blessing successfully contextualized the gospel within desperate socio-economic and religio-political contexts.

In his sermons, Cho often uses the phrase "vision and dreams" interchangeably with the term "hope." Cho states that these futuristic words are able to overcome present sufferings and "God has been using this language of the Holy Spirit to change many lives."[9] Indeed, hopelessness can be overcome only by hope. For instance, assuming that there is someone who wants to give up on life out of despair, the only

---

[5] Ibid., 20.
[6] Yonggi Cho, *March Forward to Hope* (Seoul: Seoul Logos Co., 2002), 12.
[7] Ibid.
[8] Moltmann, *The Theology of Hope*, 20-22; Moltmann, *The Crucified God*, xxi.
[9] Yonggi Cho, *The Fourth Dimension*, 46.

antidote to suicide is to find hope. During the industrialization, urbanization, and democratization after the Korean War, Cho was not involved in socio-political acts or movements. He offered hope to Koreans with his message of the Threefold Blessing, and his theology of hope greatly influenced Korean society.[10]

2. Hope and Faith

Veli-Matti Kärkkäinen claims a theological resonance between Cho's Pentecostal theology of hope and Wolfhart Pannenberg's theology of hope and faith. Both Cho and Pannenberg regard the promise of God as the basis of faith, and faith stands firm in the trust that God will fulfil his promise in the future.[11] Pannenberg understands that faith is naturally connected with hope, and the promise of God is never apart from hope.[12] According to Pannenberg, "Hope reaches beyond what is present to something that is not yet visible (Romans 8:24-25; cf 2 Corinthians 5:7; Hebrews 11:1)."[13] The Bible says that "faith is the substance of things hoped for, the evidence of things not seen (Hebrews 11:1)." Cho reinterprets the verse: "Faith is also a certificate of title of things we hope for eagerly."[14] Although hope is oriented towards the future, it can be substantiated by faith. Cho uses the word "certificate" for the ownership of hope through faith, because hope is not the subject of yearning or futuristic uncertainty any longer, but it is realized in the present by faith. Hope is oriented both towards the future and the present due to faith.

In the Threefold Blessing, Jesus is the Saviour, the Healer, and the Blesser. For Moltmann, Christian faith is primarily and essentially Christian hope.[15] However he points out that without the knowledge of

---

[10]Sang Bok Lee, "Youngsan Cho Yonggi Moksa eui Sahoigoowon Ehae [An Understanding of Rev. Yonggi Cho's Social Salvation]," *Journal of Young San Theology* 14 (2008): 57-58.
[11]Veli-Matti Kärkkäinen, "March Forward to Hope: Dr. Yonggi Cho's Pentecostal Theology of Hope," in *Dr. Yonggi Cho's Ministry and Theology II*, ed. Young San Theological Institute, 47.
[12]Wolfhart Pannenberg, *Systematic Theology vol. 3*, trans. Geoffrey Bromiley (Grand Rapids, MI: Wm. B. Eerdmans Publishing Co., 1998), 174.
[13]Ibid.
[14]Yonggi Cho, *Unleashing the Power of Faith* (Alachua, FL: Bridge-Logos, 2006), 16.
[15]Moltmann, *The Theology of Hope*, 16; Peter Althouse, *Spirit of the Last Days: Pentecostal Eschatology in Conversation with Jürgen Moltmann* (London: T&T Clark International, 2003), 176.

Christ, "hope becomes a utopia and remains hanging in the air" and without hope, faith "become a fainthearted and ultimately a dead faith."[16] Without the knowledge of Christ, hope for prosperity in the Threefold Blessing becomes similar to aspirations in shamanistic materialism.

Korean Pentecostals are convinced that they can be saved through the crucifixion of Christ; they can be healed because of his stripes (Isa 53:5; 1 Pet 2:24); and they can become rich because he became poor (2 Cor 8:9). There is no distinction between the knowledge of Christ and faith: the knowledge of Christ does not imply rational knowledge but experiential knowledge of Jesus as Saviour, Healer, and dispenser of blessings through faith. Pentecostals neither search for prosperity and physical health outside of the knowledge of Christ nor do they ignore that prosperity and physical health hinges on the prosperity of the soul. Veli-Matti Kärkkäinen evaluates Cho's theology of hope as "bold faith-expectation."[17]

Cho emphasizes hope in the unseen. His concept of hope does not operate in possibilities but is based on unconditional faith. Cho says,

> Although you may not see any evidence of it with your eyes or hears any sound with your ears, even as your future seems dark, when faith energy starts to work within you and makes you think, "it's already come about," then you become a person of faith.[18]

Cho often quotes the story of Abraham and Sarah (Gen 17:15-22) as an example of hope and faith. According to Romans 4:18-21, when Abraham and Sarah heard the promise of God, they had hope for a child even though Sarah's womb was barren. Hope diverts the present reality into a new phase: with hope, people can transfer their concerns over current matters they are struggling with to faith in the promise of God.

Cho says that God's power can be released for miracles through faith.[19] The Threefold Blessing was God's promise to Pentecostals in the

---

[16] Jürgen Moltmann, *The Theology of Hope*, 20.
[17] Veli-Matti Kärkkäinen, "March Forward to Hope: Dr. Yonggi Cho's Pentecostal Theology of Hope," 43.
[18] Yonggi Cho, *Unleashing the Power of Faith*, 16-7.
[19] Yonggi Cho, *Solving Life's Problems*, 2.

desperate situations of Korea. The hope of the Threefold Blessing or the "Pentecostal hope in Korean Pentecostal contexts," brought faith that God would fulfill this hope in their lives. Thus, in this sense, hope and faith are inseparably linked.

CHAPTER 17
THE THREEFOLD BLESSING AND MOLTMANN'S THEOLOGY OF HOPE

The Threefold Blessing of Cho and Moltmann's theology of hope developed against a background of similar social contexts and experiences of personal hardship. Comparing himself with Cho, Moltmann says, "Pastor Cho began his mission in the *Han* of the Korean people after the Korean War; I began my life in Christ in the *Han* of the Second World War and in the ruins of post-war Germany."[1] However, while both theologies focus on the theological theme of hope, there are also theological differences between them.

The publication of Moltmann's book *Theology of Hope* in 1964 influenced various types of contextual theology directly and indirectly, including Political Theology, Black Theology, Liberation Theology, Feminist Theology, and even *Minjung* Theology in Korea. When Moltmann was invited to Korea by *Minjung* and liberal theologians (mostly Moltmann's pupils or those who had studied in Germany), the socio-political aspects of Moltmann's theology were emphasized to Korean Christians. Due to theological similarities between Moltmann's theology and *Minjung* Theology, Moltmann was initially considered a liberal theologian by Korean conservative Christians as well as Pentecostals and not welcomed by either. However, as Moltmann began to dialogue with Korean Pentecostalism from the 1990s, Pentecostals were able to understand his theology from a broader perspective. In 1995, he was invited by Korean Pentecostals to conduct a seminar at the YFGC, where he did not hesitate to define the Threefold Blessing as hope for the Koreans in the post-Korean War context.[2]

---

[1] Moltmann, "The Blessing of Hope," 149.
[2] Personal interview with Jürgen Moltmann on 4 January 2012 at his house in Tübingen, Germany. See Appendix A. Interview with Dr. Jürgen Moltmann.

1. The Theological Basis of Moltmann's Hope and the Threefold Blessing

In September 1995, Dr. Jong Wha Park (one of Moltmann's PhD students and chair of the Presbyterian Church in South Korea at the time),[3] invited Moltmann for three hours of theological dialogue with Cho.[4] Moltmann then uncovered the similarities between his and Cho's biographical and theological journeys.

Both theologies have a common theological denominator, based on personal experiences of faith and the severe hardships. Using the Korean term *Han*, Moltmann identifies himself, a victim of the Second World War, with Cho who suffered extreme poverty and tuberculosis. He equates the difficult socio-economic circumstances of post-war Germany with the socio-political chaos of post-war Korea.[5] In the relationship between his theology of hope and the Pentecostal movement (including Korean Pentecostalism), Moltmann says,

> Pastor Cho began his mission in the *Han* of the Korean people after the Korean War. I began my life in Christ in the *Han* of the Second World War in the ruins of post-war Germany. Moreover, the theology of hope and the Pentecostal movement have a common spiritual root as well. This is to be found in the German revival movement that is linked with the name of the Blumhardts, father and son. This revival movement began with a healing and an exorcism which the father, Johann Christopher Blumhardt, experienced in a little village in the Black Forest. The movement continued in the prophetic and healing activity of his son, Christopher Blumhardt, in Bad Boll, near Tübingen. For Blumhardt, "healing and hoping" belonged together in just the same way as "praying and watching"—"watching" for the coming of Christ, and the "hastening to meet" Christ in his coming. Karl Barth called Blumhardt a first "theologian of hope"

---

[3]Kukmin Ilbo, one of Korean Daily News Papers, addresses the position of Dr. Jong Wha Park at that time and reports that Moltmann also gave lectures on his theology of hope to Cho and other pastors at YFGC. See http://news.kukinews.com/article/view.asp?arcid=0921286513, accessed on October 26, 2011.
[4]Moltmann, "The Blessing of Hope,"148.
[5]Ibid., 148-49.

and as a young man was deeply influenced by him. Christopher Blumhardt became the spiritual father both of the dialectical theology of Karl Barth and Eduard Thurneysen, and of the religious-social movement of Leonhard Ragaz and Hermann Kutter in Switzerland. . . . Today, among American Pentecostal theologians we find more and more followers of the forward-looking and proactive hope of Christopher Blumhardt. It is the experience of an active hope that transforms life and in anticipation reaches out into the future of Christ.[6]

Moltmann states that his theology of hope "has two roots: Christoph Blumhardt (1842-1919) and Ernst Bloch (1885-1977). I was not in Bad Boll; nor was I in Württemberg. But I was first influenced by Christoph Blumhardt before I read Ernst Bloch."[7] The German revival led by Johann Christoph Blumhardt (1805-1880) and his son, Christoph F. Blumhardt,[8] began with exorcism and healing,[9] and its main theme was "Jesus ist Sieger [Jesus is Victor]."[10] The foundational song of the Blumhardt revival movement was, "Jesus wears the glorious crown, triumphs over all his foes; Jesus conquers; all the world now his

---

[6]Ibid.,149.

[7]Jürgen Moltmann, "The Hope for the Kingdom of God and Signs of Hope in the World: The Relevance of Blumhardt's Theology Today," *PNEUMA: The Journal of the Society for Pentecostal Studies* 26, no. 1 (Spring 2004): 4.

[8]While Johann Christoph Blumhardt was ministering in the Schwabian village of Möttlingen, there were two demon possessed sisters, named Gottliebin Dittus and her sister Katharina who experienced an exorcism. For two years, Johann Christoph Blumhardt had been praying for Gottliebin Dittus who had suffered from demon possession for many years. One night in December 1843, the demon was cast out from Gottliebin but entered her sister Katharina. When the demon finally left Katharina, it shouted out "Jesus ist Sieger! [Jesus is Victor]." After the exorcism, divine healings also followed. The news of the exorcism and healing spread quickly to other regions, and within weeks, thousands of people came to Möttlingen. They were eager to receive prayer for healing from Blumhardt. It is interesting that most healings and conversions occurred after confession of sins. Also the revival is referred to as "a Bußbewegung [repentance movement]" like the Korean revivals in the early 1900s. See Simeon Zahl, *Pneumatology and Theology of the Cross in the Preaching of Christoph Friedrich Blumhardt*, 13-5; R. A. N. Kydd, "Healing in the Christian Church," in *The New International Dictionary of Pentecostal and Charismatic Movements*, ed. Stanley M. Burgess and Eduard M. Van der Maas, 700-701.

[9]Moltmann, "The Blessing of Hope,"149.

[10]Simeon Zahl, *Pneumatology and Theology of the Cross in the Preaching of Christoph Friedrich Blumhardt*, 15.

domination knows. Jesus comes with victors' might, Leads from darkness into light."[11]

Christoph F. Blumhardt was a pastor, not a theologian. He found hope in the victory of Jesus on the cross, and his hope was not lodged in human needs but in the divine promise.[12] Blumhardt had no intention to develop his theology or theoretical work, even though he studied theology in Tübingen.[13] Still, Karl Barth does not hesitate to call Christoph F. Blumhardt a theologian of hope,[14] and Moltmann acknowledges Blumhardt as the first theologian of hope.[15] Blumhardt's hope significantly influenced Moltmann's theology.

Moltmann was also influenced by Ernst Bloch, a Jewish Marxist philosopher. Although Moltmann disagrees with Barth's claim that he (Moltmann) was baptized by Bloch's *Das Prinzip Hoffnung* [the Principle of Hope],[16] he agrees that Bloch's philosophy of hope provided the basis for his "biblical hope" and his understanding of "Jewish faith in the promise and the Christian resurrection hope."[17] Bauckham argues that Moltmann developed his theology of hope through "critical dialogue with Bloch's philosophy."[18]

Through Blumhardt and Bloch's theological influences, Moltmann's theology of hope became eschatological and deeply related to the resurrection of Christ and the promise of the Second Advent. Furthermore, Moltmann understands the crucifixion and the resurrection in Trinitarian terms. The suffering of Christ on the cross was "the torment of hell" because the crucifixion was the suffering of being

---

[11]Karl Barth, *Protestant Theology in the Nineteenth Century: Its Background and History*, 645.

[12]Ibid., 648.

[13]Simeon Zahl, *Pneumatology and Theology of the Cross in the Preaching of Christoph Friedrich Blumhardt: The Holy Spirit between Wittenberg and Azusa Street* (London and New York: T& T Clark, 2010), 11.

[14]Karl Barth, *Protestant Theology*, 646. In *Protestant Theology in the Nineteenth Century*, Barth includes Christoph F. Blumhardt as one of twenty-five most influential philosophers and theologians. Ibid., 643-653.

[15]Moltmann, "The Blessing of Hope,"149.

[16]Karl Barth, *Letters 1961-1968*, trans. Geoffrey W. Bromiley (Edinburgh: T&T Clark, 1981), 175.

[17]Jürgen Moltmann, *Experiences in Theology: Ways and Forms of Christian Theology*, trans. Margaret Kohl (London: SCM Press, 2000), 92.

[18]Richard Bauckham, *Moltmann: Messianic Theology in the Making* (Hant, UK: Marshall Pickering, 1987), 7-8.

abandoned by God.[19] Unlike liberal theologians who understand the death of Christ as the death of God,[20] Moltmann recognizes the crucifixion as the death of Christ in God. The event of the cross involved the interrelationship between "Jesus and his God, between the Father and Jesus"[21] and was "the community of will of the Father and the Son."[22] Also, "By entering into death on the cross, Christ brings fellowship with God into this darkness and saves those who were lost."[23] There could be no hope for humanity and the world if the death of Christ meant the death of God.

For Moltmann, without the resurrection and the promise of the Second Advent, Christians cannot have hope in the context of the desperation of death. On the other hand, for Cho, the hopes of prosperity and healing in the Threefold Blessing are related to God's promises not only concerning the second coming of Christ but also Jesus' promises of healing and blessing. Therefore, Christ in the Threefold Blessing is not only coming to judge; he is also the healer and dispenser of blessing in this life.

2. Christ's Suffering and Hope

Moltmann's hope is based on the resurrection of Christ and the promise of the Second Advent.[24] To Moltmann, the cross is nothing but a tragedy for Christ without the resurrection.[25] Moltmann says that "the true Christian foundation for the hope of universal salvation is the theology of the cross, and the realistic consequence of the theology of the cross can only be the restoration of all things."[26] The event of the resurrection is "the dialectical event of eschatological promise": death

---

[19] Moltmann, *The Crucified God*, 150.
[20] Jürgen Moltmann, *The Trinity and the Kingdom: The Doctrine of God*, trans. Margaret Kohl (Minneapolis, MN: Fortress Press, 1993), 129-177.
[21] Moltmann, *The Crucified God*, 151.
[22] Ibid., 252.
[23] Moltmann, "The Blessing of Hope,"153.
[24] Moltmann, *The Theology of Hope*, 20-22; Moltmann, *The Crucified God*, xxi.
[25] Jürgen Moltmann, *Experiences of God*, trans. Margaret Kohl (London: SCM Press, 1980), 53.
[26] Jürgen Moltmann, *The Coming of God: Christian Eschatology*, trans. Margaret Kohl (London: SCM Press, 1996), 251.

and eternal life, God-forsakenness and the glory of God, the absence and the presence of God.[27]

In comparison with Moltmann's hope, the hope of the Threefold Blessing begins not with the resurrection and the Second Advent, but with the suffering of Christ. The hope for healing in the Threefold Blessing is related to Christ's suffering rather than his resurrection, based on Isaiah 53:5 and 2 Peter 2:24 ("By his stripes we are healed.") The resurrection and the Second Advent are the basis of hope for eternal life. Responding to this perspective, Moltmann states that "He [Jesus] healed them [the sick] not through His superior power but through His suffering."[28] In a chronological sense, Pentecostal hope begins with the suffering of Christ, which is as important as the resurrection.

Moltmann and Cho understand the gospel's application to the poor and the rich differently. Based on the scriptures Isaiah 53:4 and 2 Corinthians 8:9,[29] Cho understands that Christians can be rich because Jesus became poor to make them rich.[30] Cho relates the suffering of Christ to personal blessing. Moltmann extends the scope of the crucifixion to include socio-political matters: "To be crucified with Christ is no longer a purely private and spiritualized matter, but develops into political theology of the following of the crucified Christ."[31] Jesus became poor to liberate the poor.[32] According to Moltmann, the poor are not those with financial difficulties or who suffer from poverty. Rather, the poor include the "non-person, sub-human, dehumanized, and human fodder." The rich as the counter-term to the poor consist of "the man of violence, who makes someone else poor and enriches himself at the other's expense,"[33] like the tax collector who cheated the powerless and

---

[27]Richard Bauckham, *The Theology of Jürgen Moltmann* (Edinburgh: T&T Clark Ltd., 1995), 100-101.

[28]Moltmann, "The Blessing of Hope,"153.

[29]"He has borne our griefs and carried our sorrows" (Isa 53: 4); "Though He was rich, yet for your sakes He became poor, that you through His poverty might become rich" (2 Cor 8:9).

[30]Yonggi Cho, "Is Poverty the Will of God?" (Sunday sermon, June 11, 1989), available from http://www.fgtv.com/fgtv/f1/WF1_1_re.asp?aidnum=20341&page=7, accessed December 22, 2012.

[31]Moltmann, *The Crucified God*, 60.

[32]Ibid., 48.

[33]Jürgen Moltmann, *The Way of Jesus Christ: Christology in Messianic Dimensions*, trans. Margaret Kohl (London: SCM Press, 1999), 99-100.

abused his authority to accumulate personal wealth (Luke 1:46-54, 19:1-10).

For Moltmann, "The God of the rich is Mammon, and he is an unjust god."[34] Moltmann says, "If the title 'Christ' refers to the redeemer and liberator, then practical Christian action can only be directed towards the liberation of man from his inhumanity."[35] Moltmann understands the rich and the poor in antagonistic terms and connects Christ's redemption with liberation from unjust circumstances. In contrast, for Cho, the rich and the poor are not confrontational, especially in terms of political and social aspects.

Cho does not extend Jesus' redemption to include liberation from unjust socio-political structures. In his sermons, Cho often mentions the patriarchs, especially Abraham, as people who received abundant blessings from God.[36] Rather than the tax collector who accumulated wealth through exploitation, the rich are the Old Testament patriarchs who received blessings from God. The God of the rich is not Mammon but the same God of the poor. Cho does not consider that the matter of poverty can be resolved through social reformation, but instead through the blessings of God. It seems that Cho does not have deep theological concerns about Christian ethics for prosperity. He rarely deals with the problems of the rich among the poor theologically. However, without emphasizing Christian values and ethics for the prosperity, the prosperity gospel has inherent theological problems. First, it can justify any means of accumulating wealth. Second, the purpose of faith can be twisted so that it focuses solely on receiving financial blessings. Third, accumulation of financial blessing can become the main index of faith.

In *The Protestant Ethic and the Spirit of Capitalism*, Max Weber supports the economic activities of Christians for financial benefits and endows them with spiritual and ethical significance. Drawing on Pietist and Methodist understandings, Weber emphasizes that economic activities need to be motivated by religious values.[37] Similarly, Korean Pentecostals must combine an emphasis on prosperity with Christian

---

[34]Ibid., 100.
[35]Moltmann, *The Crucified God*, 18.
[36]Yonggi Cho, "God's Blessing and Abraham" (Sunday sermon on 08 February 2009), available from http://www.fgtv.com/fgtv/f1/WF1_1_re.asp?aidnum=21367&page=1, accessed 21 December 2012.
[37]Max Weber, *The Protestant Ethic and the Spirit of Capitalism*, trans. Stephen Kalberg (Los Angeles: Roxbury Publishing Co., 2002), 76-80.

values. Unless Pentecostals insist that prosperity is not the ultimate purpose of Christian belief, they may promote circumstances where the rich become richer and the poor become poorer.

CHAPTER 18
THEOLOGIES OF HOPE AND THE KINGDOM OF GOD

Various scholars and the Church throughout various eras have defined the Kingdom of God in their own way. Korean Pentecostals have their own understanding of the Kingdom and its implications for hope in their context. The early missionaries and Korean Christians—including Pentecostals—emphasized salvation in terms of what people are saved "from" rather than what they are saved "for."[1] Their major concern was salvation from sins. In regard to this eschatological emphasis on the future Kingdom, Veli-Matti Kärkkäinen points out that "escapism relegates Christian hope only to the future without relevance to the matters of today here on earth."[2]

Since the 1960s, during industrialization and dictatorship, the scope of salvation broadened to include not only salvation "from sins" but salvation "for" other aspects such as working for human rights, for ending exploitation, sexism, and so on. Salvation began to include within its scope socio-political acts by progressive Christians. If, for Korean progressive Christians, salvation meant liberation for social justice, and gender and social equality, it expanded for Pentecostals to include salvation *from* poverty, sickness, and sins, and *for* spiritual blessing, well-being, and prosperity.

The Kingdom of God cannot be understood only as "already but not yet," but must be extended as the present Kingdom existing "here and now." Volf argues that there must be continuity between the future Kingdom and the present world.[3] On the contrary, Land emphasizes both the continuity and discontinuity of the present and the future Kingdoms: the future Kingdom will break into the present world, which is the history of humanity.[4] Regarding the continuity of the future and present

---

[1] Harold S. Hong, Won Yong Ji, and Chung Choon Kim, eds., *Korea Struggles for Christ*, 15.
[2] Veli-Matti Kärkkäinen, "March Forward to Hope," 50.
[3] Miroslav Volf, "On Loving with Hope: Eschatology and Social Responsibility," *Transformation* 7, no. 3 (July-September 1990): 28.
[4] Steven J. Land, *Pentecostal Spirituality: A Passion for the Kingdom* (Sheffield: Sheffield Academic Press, 1993), 65.

Kingdoms, Althouse says, "The Kingdom of God breaks into the present to transform history and create anticipatory hope for the future."[5] Also, "God's Kingdom is 'already' present through the inauguration of Jesus Christ and the activity of the Spirit, but 'not yet' fulfilled, as when the presence of God will be fully revealed. As such, the vision of the future Kingdom has transformative power in the present world."[6]

For Moltmann, the future Kingdom is not to transform or change the present world for a better life, nor to fulfill individualistic desires on the earth. In the Kingdom, believers participate in the suffering of Christ and are renewed through the Spirit.[7] "Life according to the Spirit is life in love."[8] Humanity can experience the Kingdom through participating in Christ's suffering with eschatological hope and also through sharing the suffering of others on the earth. Althouse points out that the Christological pneumatology of Moltmann celebrates "the charismatic indwelling of the Spirit in the people of God, the church, and in creation itself."[9]

The Threefold Blessing embraces not only the hope for the Kingdom to come in the future but also in the "here and now" through the blessings of prosperity and healing.[10] P. H. Kim refers to Cho's healing doctrine as "an eschatological sign of the kingdom of God that is 'already' manifested and conviction of the kingdom of God that is 'not yet' completed."[11] Pentecostals do not understand the Kingdom of God merely eschatologically in relation to eternal life but also in relation to matters of this life.

There are some prominent differences between Moltmann and Korean Pentecostals. Pentecostals want hope for the visible and practical Kingdom of God in their present daily lives. Moltmann views the Kingdom of God as idealistic, metaphysical, and theological. He understands it from a Trinitarian perspective: the Kingdom is imminent

---

[5]Althouse, *Spirit of the Last Days*, 195.
[6]Ibid., 4.
[7]Jürgen Moltmann, "Pentecost and the Theology of Life," in *Pentecostal Movements as an Ecumenical Challenge*, ed. Jürgen Moltmann and Karl Josef Kuschel, 131-133.
[8]Moltmann, "The Blessing of Hope,"156.
[9]Althouse, *Spirit of the Last Days*, 195.
[10]Kim, "Paul Tillich and Dr. Yonggi Cho," 362.
[11]Ibid., 368.

in the Trinity and can be understood in the Trinitarian relationship.[12] In this sense, humanity can understand the Kingdom of God only through the economy of God. The Kingdom is "an interaction between God and the world, God and human beings or between the Trinitarian divine Persons."[13]

Furthermore, for Moltmann, the Kingdom is "the new Jerusalem" where God will dwell among "the new people of God" which he calls *"the cosmic Shekinah* [the cosmic dwelling]."[14] Therefore, the Kingdom is futuristic and eschatological. In his political theology of hope, Moltmann understands that Christian hope expects the manifestation of God's righteousness in an unjust and suffering world. Through Christ and the indwelling of the Spirit, the eschatological future becomes immersed in the present "to revolutionize the present."[15] The gospel brings "hope into an otherwise hopeless present, hope for justice and freedom and peace where injustice, oppression and conflict presently reign."[16] Further,

> Pentecostal theology needs to develop the theology of resurrection of Christ, the resurrection of the Spirit, and the resurrection from death in the future. The resurrection of Christ is the cornerstone of Christian faith because without the resurrection of Christ we would know nothing about Jesus. And the resurrection of the Spirit is important to courage to live and to be. The resurrection of the Spirit came upon the Disciples of Christ and formed into a community of sharing in Acts chapter 4, incorrectly called early Christian communists. But the resurrection of hope brings people hope to form a community where there was no differences in gender, income and where they can be accepted each other as brothers and sisters. Therefore the resurrection of hope is important for life.[17]

---

[12]Moltmann, *The Trinity and the Kingdom: The Doctrine of God*, 209-211.
[13]Moltmann, *The Coming of God: Christian Eschatology*, 330.
[14]Ibid., 317.
[15]Althouse, *Spirit of the Last*, 176.
[16]Bauckham, *The Theology of Jürgen Moltmann*, 106-07.
[17]Personal interview with Jürgen Moltmann, January 4, 2012, at his house in Tübingen, Germany. See, Appendix A. Interview with Dr. Jürgen Moltmann.

For Cho, the Kingdom does not only remain an eschatological or communal hope, but must relate to personal life and present reality. There are two aspects of the Kingdom of God: "the future aspect of kingdom" and "the present reality of the kingdom of God." [18] Additionally, "The Gospel deals not only with the hope for the eternal life and the salvation of spirit and soul but also prosperity in life and physical health and wellness that would keep the balance between spirituality and reality."[19]

Cho's messages focus on the continuity of the future and the present Kingdoms: the future Kingdom for the eternal life and the Kingdom experienced in the here and now through God's sovereignty on earth.[20] Divine healing is "a sign of the coming of the Kingdom of God to the earth"[21] because the miracle of healing is a sign of God's sovereignty in this present life.[22] Experiencing divine healing is a way to experience the Kingdom of God under his rule in this present life. In God's sovereignty, there is continuity between the present and future manifestations of the Kingdom.

Due to the influence of Cho, although the eschatological Kingdom remains paramount, Pentecostals want to experience the Kingdom of God in which there is no pain, sadness, and weeping in the "here and now." Their hope for the Kingdom of God is not a passive hope, awaiting the eschatological Kingdom while enduring current pains and sufferings. The hope that God's Kingdom and sovereignty may reach out to them in every aspect of their present lives. Pentecostals desire to experience the Kingdom of God where God's sovereignty prevails over their lives; they expect that their hardship can be removed by the power of God. Anderson points out that the "full gospel" of Pentecostal and Charismatics contains "good news for all life's problems."[23] Healing

---

[18] Yonggi Cho, *More Than Numbers: Principles of Church Growth* (Collins, Glasgow: Valley Books Trust, 1983), 78.
[19] Cho, *The Story of Fivefold Gospel*, 18.
[20] Kim, "Paul Tillich and Dr. Yonggi Cho," 362.
[21] Yonggi Cho, *Praying with Jesus* (Altamonte Springs, FL: Creation House, 1988), 50.
[22] Moon Ok Park, "An Eschatological Understanding of Dr. Yonggi Cho's Idea of Divine Healing," in *Dr. Yonggi Cho's Ministry and Theology I*, ed. Young San Theological Institute, 332.
[23] Anderson, *An Introduction to Pentecostalism*, 228.

from illness and wellbeing can be seen "as part of the essence of the gospel."[24]

Moltmann's hope and his expectation of the coming Kingdom of God do not correspond to this utopian idea for a better life:

The Christian hope is directed towards a *novum ultimum* [ultimate new], towards a new creation of all things by the God of the resurrection of Jesus Christ. It thereby opens a future outlook that embraces all things, including also death, and into this it can and must also take the limited hopes of a renewal of life, stimulating them, relativizing them, giving them direction. It will destroy the presumption in these hopes of better human freedom, of successful life, of justice and dignify for our fellow men, of control of the possibilities of nature, because it does not find in these movements the salvation it awaits, because it refuses to let the entertaining and realization of utopia ideas of this kind reconcile it with existence.[25]

Because of God's promises, Christian hope goes beyond the idea of a utopia where one can experience a more successful life, and a peaceable and more humanitarian world.[26] "The light of the resurrection illuminates the night of the cross and wants to illuminate those who are today consigned to the shadows of the cross. The cross of Christ, the community of the suffering Christ, and the sign of the oppressed creation show up the place of Christian presence."[27]

According to Moltmann, believers in the present Kingdom of God participate in the suffering of Christ with eschatological hope and by sharing the sufferings of others. They are renewed through the Spirit.[28] "Life according to the spirit [*sic*]is 'life in love.'"[29]

Moltmann's understanding of the Kingdom sheds light on certain theological difficulties within contemporary Korean Pentecostalism in relation to participation in the Kingdom of God "here and now." There is no national poverty, and the National Health Service is as developed as in some European countries. Pentecostals must think theologically

---

[24]Ibid., 228.
[25]Moltmann, *The Theology of Hope*, 33.
[26]Ibid., 34.
[27]Jürgen Moltmann, "Political Theology," *Theology Today* 28, no. 6 (1971): 23.
[28]Jürgen Moltmann, "Pentecost and the Theology of Life," in *Pentecostal Movements as an Ecumenical Challenge*, ed. Jürgen Moltmann and Karl Josef Kuschel, 131-33.
[29]Moltmann, "The Blessing of Hope," 156.

about what the Kingdom means today and how they can participate in that Kingdom. Experiencing a more prosperous life on the earth is not the way to participate in the life of the Kingdom, as Pentecostals have already experienced enough material blessings. Instead, they can share their blessings with others and care for those who are suffering and in need.

Moltmann says that hope is not the reality that exists, but the reality that is coming. It has to be sustained "in contradiction to the reality which can at present be experienced" and consequently can lead "existing reality towards the promised and hoped transformation."[30] Christian hope must be divorced from a secularized desire for a better life here on the earth that focuses on material prosperity. If the old Threefold Blessing was combined with Oral Roberts' theology and the post-Korean War context, the new Threefold Blessing needs to be a combination of Moltmann and post-second millennium Korean culture.

---

[30]Moltmann, *Theology of Hope*, 18.

Part FIVE

THE SPIRITUAL BLESSING OF THREEFOLD BLESSING

Historically, Korea was one of the strongest Buddhist and Confucian countries in Asia. Protestantism first came to Korea in the late nineteenth century. Due to disillusionment with Korean Buddhism and Confucianism from the early twentieth century, many post-war Koreans depended on their ancient Shamanism but could not always find spiritual comfort in it. Christianity and Pentecostalism grew remarkably as a source of hope in desperate and confusing situations.

CHAPTER 19
SPIRIT BAPTISM AND INFILLING IN THE THREEFOLD BLESSING

Early Korean Christians as well as Pentecostals focused on the imminent "eschatological hope of the coming of the kingdom of God."[1] Most church messages focused on the Kingdom of God, which was presented as "the new heavens and a new earth; and the former shall not be remembered or come to mind" (Isa 65:17). Koreans obtained hope to overcome the hardships they were facing in daily life: their focus shifted from their present sufferings on to the imminent, coming Kingdom of God. They were able to forget their current sufferings for a while.

1. Redefining Spirit Baptism and the Infilling of the Holy Spirit

In the socio-economic conditions after the Korean War, Pentecostals began to use the term "spiritual blessing" in relation to the Threefold Blessing theology. The spiritual blessing included regeneration and post-conversion life in the Holy Spirit. It was not intended to deemphasize the eschatological hope for salvation but rather to emphasize life in the Spirit. Cho distinguishes regeneration and the baptism in the Spirit this way:

> We can see that regeneration and the baptism with the Holy Spirit are two distinctly different experiences. Regeneration is the experience of receiving the life of the Lord by being grafted into the body of Christ through the Holy Spirit and the Scriptures. The baptism of the Holy Spirit is the experience in which Jesus fills believers with the power of God for ministry, service and victorious living.[2]

---

[1] Harold S. Hong, "General Picture of the Korean Church, Yesterday and Today," in *Korea Struggles for Christ*, ed. Harold S. Hong, Won Yong Ji, and Chung Choon Kim, 18.

[2] Yonggi Cho, *The Holy Spirit My Senior Partner* (Milton Keynes, UK: Word Ltd., 1989), 103.

The Holy Spirit is involved not only in the process of salvation (1 Cor 12:3) but also in everyday life. Cho often uses Acts 19:1-6[3] to emphasize the necessity of the baptism with the Holy Spirit after conversion, because the new birth is considered insufficient.[4]

Before the modern Pentecostal movement, "baptism in the Spirit" was used by members of the Wesleyan tradition, the Holiness movement, and the radical evangelical movement in different ways. The Wesleyan tradition emphasizes "the role of the Spirit" in sanctification following conversion. Based on the Wesleyans, the Holiness tradition understands Spirit baptism as an experience of sanctification. Evangelical preachers such as Charles Finny, D. L. Moody, and Reuben Torrey regarded baptism in the Spirit as an "enduement of power for witness and service."[5] From a Holiness perspective, believers' hearts are purified and empowered for service through Spirit baptism.[6] To radical evangelicals, "the gift of the Spirit is subsequent to repentance" and "an additional and separate blessing."[7] Later, classical Pentecostals adopted Holiness teaching on Spirit baptism.

Cho adopted the classical Pentecostal teaching that Spirit baptism is "the empowerment of the Spirit for service."[8] He also insists that the Spirit is more than "the Spirit of being born again" or "the Spirit of power" but "a Person [who wants] intimate fellowship and communication" with believers.[9] The Spirit teaches Christians how to follow the Lord as well

---

[3] "He said to them, 'Did you receive the Holy Spirit when you believed?' So they said to him, 'We have not so much as heard whether there is a Holy Spirit.' And he said to them, 'Into what then were you baptized?' So they said, 'Into John's baptism.' Then Paul said, 'John indeed baptized with a baptism of repentance, saying to the people that they should believe on Him who would come after him, that is, on Christ Jesus.' When they heard this, they were baptized in the name of the Lord Jesus. And when Paul had laid hands on them, the Holy Spirit came upon them, and they spoke with tongues and prophesied" (Acts 19: 2-6, NKJV).

[4] Yonggi Cho, *Born to be Blessed* (Seoul: Seoul Logos Co., 1993), 119. See also Yonggi Cho, *Sung Ryeoung Lon* [Pneumatology] (Seoul: Seoul Malsseum Sa, 1998), 99.

[5] Menzies, "David Yonggi Cho's Theology of the Fullness of the Spirit," 178-79.

[6] Donald W. Dayton, *Theological Roots of Pentecostalism*, 94.

[7] A. J. Gordon, *The Ministry of the Spirit* (Philadelphia, PA: American Baptist Publication Society, 1895), 68-70.

[8] Menzies, "David Yonggi Cho's Theology of the Fullness of the Spirit," 179.

[9] Cho, *Successful Home Cell Groups*, 116.

as empowering them in their Christian lives.[10] Believers must allow "a greater place for the Holy Spirit" to have deeper fellowship with the Spirit.[11] He insists that the Spirit continues "the work of Jesus Christ;" believers can experience "the presence and work of Christ" through the Spirit.[12]

According to Land, through the Holy Spirit, Jesus could be present in wonders, signs, and salvation for the early church and Pentecostals. Living in the Holy Spirit is living in the Kingdom of God.[13] Cho understands the Greek term κοινωνία (*koinonia*) related to the Holy Spirit (2 Cor 13:14) as communion, partnership, or fellowship with the Spirit.[14] "We cannot expect church growth without the presence of the Holy Spirit as a living person of God. During the early days of my ministry, I did not know clearly that the Holy Spirit was a person."[15] When he came to understand the Holy Spirit as his senior partner and counselor, his ministry became successful.[16] Having fellowship with the Spirit means mutual recognition between the Holy Spirit and human beings.[17]

Unlike classical Pentecostals and Holiness groups, Cho relates post-conversion baptism in the Spirit more to personal fellowship with the Spirit than to sanctification. The spiritual blessing in the Threefold Blessing involves being baptized with the Spirit to have a deeper relationship with God, which requires the severance of association with indigenous religions and pagan beliefs.

Cho also says, "When we know that the Holy Spirit is a person, our life of faith makes a big leap. Our life changes for the better when we share a deep personal fellowship with the Holy Spirit. I realized that the

---

[10]Cho, *The Holy Spirit My Senior Partner*, 85.
[11]Cho, *Born to be Blessed*, 119.
[12]Cho, *Salvation, Health and Prosperity*, 30.
[13]Steven. J. Land, *Pentecostal Spirituality: A Passion for the Kingdom* (Sheffield: Sheffield Academic Press, 2001), 64.
[14]Cho, *Sung Ryoung Lon* [Pneumatology], 9-10.
[15]Myung Sung Hoon and Hong Young Gi, eds., *Charis and Charisma: David Yonggi Cho and the Growth of Yoido Full Gospel Church* (Oxford: Regnum Books International, 2003), 51-52.
[16]Ibid., 51.
[17]Yonggi Cho, *Successful Home Cell Groups* (North Brunswick, NJ: Bridge Logos Publishers, 1999), 116.

Holy Spirit wants a deep personal relationship with Christians."[18] Cho understands the baptism in the Spirit as an ongoing experience rather than a mere post-conversion crisis event.

The "infilling of the Holy Spirit" and "baptism in the Spirit" are often used interchangeably without distinction by Pentecostals. Those influenced by Cho prefer to use the term "infilling of the Holy Spirit" rather than "baptism in the Spirit" because the latter refers to "the initial Spirit-filling"; the former implies "the subsequent and repetitive infilling of the Spirit."[19]

New Testament scholars understand the outpouring of the Spirit mainly in soteriological and eschatological terms. Robert P. Menzies views the Pentecostal event of Acts 2 as the fulfillment of "the promise of the Father" (Joel 3:1-5).[20] James Dunn finds Menzies's soteriologial emphasis on the Spirit event dubious, suggesting that he overlooks its eschatological significance.[21] Dunn insists that, through the descent of the Spirit at the Jordan River, Jesus entered into "the new age and covenant."[22] The new age means the "the age of the Spirit." At that time Jesus was anointed with the Spirit as "Messiah and Servant" (Luke 3:22, 4:18; Acts 4:27).[23] He insists that Jesus brought the eschatological Kingdom into the present through the outpouring of the Spirit at the Jordan.[24] Scholars like G. Haya-Prats, H. Gunkel, E. Schweizer, and more recently James Shelton and Roger Stronstad, write that "Luke consistently portrays the Spirit as the source of power for service."[25]

From a missiological perspective, the empowerment of the Spirit is understood in terms of the *missio Dei*. In his article "The Revelation of

---

[18]Hoon and Gi, *Charis and Charisma*, 52.
[19]Kim, *History and Theology of Korean Pentecostalism*, 255-256.
[20]Robert Menzies, *The Development of Early Christian Pneumatology* (Sheffield: Sheffield Academic Press, 1991), 203.
[21]James D. G. Dunn, "Baptism in the Spirit: A Response to Pentecostal Scholarship on Luke-Acts," *Journal of Pentecostal Theology* 3 (1993): 21-22.
[22]James D. G. Dunn, *Baptism in the Holy Spirit: A Re-examination of the New Testament Teaching on the Gift of the Spirit in relation to Pentecostalism today* (London: SCM Press Ltd., 1984), 41.
[23]Ibid., 41-42.
[24]Dunn, "Baptism in the Spirit," 18.
[25]William W. Menzies and Robert Menzies, *Spirit and Power: Foundations of Pentecostal Experience* (Grand Rapids, MI: Zondervan Publishing House, 2000), 70.

the Holy Spirit in the Acts of the Apostles," Roland Allen describes the work of the Spirit in missiological terms: "His nature is missionary, His work is missionary."[26] Early Pentecostals regarded *glossolalia* as missionary tongues (*xenolalia*) to enable missionaries to communicate the gospel in other nations; the Holy Spirit was considered the Spirit of power for evangelism.[27]

The spiritual blessing in the Threefold Blessing does not adhere merely to the traditional Pentecostal understanding of empowerment for service or witness but includes "physical and other life matters,"[28] influencing the physical, mental, and emotional dimensions of life. Traditionally, the teachings of mainstream Korean Christianity were sinner-oriented. In contrast, Pentecostals proclaim hope and blessings to those experiencing current hardships. The sick start a new life through divine healing, and the desperate gain hope to change their lives through the Spirit. The Spirit's empowerment changes individual lives from hopelessness to hope. C. B. Johns says, "Transformation may occur in many forms. It may occur as deliverance from the demonic. It may occur as the new birth to salvation. It may occur as healing. It may occur as sanctification of the affections. And it may occur as being filled with the Holy Spirit."[29]

Menzies says "the term fullness points beyond that initial moment to the pattern of life that follows. It seems to speak of the Spirit-filled life."[30] Spiritual blessing involves a deep fellowship with the Spirit in everyday life rather than merely to be saved spiritually. Through repetitive infilling of the Spirit in daily life, Korean Pentecostals expect both sanctification and ongoing transformation. Johns says,

For Pentecostals, healing and deliverance are constitutive aspects of the gospel. They are means whereby the "good news" is proclaimed in both the physical and spiritual dimensions of reality. Such manifestations are reflections of the power of the gospel for the whole person and for the whole of the cosmos.[31]

---

[26]Roland Allen, "The Revelation of the Holy Spirit in the Acts of the Apostles," *The International Review of Mission* 7 (1918): 161.
[27]Anderson, *Spreading Fires*, 40-42.
[28]Ma, "David Yonggi Cho's Theology of Blessing," 196-97.
[29]Johns, "Healing and Deliverance," 47.
[30]Menzies, "David Yonggi Cho's Theology of the Fullness of the Spirit," 181.
[31]Johns, "Healing and Deliverance," 45.

A gospel focused only on spiritual salvation would not be "good news" to post-war Pentecostals because it would not address their struggles. Currently, baptism in the Spirit merely in its spiritual dimension is not appealing: Pentecostals want the empowerment of the Spirit repeatedly, with ongoing spiritual gifts and a fulfilling life in every aspect—by the Spirit. About 400,000 Korean Christians visit a prayer mountain each year, praying and fasting not only for their physical and financial problems but also to deepen their spirituality.[32]

Through receiving spiritual gifts, they are able to experience the sovereignty of God and the influence of his Kingdom upon their lives. The spiritual gifts they practice provide them with evidence of the eschatological coming of the Kingdom of God.

2. Charismata and the Spiritual Blessing

New Testament scholars typically understand the Greek word χαρίσματα (*charismata*) as referring to "the gifts of the Spirit," the way it has been understood by Christian believers and churches. However, the lexical meaning of χαρίσματα (Rom 12:6) is not "the gifts of the Spirit" but simply "gifts." In 1 Corinthians 12:1 and 14:12, English translations mention "spiritual gifts," but the Greek word is πνευματικῶν [spiritual] rather than χαρίσματα. "Gift" was added when the Greek text was translated into English. According to Fee, in Romans 1: 11, the adjective πνευματικὸν was translated "spiritual gifting."[33] Elsewhere, "gift" is used in different ways. In Ephesians 4: 7, it is used to refer to "the gift of Christ" (τῆς δωρεᾶς τοῦ Χριστου), and in 1 Peter 4: 10 it is used to translate χάρισμα. Thus, there are many ideas associated with spiritual gifts in the New Testament, but there is no term that particularly translates "the gifts of the Spirit."[34]

Fee discusses the Pauline understanding of spiritual gifts. Referring to Paul's teaching in 1 Corinthians and Romans, he points out that in 1 Corinthians 12: 4, χαρίσματα refers to "Spirit manifestations," while in

---

[32]Hurston, *Growing the World's Largest Church*, 58-61.
[33]Fee, *God's Empowering Presence*, 606.
[34]Benny C. Aker, "Charismata: Gifts, Enablements, or Ministries?" *Journal of Pentecostal Theology* 11, no. 1 (2002): 53-54.

Romans "gifts" should be understood as "gifts of God which are effectively brought into the life of the community by the Spirit."[35] Pentecostals widely accept the term χαρίσματα as referring to the gifts of the Spirit. From an ecclesiological perspective, the experience of the Spirit and spiritual gifts were regarded as "the key to the expansion of the early church."[36]

For Pentecostals, the issue of the gift of speaking in tongues has been more controversial than the ongoing debate about whether χαρίσματα should be translated as "spiritual gifts" originating from the Spirit or from God. When the Azusa Street Revival broke out, participants were convinced that speaking in tongues was *xenolalia* or "missionary tongues." With their new spiritual gift of speaking in tongues, early Pentecostals assumed that they could communicate the gospel to foreign populations. The gift of tongues included "the purpose of calling them to a specific people" to spread the gospel.[37] William Seymour encouraged Azusa Street Pentecostals to depart for the world immediately,[38] and some went to foreign lands within weeks of the revival breaking out.[39] It did not take long for them to realize their misconception about speaking in tongues.[40]

According to Max Turner, in Acts 2:1-13, Luke considers speaking in tongues as "*xenolalia*: the speaking of actual foreign languages" because in Acts 2: 6, Luke mentions that everyone heard the gospel in their own dialect.[41] In contrast, Paul seemingly did not understand tongues-speaking as *xenolalia* or recognizable languages. In 1 Corinthians 14: 13, he mentions the necessity of interpretation for tongues-speaking, and in verse 14, he says that praying in tongues is beneficial for the human spirit but unfruitful for the mind. "Five

---

[35]Fee, *God's Empowering Presence*, 606-607.
[36]Paul A. Pomerville, *Introduction to Missions: An Independent-Study Textbook* (Irving, TX: ICI University Press, 1987), 95-97; Allan Anderson, "Toward a Pentecostal Missiology for the Majority World," represented in the International Symposium on Pentecostal Missiology at Asia-Pacific Theological Seminary in Baguio City, Philippines, January 29-30, 2003, 3.
[37]A. E. Dyer, "Introduction," in *Pentecostal and Charismatic Studies*, ed. William K. Kay and Anne E. Dyer (London: SCM Press, 2004), 211.
[38]Anderson, *Spreading Fires*, 40-41.
[39]Daniel H. Bays, "Indigenous Protestant Churches in China, 1900-1937: A Pentecostal Case Study," in *Indigenous Responses to Western Christianity*, ed. Steven Kaplan (New York: New York University Press, 1995), 128.
[40]Synan, *The Holiness-Pentecostal Tradition*, 101.
[41]Max Turner, "Spiritual Gifts Then and Now," *Vox Evangelica* 15 (1985): 17.

intelligible words to instruct others are better than ten thousand words in a tongue" (v. 19). In other words, Paul does not consider tongues as *xenolalia* for two reasons. First, the event of speaking in tongues at Pentecost which broke down the linguistic barrier for evangelism was no longer expected to occur in the early churches. Paul makes no mention of such a comparable ecumenical linguistic event in his letters. Second, Paul is concerned about the individual use and value of the gift of tongues, which is not the main concern of Luke in Acts. Paul points out that the function of tongues is not for evangelism, but to edify believers (1 Cor 14:4).

Early Pentecostals understood tongues in the New Testament as the means "to preach the gospel to the nations."[42] The phenomenon of their mission work needs to be understood not merely in relation to their assumption about tongues but also as their zealous response to the world mission movement in the early twentieth century. In 1908, J. Roswell Flower, an early American Pentecostal leader, wrote, "When the Holy Spirit comes into our hearts, the missionary spirit comes in with it; they are inseparable."[43]

The more crucial controversy about tongues is whether it is the initial evidence of Spirit baptism or merely one spiritual gift, rather than whether it is *xenolalia* or *glossolalia*. Classical Pentecostals, especially those affiliated with the American Assemblies of God, insist that "the baptism of believers in the Holy Spirit is witnessed by the initial physical sign of speaking with other tongues as the Spirit of God gives them utterance."[44]

Other scholars and Pentecostals disagree. The earliest Korean Pentecostals followed all beliefs of the American Assemblies of God.

---

[42]Frank D. Macchia, "Babel and the Tongues of Pentecost: Reversal or Fulfillment? A Theological Perspective," in *Speaking in Tongues: Multi-Disciplinary Perspectives*, ed. Mark J. Cartledge (Milton Keynes: Paternoster Press, 2006), 48-49.

[43]Gary B. McGee, "Pentecostals and their Various Strategies for Global Mission: A Historical Assessment," in *Called and Empowered: Global Mission in Pentecostal Perspective*, ed. M. A. Dempster, B. D. Klaus and D. Petersen (Peabody, MA: Hendrickson Publishers Inc., 1991), 206; Allan Anderson, "Toward a Pentecostal Missiology for the Majority World," 2-3.

[44]The Assemblies of God USA, "Statement of Fundamental Truths," http://ag.org/top/Beliefs/Statement_of_Fundamental_Truths/sft_full.cfm#8, accessed December 27, 2011.

The KAG no longer accepts tongues as the initial physical evidence of Spirit baptism. On May 20, 2008, after the unification of the three divided groups of Korean Pentecostals[45] the KAG omitted the clause which specified tongues-speaking as the initial evidence of Spirit baptism.[46] Based on Acts 2:4, 10:45-46, and 19:6, speaking in tongues is referred to in the constitution of the KAG as "the common evidence of the baptism in the Spirit," explaining that in the past, on the Day of Pentecost, tongues-speaking manifested as 'the initial physical sign of the Spirit baptism.'[47] Cho understands tongues as "the typical external sign of the Spirit baptism"; the purpose of practicing tongues daily is to have a deeper fellowship with God.[48]

The KAG has become more flexible about tongues-speaking for two reasons. First, the initial evidence doctrine of tongues became one of the major issues in the disputes with mainstream Christian denominations. Second, Pentecostals have more interest in experiencing the fullness of the Spirit in daily life by practicing the spiritual gifts, including tongue-speaking rather than in an ongoing debate about whether or not speaking in tongues is the initial evidence.

Korean conservatives and non-Pentecostal scholars have compared the enthusiastic praying in tongues of Pentecostals with the ecstatic phenomenon of Shamanism.[49] Cox argues that the positive elements of Shamanism influenced Pentecostalism and calls Pentecostalism a form of Christian Shamanism.[50] Despite the objections of Pentecostals themselves, Cox says, "Yoido Full Gospel Church of Seoul involves a massive importation of shamanic practices into a Christian ritual."[51] He understands Korean Pentecostalism from the perspective of the phenomenology of religion. He regards the shamanistic enthusiasm of

---

[45]With regard to the division of the Korean Assemblies of God, see the constitution of the Korean Assemblies of God, pp 14-23 available as a PDF file at http://www.aogk.org/?mid=aogk_law, accessed on 27 December 2011.

[46]http://www.aogk.org/?mid=law0 [the official website of the Korea Assemblies of God] and http://ag.org/top/Beliefs/Statement_of_Fundamental_Truths/sft_short.cfm[the official website of Assemblies of God USA], accessed on 26 December 2011.

[47]Gidokgyo Daehan Hananim eui SeungHoi [the Korean Assemblies of God], *Gyodan Heonbeob* [Denomination Constitution] (Seoul: Eumji, 2008), 32.

[48]Cho, *Sung Ryoung Lon* [Pneumatology], 166-68.

[49]Cox, 221-24.

[50]Ibid., 226-27.

[51]Ibid., 226.

Koreans as primal spirituality and suggests that this is deeply immersed in the spirituality of Korean Pentecostalism.[52] However, Moltmann says, "There is not a real relationship between Korean Pentecostalism and Korean shamanism. Korean Pentecostalism is more related with the work of the Holy Spirit than shamanism."[53]

Indeed, most ordinary Koreans did not experience any spiritual manifestation or spiritual gifts (χαρίσματα) in the biblical sense in their indigenous religions. In fact, Confucianism is a kind of philosophy rather than a religion, and Buddhism emphasizes meditation rather than focusing on spiritual experience. Both the Buddhist and Confucian scriptures are written in Chinese characters which ordinary Koreans do not understand.[54] Korean Buddhists and Confucians could only listen and follow what Buddhist monks and Confucian scholars taught. As time went by, both religions appropriated Shamanism. Subsequently, Koreans experienced shamanic spirituality indigenized in those religions rather than Buddhist or Confucian spirituality. For instance, *gut* [shamanic ritual] was often performed by Buddhist monks as well as by shamans.

Accustomed to shamanistic spiritual manifestations, Korean mainstream believers did not welcome Pentecostal spirituality due to its similarity with shamanistic enthusiasm, and tried to deshamanize all "shamanic-like" elements in their Christianity.[55] Korean Presbyterians devotedly followed the teaching of Calvin and the early church fathers such as Augustine, Chrysostom, and Pope Leo the Great, who believed that tongues and other spiritual gifts had ceased after fulfilling their purpose of extending the church throughout the nations.[56] Supernatural signs and other manifestations of the Spirit were often regarded as mysterious or shamanic elements which should not be practiced in Korean Christianity. Nevertheless, Korean Pentecostals' eagerness for

---

[52]Ibid.; *Fire from Heaven*, 222-27.
[53]Personal interview with Jürgen Moltmann, January 4, 2012, at his house in Tübingen, Germany. See, Appendix A. Interview with Dr. Jürgen Moltmann.
[54]Nowadays, there are some portions of Confucian and Buddhist scriptures translated in Korean, but not the entire scriptures.
[55]Min, *Hankook Gidokgyo Gyohoi Sa* [the History of Korean Christianity], 438; Anderson, *An Introduction to Pentecostalism*, 137; Dayton, *Theological Roots of Pentecostalism*, 116-117.
[56]Turner, "Spiritual Gifts Then and Now," 51.

χαρίσματα did not diminish but spread to other denominations. After independence from Japan in 1945, large crusades, revivals in individual churches, and the Prayer Mountain Movement [57] began to prevail throughout the nation. About 200,000 people come to *Ohsanri Choijasil Ginyeom Geumshik Gidowon* [Ohsanri Ja Sil Choi Memorial Fasting Prayer Mountain], established by YFGC, annually. These include Presbyterians (46%), Assemblies of God (33%), Methodists (10%), Holiness (5%), Baptists (2.4 %) and others (3.6%).[58] Many Christians have experienced Spirit baptism and spiritual gifts, including tongues-speaking and healing; other manifestations of the Spirit have become more common.

The spiritual blessing in the Threefold Blessing has three elements. The first refers to salvation. In his book *Ohjungbokeum kwa Samjungchukbok* [The Fivefold Gospel and the Threefold Blessing], Cho deals with the Threefold Corruptions which are spiritual death, environmental curse, and physical death caused by the fall of humanity.[59] According to him, these corruptions were produced by humanity's disconnection with God, and salvation involves the restoration of this relationship with God in order for human beings to become the children of God who deserve to receive his blessings. Therefore, salvation is the most important blessing in the Threefold Blessing and the starting point for receiving other blessings from God.[60] In other words, salvation is the primary blessing which is prior to other blessings in the Threefold Blessing. The second element is the repetitive infilling of the Holy Spirit. The experience of Spirit baptism was a totally new and sensational experience to Korean Christians who had grown up against the background of Buddhism, Confucianism, and Shamanism. They had never experienced the spirituality of Christianity nor the empowerment of the Holy Spirit in these indigenous religions. Through Bible study and

---

[57]In 1945, there were two prayer mountains in Korea: the first prayer mountain, Taehan Christian Prayer Mountain, was established by Jaehun Yoo, and Yongmum Prayer Mountain by Elder Woon Mong Ra. After independence, the number of prayer mountains increased remarkably to 207 in 1975, 462 in 1988, and 500 in 1994. See Eim, "South Korea," 240-243.

[58]Gook Jae Shin Hak Yeon Goo Won [International Theological Institute], *Hananim euy Sunghoi GyoHoiSa* [Church History of Assemblies of God], 271-72.

[59]Cho, *Ohjungbokeum kwa Samjungchukbok* [The Fivefold Gospel and the Threefold Blessing], 254-256.

[60]Ibid., 253-259.

messages from preachers, believers were able to learn about Christianity and have more Bible knowledge, but were not able to experience the spiritual empowerment of the Holy Spirit because this could not be theoretically explained or taught.

Since the Korean revivals broke out, Korean Pentecostals have eagerly focused on prayers. They have prayed in the early morning and during the night to receive the Holy Spirit. Moltmann says, "the petitions and groanings for the coming of the Spirit are . . . the first signs of the Spirit's life."[61] In fact, Spirit baptism was normative in the early Church because it was the fulfillment of Christ's promise (Acts 1: 4-5), and Peter and Paul urged the early Christians to be baptized in the Spirit (Acts 8:12, 11:15-6, 19:6).[62] Like the early Christians, being baptized with the Spirit is normative to Korean Pentecostals. They often go to the Prayer Mountain and practice fasting in order to be filled by the Spirit.

This eagerness for the Spirit has become the central feature of Korean Pentecostal spirituality. As Cho has referred to the Spirit as his senior partner,[63] Pentecostals want not only to experience the Holy Spirit once for all but to cooperate with him in their daily lives. F. L. Arrington differentiates between the terms indwelling, baptism, and infilling with reference to the Holy Spirit. According to him, indwelling refers to regeneration through salvation because no one can say "Jesus is Lord" without the Spirit (1 Cor 12:3); Spirit baptism means a definite spiritual experience following salvation, while infilling with the Spirit is being repeatedly filled with the power of the Spirit.[64] This repeated experience of infilling of the Spirit is the core and one of the prominent characteristics of Korean Pentecostalism.

The third element of the Threefold Blessing is the new life in the Holy Spirit. Unlike other global expressions of Pentecostalism, Korean Pentecostalism began with a repentance movement. One of the prominent differences between Pentecostalism and Shamanism is the focus on repentance from sins. As there are no values or ethics for life

---

[61] Moltmann, "A Pentecostal Theology of Life," 4.
[62] French L. Arrington, "Indwelling, Baptism, and Infilling with the Holy Spirit: A Differentiation of Terms," *PNEUMA: The Journal of the Society for Pentecostal Studies* 3 (November 1981): 6.
[63] Cho, *The Holy Spirit My Senior Partner*.
[64] Arrington, "Indwelling, Baptism, and Infilling with the Holy Spirit," 1-10.

contained within Shamanism, it is impossible to expect moral transformation through repentance there. Koreans came to believe that certain behavior which had been accepted culturally and traditionally was regarded as sin within the Christian value system. For example, keeping a concubine was widely practiced in Korean society based on Confucianism and was not considered wrong. Even the king had multiple concubines. However, Koreans recognized it as a sin when they encountered Christianity, and deeply repented of it. When overwhelmed by the Spirit, they repented of all kinds of sins. This brought an ethical and moral transition for Koreans influenced by the Spirit.

Mainstream Korean Christianity did not give a warm reception to the manifestations of the Spirit because they did not have sufficient theological knowledge to distinguish between Pentecostal spirituality and shamanic enthusiasm. Moltmann says,

Where the Holy Spirit is, there God is present in a special sense, and we experience God through our lives or through that which is brought forth fully alive from deep within. We experience the abundant, full, healed, and redeemed life with all of our senses.[65]

Korean Pentecostals experience the rule of God physically through the manifestations of the Spirit. By experiencing these, they are able also to recognize the presence of the Spirit in their lives. The experience of the Spirit and spiritual gifts such as divine healing and speaking in tongues are the physical evidence that the Holy Spirit is with them; through these experiences, they can be more confident of the ministry of the Spirit in their lives.

Moltmann interprets the *charismata* as "the living energies of the Holy Spirit" and says that *charismata* are "sent by the risen, living and present Christ into the community of his people and into the world."[66] Hermeneutically, the terms Spirit and power have been used interchangeably. According to Gordon D. Fee, "The presence of the Spirit means the presence of power (1 Thessalonians 1:5; 1 Corinthians 2:4; Galatians 3:5; Romans 1:4; Ephesians 3:16; 2 Timothy1:7),"[67] and other scriptures, especially in the epistles of Paul, "refer to the powerful working of the Spirit in the lives of believers."[68] This means that

---

[65]Moltmann, "A Pentecostal Theology of Life," 4.
[66]Moltmann, "The Blessing of Hope,"150.
[67]Fee, *God's Empowering Presence*, 35.
[68]Ibid., 36.

experiencing "χαρίσματα" is a form of communication with God, and with this communication Korean Pentecostals have experienced a transformation of their lives.

Calvin says the Holy Spirit is the *fons vitae*, the fountain of life.[69] Based on Titus 3:5, he emphasizes "newness of life" by the Spirit after receiving salvation.[70] Wesley makes a distinction between the first and second salvation: the former is regeneration through repentance and the latter includes "prevenient grace, justification and sanctification." [71] Unlike Calvin and Wesley, Cho does not separate sanctification and justification. The primary reason for this perspective is that sanctification and justification through the Spirit does not always occur in chronological order. In comparison with Wesley's soteriology, the spiritual blessing in the Threefold Blessing means both salvation and living a new life in the Spirit. Cho remembers,

The first grace we received when we entered the first room with the sign, "As Your Soul Prospers," was the grace of salvation. After breaking our soulish nature, we learned to obey direction and guidance of the Holy Spirit. The breaking period was painful and difficult, but through that painful process our faith grew and our understanding of the providence of God deepened. . . . By nailing ourselves daily to the cross we can learn the secret of full obedience to the leading of the Holy Spirit.[72]

This means that Christians can start a new life by the leading of the Spirit. Moltmann says that "the mission of the Holy Spirit is the mission of new life, and that is more."[73] Also,

The sending of the Holy Spirit is the revelation of God's indestructible affirmation of life and his marvellous zest for life. The Synoptic Gospels tell us that wherever Jesus is, there is life:

---

[69]Calvin, *Institute of the Christian Religion*, 860-63; Moltmann, *The Spirit of Life: A Universal Affirmation*, trans. Margaret Kohl (London: SCM Press, 1999), 35.
[70]Calvin, *Institute of the Christian Religion*, 861.
[71]Edward H. Sugden, ed., *Wesley's Standard Sermons* Vol. I (London: The Epworth Press, 1951), 36.
[72]Cho, *Salvation, Health and Prosperity*, 49.
[73]Moltmann, "Pentecost and the Theology of Life," 129.

there the sick are healed, those who mourn are comforted, outsiders are accepted and the demons of death are cast out. Acts and the apostolic letters tell us that where the Holy Spirit is present there is life: there joy rules over the victory of life against death, and there one experiences the power of eternal life.[74]

After the Korean War, most Koreans felt powerless physically and spiritually due to their financial hardship, sickness, and the decline of the influence of Buddhism and Confucianism. At that time, Koreans needed the empowerment of the Spirit not only for service or witness but also to enable them to have victory in every aspect of their lives by the leading of the Holy Spirit. Even today, many Christians live powerless lives. Cho insists that the reason today's Christians are powerless and sick is not because they do not have the experience of being born again, but because they are not filled with the Holy Spirit.[75] Moltmann says, "The Spirit is more than one gift among other gifts: the 'Holy Spirit' is the boundless presence of God awakened in our lives, filled with vitality, and gifted with spiritual powers."[76]

Cho's sermons are also positive and hope-centered. Cho preaches hope to those who are desperate and the "can do spirit" to those who think they cannot do. Historically, the "can do spirit" was a socio-economic movement during the period of economic development between the 1960s and 1980s. The government propaganda slogan, *Hal Soo It Da* (I can do it), was pasted on the walls in classrooms, public offices, army camps, and wherever people gathered. Pentecostal preachers, including Cho, vividly participated in this movement with messages based on Mark 9:23.[77]

Theologically, the "can do spirit" is a response to *Han* in Korean contexts. As noted previously, *Han* is accumulated when people cannot do anything about the problems they are facing. For instance, Koreans used to accept extreme poverty and diseases as their *Han* because they could not do anything to solve these problems. Yet Pentecostal preachers,

---

[74]Ibid.
[75]Cho, *The Holy Spirit My Senior Partner*, 103.
[76]Moltmann, "A Pentecostal Theology of Life," 4.
[77]"If you can?" said Jesus. "Everything is possible for him who believes" (Mark 9:23, NIV)."

including Cho, preached that it was possible to overcome these problems through Christ and the Holy Spirit; they preached hope to the hopeless, the "can do spirit" to defeatism, and the power of the Spirit to the powerless.

Wonsuk Ma identifies four characteristics of Cho's sermons: 1) Bible-centered; 2) spiritual experience-centered; 3) Holy Spirit-centered; and 4) God's sovereignty-centered.[78] In addition, Ma writes,

> ... earlier messages of Yonggi Cho to the suffering masses after the devastating Korean War were constructed around two emphases: 1) God's power to heal and solve human problems through the Holy Spirit; and 2) Human faith in God's miracle power. He is in fact a product of the miracle-faith principles. This combination resulted in a message of hope even in this world. The "can-do" spirit is the immediate consequence.[79]

Salvation in the New Testament often focuses on the new creation.[80] For Cho, the new creation does not mean only eternal life over against death and judgment but also a present infusion of vitality and power through the Spirit. Without the Holy Spirit, both the service and life of Pentecostals cannot be dynamic and powerful. Life in the power of the Spirit is a contradistinction to desperation, lethargy, defeatism and the cannot do spirit. The Spirit's empowerment is not restricted to the spiritual dimension but extends to the horizon of practical living. Thus, Pentecostals are given hope to live in the power of the Spirit. In this sense, the powerful life in the Spirit gives them new hope in their hopeless situations. The new creation is the means for them to become new people with a can do spirit through the Holy Spirit. By practicing the gifts of the Spirit, they can experience the miraculous power of God in daily life.

---

[78]Ma, "The Effect of Rev. Cho's Sermon Style," 160-166.
[79]Wonsuk Ma, "Toward an Asian Pentecostal Theology," *Asian Journal of Pentecostal Studies* (January 1998): 9-10.
[80]Moltmann, "A Response to My Pentecostal Dialogue Partners," 62.

CHAPTER 20
PROSPERITY AND HOPE IN THE THREEFOLD BLESSING

After the Korean War, the biggest socio-political concern was addressing the issue of national poverty. Romans 14:17 says, "The Kingdom is not a matter of eating and drinking, but of righteousness, joy and peace in the Spirit," but the matter of food was an existential matter and a prime concern for every individual and Korean society in post-war Korea. To Pentecostals, eating well is as important as the prosperity of the soul. Liberation from extreme poverty was a primal hope.

Pentecostalism is a grassroots movement that is more appealing to the impoverished than the privileged around the world.[1] It has also taken root among the poor and the sick. Cho was a typical Korean struggling with extreme poverty. Due to his own experience of poverty, he emphasized prosperity in Christ. In the Threefold Blessing, consequently, prosperity is as significant as healing and salvation.

Cho's prosperity theology was criticized for a long time by conservative Christians in Korea. Conservative churches and theologians did not welcome Pentecostalism since they thought that asking blessings from God was unbiblical and reflected shamanistic influences. They called the faith of Korean Pentecostalism *kibock sinang* and regarded it as heretical. Gordon Fee criticizes the theology of wealth and health as the "alien gospel of the cult of prosperity."[2] Cho has been criticized both as "a preacher of a North American prosperity gospel" and "a Pentecostal shaman."[3]

Prosperity theology was not a part of early Pentecostalism in North America or Korea due to Pentecostalism's eschatological emphasis. It emerged with American healing evangelists during the 1940s and 1950s. Most prominent American evangelists and those involved in the Word of Faith (Positive Confession) movement (such as T. L. Osborn, W. J. Baxter, David Nunn, Jimmy Swaggart, Kenneth Hagin, Kenneth

---

[1]Cox, *Fire From Heaven*, 119.
[2]Anderson, "The Contextual Pentecostal Theology of David Yonggi Cho," 105.
[3]Ibid., 118.

Copeland, and others) were influenced by E. W. Kenyon (1867-1948).[4] They were very active in writing books. Kenneth Hagin wrote *Redeemed from Poverty, Sickness, and Spiritual Death* in 1966[5] and *How God Taught Me about Prosperity* in 1985.[6] Kenneth Copeland wrote *Prosperity: The Choice Is Yours* in 1992[7] and *The Laws of Prosperity* in 1995.[8] Other evangelists have also authored books about the prosperity gospel. They are convinced that financial blessing for believers is the will of God and is biblical.

Furthermore, they teach that financial problems can be solved by faith and that those who donate to Christian missions and ministries, mostly their own missions and ministries, will receive blessings from God in return. According to the seed faith doctrine of Oral Roberts, a donation is a seed that will grow with God's favor and then will be given back to the donor. Roberts calls this theology the "Blessing-Pact."

Through the influence of the Word of Faith movement, positive thinking and speaking also became significant in relation to prosperity theology. American evangelists preached and wrote about positive thinking and using positive words in order to solve physical and financial problems.[9] The influence of Oral Roberts on the prosperity theology of Cho is prominent. Oral Roberts started teaching prosperity theology in 1947; Cho obtained Roberts's books and sermons from American missionaries in Korea.

Although the influence of the North American health and wealth movement on Cho's prosperity theology cannot be overlooked, there are at least three significant differences between them. First, Cho's prosperity gospel is set in the Korean context. In its beginning, Cho's

---

[4]R. M. Riss, "Kenyon, Essek William," in *The New International Dictionary of Pentecostal and Charismatic Movements*, ed. Stanley M. Burgess and Eduard M. Van der Maas, 819-820.

[5]Kenneth Hagin, *Redeemed from Poverty, Sickness, and Spiritual Death* (Tulsa, OK: Faith Library Publications, 1966).

[6]Kenneth Hagin, *How God Taught Me about Prosperity* (Tulsa, OK: Faith Library Publications, 1985).

[7]Kenneth Copeland, *Prosperity: The Choice is Yours* (Tulsa, OK: Harrison House, 1992).

[8]Kenneth Copeland, *The Laws of Prosperity* (Fort Worth, TX: Kenneth Copeland Publications, 1995).

[9]Kenneth Copeland, "Prosperity," in *Pentecostal and Charismatic Studies*, ed. William Kay and Anne E. Dyer, 255-258.

prosperity theology was contextualized among the mostly urban poor and needy. In contrast, the health and wealth movement in the United States was promoted by middle-class Christians.[10] Anderson insists that it is inaccurate to interpret Cho's views about prosperity and poverty from "the context of western wealth and materialism" since Cho's prosperity theology is based on "his [Cho's] own Korean context of poverty, Japanese occupation, and the Korean War."[11] Regarding the relation between the Korean economy and the Pentecostal movement, with its emphasis on prosperity, Cox suggests that Korean Pentecostalism contributed to the economic growth of Korea.[12] Prosperity theology in America was a reflection of Christian materialism, but prosperity in Christ gave hope to Koreans in their desperation. Anderson concludes that Cho's prosperity theology cannot be identified with Western prosperity theology.[13]

Second, Cho's prosperity theology is interwoven with Korean primal religiosity or *kibock sinang*. A goal of Korean indigenous religions, regardless of whether they are high or low, is faith for blessings. Anderson affirms, "Pentecostal converts and local preachers began to relate their messages of the transforming power of the gospel to their own religious worlds, creating continuity between certain aspects of the old religions and the new form of Christianity."[14] Korean Pentecostalism is one example of this. Traditionally, Koreans believed that they could obtain blessings through their religious activities or faith: their experience of blessings or misfortunes depended on how they practiced ancestor worship in Confucian culture, how they performed shamanic rituals, or how sincerely they prayed to nature gods in Shamanism and Buddha in Buddhism. This tendency to integrate religion with the acquisition of blessings is not exceptional to Christianity in Korea. Just as Shamanism is more concerned about personal matters such as wealth, health, and success rather than social matters, so most Korean Pentecostals are more interested in personal matters than socio-political

---

[10]Coleman, *The Globalisation of Charismatic Christianity*, 28.
[11]Anderson, "The Contextual Pentecostal Theology of David Yonggi Cho," 116.
[12]Cox, *Fire From Heaven*, 236; see also Lee, "Influence of Dr. Cho's God Is So Good-Faith in the Korean Churches," 74.
[13]Anderson, "The Contextual Pentecostal Theology of David Yonggi Cho," 104.
[14]Anderson, *Spreading Fires*, 238.

issues. Young Hoon Lee says that due to this shamanistic influence on Korean Christianity, Korean Christians selfishly pray for personal prosperity as well as the solution of personal problems rather than social matters.[15] In this sense, prosperity in the Threefold Blessing is influenced by *kibock sinang*.

Third, Cho's prosperity gospel is related to evangelization. In his sermons, Cho deals mainly with such topics as faith, prayer, prosperity, happiness, spiritual growth, based on the Threefold Blessing.[16]

Hwa Yung says that for Cho, "prosperity is not just about financial success."[17] Indeed, Cho's use of the word "prosperity" includes financial and spiritual prosperity. His prosperity message is always linked to the *Kerygma*. Due to extreme poverty and illness after the Korean War, Koreans were not so much interested in the eschatological message of the gospel but in messages that related directly and practically to their lives.[18] Because Cho's teaching of prosperity appealed to many Koreans,[19] his Pentecostal messages proved to be successful evangelistically. Consequently, through indigenization with Korean primal spirituality and contextualization into the post-Korean War contexts, Cho's message gave hope to Koreans and hastened the process of evangelization.

---

[15]Lee, *The Holy Spirit Movement in Korea*, 13.
[16]Hong, "The Influence of Rev. Cho's Church Growth on Korean Society," 203.
[17]Yung, *Mangoes or Bananas?*, 210.
[18]Anderson, "The Contextual Pentecostal Theology of David Yonggi Cho," 115.
[19]Yung, *Mangoes or Bananas?*, 210.

CHAPTER 21
HEALING AND HOPE IN THE THREEFOLD BLESSING

Praying for and preaching on divine healing are less controversial and more acceptable to Korean Christians than speaking in tongues.[1] From 1978 to 1985, pastors at ten major Protestant churches preached over 1,300 sermons on divine healing.[2]

Why did Koreans need divine healing more than other spiritual gifts? In the post-Korean War period, most had no access to medical care due to the lack of hospitals and doctors and extremely high healthcare costs. Divine healing was their only hope. They came to church to experience divine healing.

Besides socio-economic factors, divine healing is significant to Korean Pentecostals from three perspectives. First, divine healing is considered part of Christ's redemption. In Cho's holistic salvation, the cross not only saves the soul but saves human beings from physical and financial sufferings. Cho believes that diseases are caused by a curse from God or the devil, so divine healing is an essential aspect of redemption.[3] Healing is based on the suffering of Christ on the Cross. Cho says, "Jesus paid the price for our healing at Calvary."[4]

After observing Korean Pentecostal services, Cox identified divine healing with disease-curing exorcism in Korean shamanic rituals.[5] Hollenweger considers Cho as "a Pentecostal Shaman par excellence."[6] However, Myung Soo Park argues that both Hollenweger and Cox are making hasty generalizations by equating the Holy Spirit with the

---

[1] Kim, "Korean Religious Culture and its Affinity to Christianity," 126. According to the Korea Gallup Polls, in 1984, 38.1 percent of 314 Korean Protestant respondents said that they personally had experienced faith-healing.[footnote?] In 1989, 37.6 percent of 383 respondents had experienced divine healing.

[2] Kim, "Korean Religious Culture and Its Affinity to Christianity," 126.

[3] Anderson, "The Contextual Pentecostal Theology of David Yonggi Cho," 117. Also, Cho, *How Can I Be Healed?*, 29.

[4] Hurston, *Growing the World's Largest Church*, 140.

[5] Kim, "Korean Religious Culture and its Affinity to Christianity," 121.

[6] Hollenweger, *Pentecostalism*, 100.

shamanistic spirit.[7] Dayton argues that Cho's healing and prosperity message is not influenced by Shamanism but rather is derived from the contemporary and proto-Pentecostal movements.[8]

Examining the relationship between divine healing and redemption, Turner states,

> For the New Testament writers, the healings were not externally attesting signs, but part of the scope of the salvation announced, which reached beyond merely spiritual to the psychological and physical . . . essentially the healings belonged as part of the firstfruits of the kingdom of God, and so as part of the message of salvation which the church announced.[9]

Second, healing is an aspect of the gospel that greatly contributes to evangelism. Cheryl Bridges Johns says,

> Healing and deliverance are constitutive aspects of the gospel. They are means whereby the "good news" is proclaimed in both the physical and spiritual dimensions of reality. Such manifestations are reflections of the power of the gospel for the whole person and for the whole of the cosmos.[10]

Pentecostalism is more practical and experiential than theoretical. Thus, for Pentecostals, the gospel cannot be good news if it does not include this practical and experiential dimension. Through the experience of divine healing, people are overwhelmed by the power of the Spirit and willingly accept the gospel. They experience the presence of God and open their hearts. For Cho, "healing is central to the Gospel. Healing is normative in the Kingdom of God. Healing is a key to evangelization. Miracles and healing can facilitate the spreading of the Gospel."[11]

---

[7]Park, "David Yonggi Cho and International Pentecostal/Charismatic Movements," 221.
[8]Dayton, "The Good God and the Theology of Blessing," 48.
[9]Turner, "Spiritual Gifts Then and Now," 37.
[10]Johns, "Healing and Deliverance," 45.
[11]Cho, *How Can I Be Healed?*, 101.

Many YFGC members have experienced healing. Once they do so, they turn into enthusiastic lay evangelists. During a Sunday service, Cho proclaimed that God was healing a woman, Inja, who had suffered skin trouble for years. Cho asked her to stand up in faith. Inja stood up in faith and received prayer, and testified that she was completely healed. She became a cell group leader and brought sixty non-believers to Christ. She says the key to her evangelism is "to tell others what Jesus has done" in her life.[12] Like Inja, many who receive divine healing become testimonies of God's healing power, which leads directly to evangelism.

Third, divine healing in the Threefold Blessing includes the healing of *Han*. (As stated earlier, without dealing with this distinctive national emotion, no religious and social movement can be successful because Koreans are people of *Han*. They live and die with it.)[13] In 1978, the rate of conversion to Christianity was four times higher than the birth population rate.[14] This suggests that Koreans were finding hope to deal with their *Han*. In Pentecostalism, the contextualized theology of the Threefold Blessing provided a solution to the *Han* of the people. Anderson argues that Cho's teaching on the Threefold Blessing was the "theological counteraction to the *Han*" in the post-Korean War contexts.[15]

According to Chong Hee Jeong, "Shamanism not only gave Koreans a concept of a High God but through its rituals it offered help and salvation from worldly suffering and pain of *Han* and it ensured health, fertility and success," and "Korean Pentecostalism has a similar ritual function within the same culture of *Han*."[16] Dong Soo Kim also says that Cho's message of the Threefold Blessing helped Koreans to escape from their *Han*.[17]

Perhaps Pentecostal practices such as loud praying with tears, singing hymns and gospel songs along with clapping of hands, tongues-speaking, and sharing personal testimonies in public, allows Koreans to

---

[12] Hurston, *Growing the World's Largest Church*, 171.
[13] Suh, "Liberating Spirituality," 33.
[14] Kennedy, *Dream Your Way to Success*, 229.
[15] Anderson, "The Contextual Pentecostal Theology of David Yonggi Cho," 115.
[16] Chong Hee Jeong, "The Formation and Development of Korean Pentecostalism from the Viewpoint of a Dynamic Contextual Theology" (PhD diss., University of Birmingham, 2001), 201.
[17] Kim, "The Healing of *Han* in Korean Pentecostalism," 133.

release their *Han*. The real solution to the problem of *Han* is not merely temporary release, but permanent healing through blessings from God.

CHAPTER 22
KERYGMA IN THE THREEFOLD BLESSING

In the Old Testament scriptures, the fall of humanity brought thorns and thistles from the ground. Humans have to work hard to eat. Throughout the Bible, God promises that those who obey him and keep his words will be prosperous and successful on the earth. In the Threefold Blessing, Korean Pentecostals affirmed this promise of God as hope in economically deprived circumstances.

In the Old Testament, the gospel is related to the phrase בְּשׂוֹרָה טוֹבָה (*besora toba*), meaning "good news" (2 Sam 18:27; 2 Kings 7:9). It refers to "the word of God," "Good is the word" (Isa 39:8), and "the mouth of God" (פִּי יְהוָה דִּבֵּר; Isa 40:5).[1] In Greek, the word *gospel* is εὐαγγέλιον (*euangelion*), and its cognate verb is εὐαγγελίζομαι (*euangelizomai*), meaning "to bring glad tidings." In Jewish and rabbinic sources, the word of God proclaimed by the prophets is closely interwoven with the message of God's salvation.[2] In the Synoptic Gospels, Jesus firmly links the good news to the Kingdom of God. Paul uses *gospel* in various ways: "the preaching of Christ" (2 Cor 4:6; 5:16); the "the word of reconciliation" (2 Cor 5:17-21); and "the message of justification" or "the gospel of the righteousness of God" (Rom 1:16-17).[3]

The social aspect of the gospel is emphasized both by Christian socialists and theologians such as C. F. Blumhardt, H. Kutter, L. Ragaz, A. Stoekker, and A. von Harnack. In Liberation Theology, the gospel also acquires an ethical-political aspect.[4]

It is important to consider who Christ is in the Threefold Blessing and what kind of gospel it represents. Certainly, Christ is the Savior, Healer, and dispenser of blessings. The Threefold Blessing of salvation, prosperity, and healing responded to the spiritual and contemporary

---

[1] Erwin Fahlbusch, Jan Milic Lochman, John Mbiti, Jaroslav Pelikan, Lukas Vischer, Geoffrey W. Broiley, and David B. Barrett, eds., *The Encyclopedia of Christianity Vol 2.*, "Gospel," 446.
[2] F. L. Cross, *The Oxford Dictionary of the Christian Church*, 3rd ed., s.v. "Gospel" (Oxford: Oxford University Press, 2005), 697-698.
[3] Fahlbusch et al., "Gospel," 446-449.
[4] Erwin Fahlbusch et al., "Gospel," 446-449.

material issues and gave Pentecostals the hope they needed in their hopeless situations. The gospel also cannot really be good news without addressing the problems people are struggling with. For the poor, the promise of prosperity is good news and the hope they need for healing the sick and saving the lost.

Conservative Christians influenced by Confucian beliefs regarded prosperity as an inferior value, an aspect of Shamanism, and unworthy of Christianity as a high religion. They emphasized eschatological hope rather than hope for present matters. Yet it is questionable whether hope can be hope without a focus on existential matters of this life. From a Pentecostal perspective, unless hope contains both elements, it is detrimental to Christian growth.

The soteriology of Korean Pentecostalism is holistic, so Pentecostals' hope is also holistic. It is interwoven with present and future soteriological needs: their hope is focused both on the present and the future. In contrast, Moltmann says,

> That we do not reconcile ourselves, that there is no pleasant harmony between us and reality, is due to our unquenchable hope. This hope keeps man unreconciled, until the great day of the fulfillment of all the promises of God. It keeps him *in statu viatoris* [on the pilgrimage], in that unresolved openness to world questions which has its origin in the promise of God in the resurrection of Christ and can therefore be resolved only when the same God fulfills his promise.[5]

Due to his eschatological perspective on hope, Moltmann suggests that the life of believers is not set at the high noon of day, but "at the dawn of a new day where night and day" coexist. Thus, "the believer does not simply take the day as it comes, but looks beyond the day to the things which according to the promise of him who is the *creator ex nihilo* [Creator out of nothing] and raiser of the dead are still to come."[6]

Korean Pentecostals are not content to look towards the dawn of a new day while they remain cold and hungry. With the Threefold Blessing, they expect to live in the high noon of day. They want to experience the

---

[5]Moltmann, *The Theology of Hope*, 22.
[6]Ibid., 31.

fulfillment of their hope in the here and now. In his Epistles, Paul regards the Kingdom of God as "already but not yet." In contrast, for Pentecostals, the Kingdom must be both "already but not yet" and "here and now." It is not to be experienced only in its eschatological dimension: the Kingdom must have practical, present relevance. They want to experience the power of God for salvation *and* as help in their present sufferings. Therefore, the *Kerygma* has to be relevant both to the future and the present.

The focus on the present reality of the eschatological Kingdom has been controversial between Pentecostals and mainstream Christians, especially in relation to the influence of Shamanism. As "the religious soil of Korea,"[7] the contribution of Shamanism to Pentecostalism cannot be overlooked: the influences of shamanistic practices is apparent in such practices as dawn prayer, praying on mountains, and the emphasis on present blessings. At the same time, Pentecostalism was contextualized without shamanistic beliefs such as polytheism and ancestor worship.

The Threefold Blessing theology was contextualized successfully into three major Korean contexts: spiritual, socio-economic, and well-being. It was successful because it met the needs of the Korean context after the war. Young Hoon Lee argues that the instability of Korean society led people to accept the Holy Spirit movement as they desperately searched for spiritual satisfaction and stability.[8] Thus, the *Kerygma* of the Kingdom has to be relevant both to the present and the future.

The rule of God is not restricted to the eschatological Kingdom but predominates over heaven and earth. God's dominion and Kingdom have to be a present reality in the whole universe, in time and in space. Pentecostals seek a Kingdom with rest for the here and now in the context of their sufferings.

The present reality of the Kingdom is better understood from a soteriological rather than eschatological perspective. Nevertheless, the Kingdom here and now cannot be understood apart from the future Kingdom: the Kingdom's present reality is an expression of the

---

[7]Suh, "Liberation Spiritual in the Korean *Minjung* Tradition," 31.
[8]Young Hoon Lee, "The Korean Holy Spirit Movement in Relation to Pentecostalism," in *Asian and Pentecostal: The Charismatic Face of Christianity in Asia*, ed. Allan Anderson and Edmond Tang, 520.

eschatological Kingdom of God with its focus on righteousness, justice, and blessing. J. D. Johns writes,

At the core of the Pentecostal worldview is affective experience of God which generates an apocalyptic horizon for reading reality. In this apocalyptic horizon the experience of God is fused to all other perceptions in the space-time continuum. The fusion holds all things in a dialectic tension between the already and the not yet.[9]

The power and presence of the Spirit makes it possible to experience God's future Kingdom in the here and now. Through the Spirit, Pentecostals experience the rule of God and his presence. Cho believes that through the Spirit, the Kingdom of God can be realized not only spiritually but also existentially. It offers a new soteriological hope for this present life.

Soteriologically, the Threefold Blessing needs to be understood as salvation for the soul *and* salvation from contemporary hardships. Pentecostals accept salvation through the atonement as ongoing in the here and now through the Spirit.[10] This Pentecostal soteriology is not identical to that of radical Christians. Pentecostal soteriology does not focus on social change or political reform. Pentecostals believe in salvation from hardships through receiving blessings from God. As children of God, they expect to receive blessings on this soteriological understanding.

The Threefold Blessing of salvation, prosperity, and health was not the reality for Koreans in the post-Korean War context. They also were inconsistent with reality throughout the history of *Han* the Koreans had passed through. However, the Threefold Blessing was proclaimed as the promise of God to Pentecostals and became a contextual theology of hope in such a desperate situation.

Anderson insists that "for Cho, the message of Christ and the power of the Holy Spirit was a personal contextual message that gave hope to a suffering and destitute community,"[11] and his message of hope solved

---

[9] Jackie David Johns, "Pentecostalism and the Postmodern Worldview," *Journal of Pentecostal Theology* 7 (1995): 87.
[10] Lee, "Influence of Dr. Cho's God," 72.
[11] Anderson, "The Contextual Pentecostal Theology of David Yonggi Cho," 115.

the *Han* of Koreans.[12] Through the message of the Threefold Blessing, Pentecostals obtained hope for the future and were able to change their negative and defeatist mentality.[13] Moltmann says that "the hope of the gospel has a polemic and liberating relation not only to the religions and ideologies of men, but still more to the factual, practical life of men and to the relationships in which this life is lived."[14] As there are no sufferings nor sorrow but only joy and prosperity in God's Kingdom, Pentecostals focus their hope on the present Kingdom. Without hope for the present reality, the future hope of an eschatological Kingdom merely seems to offer the endurance of present suffering. Thus, the Threefold Blessing includes the present experience of the coming Kingdom as well as the gospel of the Kingdom in the here and now.

---

[12]Ibid., 114.
[13]Gook Jae Shin Hak Yeon Goo Won [International Theology Institute], *Hananim euy Sunghoi GyoHoiSa* [Church History of Assemblies of God], 258.
[14]Moltmann, *Theology of Hope*, 330.

Part SIX

THE THREEFOLD BLESSING IN PRESENT AND FUTURE PERSPECTIVES

The Threefold Blessing must continue to contextualize in order to survive in Korea's evolving society, politics, and economics. The former needs of poverty, ill health, and poor systems no longer exist. Perceived needs for God's blessings are also changing.

The Threefold Blessing cannot continue to give hope to Korean Pentecostals unless it is reinterpreted and recontextualized from ecclesiological, eschatological, and soteriological perspectives. However, the Threefold Blessing, with salvation, healing, and provision at its core, will be just as relevant today if it can be renewed and recontextualized in the current situation.

CHAPTER 23
CHANGING CONTEXTS: CURRENT KOREAN PENTECOSTALISM

Young Hoon Lee divides the history of Pentecostalism in Korea into six two-decade periods. His sixth period began in 2000, reflecting the remarkable changes in Korean society and the church.[1] Three shifts should be noted.

First, changes in Korean society, politics, and economy must not be overlooked as change factors that have affected and shaped Christianity.[2] In 1998, a dramatic political reversal in South Korea's diplomatic approach towards North Korea changed its hard-line policy to an appeasement policy called *Haet Byet Jeong Chaek* (the Sunshine Policy). On April 4, 1998, Kim Dae-jung (1924-2009), Korea's President from 1998 to 2003, delivered a speech at the School of Oriental and African Studies, London University, using the term *Haet Byet Jeong Chaek* for the first time. The policy contained three fundament diplomatic principles: 1) "Non-tolerance of military threat or armed provocation"; 2) "the official abandonment of the idea of unification by absorption and the negation of any other measure to undermine or threaten North Korea"; and 3) "the promotion of exchanges and cooperation through resumption of the 1991 Agreement on Reconciliation, Non-aggression and Exchanges and Cooperation."[3] With this decision, national systems had to be changed, including the military, trade, diplomatic policies for the North and other neighboring countries, how to deal with North Korean refugees, and so on.

Second, YFGC's leadership transferred from Cho to his successor, Young Hoon Lee. From 2005, in a series of interviews and official statements, Cho had officially begun to announce his plans for retirement

---

[1] The first period (1900-1920), the second (1920-1940), the third (1940-1960), the fourth period (1960-1980), the fifth period (1980-2000), and the sixth period (2000-present). See Young Hoon Lee, *The Holy Spirit Movement in Korea*.

[2] Lee, *The Holy Spirit Movement in Korea*, 119.

[3] Chung In Moon, "The Sunshine Policy and the Korean Summit: Assessments and Prospects," *East Asian Review* 12, no. 4 (Winter 2000): 6-7.

in 2008.[4] In November 2006, the elders' council elected Young Hoon Lee in a secret ballot. He officially succeeded Cho on May 21, 2008.[5]

Third, social changes affected the church's role in social responsibility, world mission, its leadership for Korean Pentecostalism, and its response to environmental issues.[6] The development of the Korean economy and the welfare system removed national poverty and offers good national health care.[7] As mentioned previously, in the post-Korean War context of poverty and hardships, the Threefold Blessing developed as "good news" and the YFGC grew rapidly.[8] Today, most Pentecostals do not belong to the lower socioeconomic class. In today's healthier socio-economic context, pursuing personal blessings can become a form of Christian materialism. Wonsuk Ma points out that Pentecostals need to examine whether their pursuit of blessings is "self-serving" or "kingdom-serving."[9]

1. New Church Roles in Social Responsibility

Traditionally, Pentecostals have avoided socio-political issues. Their tendency has been "to accept present oppressive conditions or to promote a health and wealth gospel that makes material gain a spiritual virtue."[10]

Latin American Pentecostals have addressed socio-political matters, although their participation in socio-political issues is not always welcomed by Pentecostal leaders concerned about a loss in their spiritual focus. Manoel de Mello, the founder of the Pentecostal denomination Brazil for Christ, states that "the gospel cannot be proclaimed fully

---

[4]Lee, *The Holy Spirit Movement in Korea*, 126.
[5]Ibid. For the date of Lee's installation, see
http://pastorlee.fgtv.com/p3/02_view.asp?NUM=35&page=5&vnum=34, accessed June 15, 2012.
[6]Lee, *The Holy Spirit Movement in Korea*, 120.
[7]According to the World Bank, Korea's GDP reached $1.116 trillion in 2011. For more on the economic growth of Korea, see the World Bank, "Korea, Rep," available from the World Bank [database online], http://data.worldbank.org/country/korea-republic, accessed March 19, 2013.
[8]Yonggi Cho, *My Church Growth Stories* (Seoul: Seoul Logos Co., 2006), 157.
[9]Ma, "Dr. Yonggi Cho's Theology of Blessing," 191.
[10]Allan Anderson, "A Time to Share Love: Global Pentecostalism and the Social Ministry of David Yonggi Cho," *Journal of Pentecostal Theology* 21 (2012): 153.

without denouncing injustices committed by the powerful."[11] In Chile, Pentecostals who resisted Augusto Pinochet's dictatorship were "harassed, tortured, and even killed."[12] In the Philippines, Eddie Villanueva, the founder of Jesus is Lord Church, the largest Pentecostal church in the country, is active in politics. He was one of the strongest political opponents of the Gloria Arroyo government and led a petition for Arroyo's impeachment. He became a presidential candidate in 2004 and 2010.[13]

In contrast, Cho's social theology is "more implied than expressed."[14] Though he does not focus on socio-political issues in his writings and sermons, the contributions of Cho and the YFGC on behalf of the community may be greater than any other Christian organization in Korea. Since the 1980s, Cho and the YFGC have supported social welfare centers and engaged in international relief work around the world. From 1982 to 1986, they built a church, gymnasium, and houses designed for the disabled, which Cho donated to Holt Children's Service Inc.[15] Between 1984 and 1997, YFGC developed a medical program for patients with cardiac disease, offering free surgeries. (2,358 cardiac patients underwent successful surgical operations.) In 1990, they funded surgeries for children with cardiac problems by running a paper-recycling scheme named *Peji Soojip Oondong* (Campaign for Recycling Collection), in which most YFGC church members participated.

In December 1985, Cho started a relief scheme for underprivileged teenagers and marginalized senior citizens. In January 1986, he established a special committee, *Elim Bokji Yisahoi* (The Board of Directors of Elim Welfare), and in July 1988, they completed *Elim Bokji Town* (Elim Welfare Town) with a vocational school for youth and a nursing home for seniors. He added the *Elim Sungyowon* (Elim nursery) in 1994 and the *Elim Yoyangwon* (Elim Sanatorium) in 1997.

---

[11] Murray W. Dempster, "Pentecostal Social Concern and the Biblical Mandate of Social Justice," 129; Anderson, "A Time to Share Love," 153.
[12] Anderson, *An Introduction to Pentecostalism*, 67.
[13] Anderson, "A Time to Share Love," 157.
[14] Ibid., 159.
[15] In 1955, Holt Children Services Inc. was begun by Bertha (1904-2000) and Harry Holt (1904-1964) with the adoption of eight Korean War orphans in Korea. It has become a world-renowned and professional organization in terms of international and domestic adoption as well as provision of social welfare. Its official website is available from http://www.holt.or.kr/holten/main/view.jsp?c_no=001001, accessed February 14, 2013.

In 1992, a food aid program called *Eunhaeeui Bbang Nanoogi Oondong* (Bread of Grace Sharing Campaign) provided foodstuffs for Cambodia, Vietnam, Mozambique, Bangladesh, and other undeveloped countries.[16]

The sudden development of the North Korea Mission reflected the radical change of the political situation in the Korean Peninsula from 1998. Through various campaigns including broadcast media, the South Korean government tried to change the country's stance toward North Korea from archenemy to siblings. Due to its teaching on love for one's neighbors as well as one's enemy, the church became "the best agent" to bring about this change among South Koreans.[17]

The YFGC responded positively to the new political climate of the Sunshine Policy. The soft-line government policy initiated a radical change in the YFGC's mission to the North. In January 1999, Cho established the *Hankook Sunhan Samaliainhoi* (Korean Good Samaritans, renamed that June as *Sunhan Salamdeul* or Good People.) It focused on international relief work including relief for refugees from North Korea. In 2000, 1,500 tons of fertilizer and ninety-five tons of corn seed were sent to North Korea through the organization. In December 2000, Cho opened *Kyoungshinjin Byoungwon* (Kyoungshinjin Hospital) on the border of China and North Korea. *Jayoo Simin Daehak* (Free Citizen College) was started in February 2002 to help North Korean refugees settle in South Korea.

2. New Church Roles in Hope for the Reunification of Korea

The reunification of South and North Korea presents one of the biggest challenges for Korea in its history. No one knows if or when it will happen. The Korean church would play an important role, similar to that of the German church during Germany's reunification.

To hasten the reunification, the church must develop a theological basis for reconciliation. If it does occur, the reunification will be Korea's most significant event of the twenty-first century politically, theologically, ecclesiologically, and missiologically. The event would

---

[16] The official website of the YFGC provides the entire history of the church with describing detail monthly events from its beginning in 1958 up to now, available from http://yfgc.fgtv.com/y1/04_0301.asp, accessed May 24, 2012.

[17] Lee, *The Holy Spirit Movement in Korea*, 120.

change every aspect of Korea: its society, culture, politics, economy, and even the everyday lives of Koreans. The function and mission of the church will also be transformed by the new paradigm of unification and reconciliation.

Two significant characteristics of Pentecostalism are ecumenism and reconciliation, which broke down denominational and racial barriers within Christianity. The situation in Korea is more complex than the German reunification, and offers less favorable conditions for reunification. Both sides were deeply hurt as family members were either killed or lost during the Korean War. Since, both sides have continued to build up their armaments. Military duty is mandatory, and sometimes soldiers are killed in regional border conflicts. Thus, somehow reconciliation between the South and the North must be carried out before reunification can happen.

In American Pentecostalism at Azusa Street, Frank Bartleman testified that "the color line was washed in the blood [of Jesus]."[18] The revival challenged racial segregation. Pentecostal efforts for reconciliation between ethnic groups, sexes, denominations, and races has continued. In October 1994 in Memphis, the Pentecostal Fellowship of North America (PFNA) and its members apologized to black Pentecostal bodies for racial segregation they perpetuated in the past and dissolved the PFNA. They established the Pentecostal/Charismatic Churches of North America (PCCNA) with a governing board of six African-Americans and six whites.[19] Manuel Gaxiola-Gaxiola argues that the Memphis meeting did not merely dissolve racial segregation by the white Pentecostal bodies but allowed all ethnic groups of Pentecostals in the world, including Blacks, Latinos, Anglo-Saxons, and Asians, to be "a part of the [Pentecostal/Charismatic] movement."[20]

---

[18]Frank Bartleman, *Azusa Street: The Roots of Modern-Day Pentecost* (South Plainfield, NJ: Logos, 1980), 54; Wonsuk Ma, "Asian (Classical) Pentecostal Theology in Context," in *Asian and Pentecostal: The Charismatic Face of Christianity in Asia*, ed. Allan Anderson and Edmond Tang, 82.
[19]Frank D. Macchia, "From Azusa to Memphis: Evaluating the Racial Reconciliation Dialogue among Pentecostals," *PNEUMA: The Journal of the Society for Pentecostal Studies* 17, no. 2 (Fall 1995): 203.
[20]Manuel Gaxiola-Gaxiola, "Roundtable: Racial Reconciliation—From Azusa to Memphis: Where Do We Go from Here? Roundtable Discussion on the Memphis Colloquy," *PNEUMA: The Journal of the Society for Pentecostal Studies* 18, no. 1 (Spring 1996): 125.

Similarly, Korean Pentecostalism can support conditions for the reunification of Korea by following this Pentecostal tradition of reconciliation. Throughout its history, the Korean Pentecostal movement has broken down the strong class and gender barriers of Confucian society. For reunification, Korean Pentecostalism must provide a hope beyond personal material blessing or physical health.

The YFGC's current mission to the North is significant in at least three ways. First, it reminds Christians in the South that North Koreans are not their enemies but their brothers and sisters. During the Cold War and the military dictatorship in South Korea, North Koreans were regarded as major enemies. Through YFGC's mission, South Korean believers have opened their hearts to recognize and restore brotherly love to North Koreans.

Second, the mission is an attempt to bring about reconciliation between the North and the South through Christ. During the Korean War, Koreans killed one another and destroyed each other's properties. Thus, reunification cannot happen without reconciliation. Moltmann points out that churches in East and West Germany reconciled before reunification was achieved. Based on reconciliation and the restoration of love, German Christians and others Germans began to rebuild their relationships before reunification. While Korea can learn some lessons from the German example, it has to find its own way of reconciliation because of the contextual differences.[21] Unlike the German church and government, the Korean church and both Korean governments are not yet ready for reunification.

What is the current responsibility of the Korean church? Lee sees the Korean church as the "the best agent" to bring about this historical event.[22] The church can do what the government of South Korea cannot do because of political reasons, expressing its love in practical ways and attempting to rebuild confidence between the two communities through Christ. In February 2004, the YFGC built a soybean oil factory in Pyongyang, the capital city of North Korea, not to generate profits for the church but to offer job opportunities to North Koreans.[23]

---

[21]Personal interview with Jürgen Moltmann, January 4, 2012, at his house in Tübingen, Germany. See, Appendix A. Interview with Dr. Jürgen Moltmann.
[22]Lee, *The Holy Spirit Movement in Korea*, 120.
[23]http://www.goodpeople.or.kr/goodple/goodple_history.asp, accessed May 24, 2012.

Third, the North Korean mission gives hope for the evangelization of North Korea. Pentecostalism began when revival movements broke out in North Korea. However, when North Korea became a communist state soon after independence from Japanese rule, Christians in North Korea were persecuted. Since the Korean War broke out in 1950, the North and South have engaged in a fierce arms race. Despite diplomatic efforts, the North Korean nuclear weapon issue has not been resolved. Occasional regional conflicts happen near the border between the North and the South. The ecclesiological change since the beginning of the new millennium, especially with regard to the North Korea mission, gives hope for the possibility of peace as well as the future reunification of Korea.

3. New Church Roles in Social Transformation

Considering his strong Confucian background, Cho's social influence is significant in terms of social relief work and empowering women in church leadership. Following the suggestion of Jashil Choi, from the early 1960s, Cho began to train lay women and appoint them as cell group leaders.[24] This transformation in the social status of women in the church, especially in a strong male-oriented society, is revolutionary.[25] Prior to this, women leadership was not considered in the church: most churches were entirely led by men, influenced by 1 Corinthians 14:34 ("Women should remain silent in the churches," NIV) and their male-dominated culture.

By January 2009, most of the cell leaders of YFGC's 14,888 home cell units were women.[26] Anderson regards this social transformation as "a ground-breaking change."[27] As Anderson says, Cho's social theology is not explicit but rather implicit.[28] Cho's social theology and concerns about social matters are not as prominent as in *Minjung* theology. He has been criticized for giving priority to evangelization and church growth over concern for social matters because his social theology has not been developed systematically. The theology of the Threefold Blessing still

---

[24] Anderson, "A Time to Share Love," 162.
[25] Ibid.
[26] Lee, *The Holy Spirit Movement in Korea*, 107.
[27] Anderson, "A Time to Share Love," 162.
[28] Ibid., 159.

focuses on personal blessings. However, due to YFGC's financial capacity and large membership, its social relief work surpasses the work of other Christian churches or groups. Cho and the YFGC continue to lead the way in social transformation and give hope to the Korean people.

CHAPTER 24
RENEWING THE THREEFOLD BLESSING IN THE CURRENT CONTEXT

The existing scope of Cho's Threefold Blessing theology is not broad enough to include society or the environment. In his writings and sermons, Cho emphasizes divine healing, well-being, and blessings for individuals. In contrast, Anderson says, "Pentecostals do not always separate the spiritual from the physical, but they integrate them in a holistic whole that leads to involvement in social issues and politics."[1] Although Cho's theology claims to be holistic, he has not developed a soteriology that includes socio-political issues. Healing in the Threefold Blessing does not include a social element. Blessing is limited to individual prosperity, and well-being is understood as individual welfare rather than environmental care.

In 2005, Cho expanded the scope of his theology of salvation to include human society, nature, and the whole ecosystem, according to Moon Chul Shin.[2] During a kick-off service for the year on January 4, 2005, Cho acknowledged that his ministries focused on personal salvation and were not concerned about social matters. He promised to show more concern for relief of the poor, support for senior citizens who live alone, and assistance for child breadwinners.[3] "We have had a narrow perspective so far. With open heart and faith, we need to work hard to remove the social evil in our society and to start a movement in order to protect our environment as well as evangelize the lost this New Year" [translation mine].[4] He confessed, "I did not pray enough for the politics of my country. I have understood the theology of the cross from

---

[1] Anderson, "A Time to Share Love," 154.
[2] Moon Chul Shin, "Young San eui Saeng Tae Shin Hak [Yonggi Cho's Eco-Theology]," in *Young San eui Mokhoiwya Shin Hak I* [Younggi Cho's Ministry and Theology], Gook Jae Shin Hak Yeon Goo Won [International Theological Institute] (Gunpo: Hansei University Press, 2008), 398.
[3] Heung Kil Jang, "Youngsan Cho Yonggi Moksaeui Sahoi Goowonae Gwhanhan Shiyak Sungseo Yoonlijeok Pyungga [Ethical Critic for the perspective of Rev. Yonggi Cho about Social Salvation based on the New Testament]," *Journal of Young San Theology*, no. 17 (2009): 67.
[4] Shin, "Young San eui Saeng Tae Shin Hak [Yonggi Cho's Eco-Theology]," 398.

a narrow perspective. I have disregarded social vices and had no concern about natural disasters" [translation mine].[5] He added that salvation was not only for humanity, but includes the world, society, and even the environment.[6]

Moltmann evaluates this change in Cho's soteriology as a "marvellous turning point."[7] Traditionally, Christians have understood creation from a Trinitarian perspective, that all things are created by God the Father "through the Son in the power of the Holy Spirit" and exist in God.[8] Moltmann argues that, in order to emphasize God's transcendence, the Western church merely stressed the first aspect, that all things are created by God, rather than the latter, that they exist in God and God also is in them. They distinguish and separate "God the Creator from the world as His creation.[9] Moltmann emphasizes both God's transcendence and immanence in His creation. "The presence of God [is] immanent in the world and present in all things."[10] Stanley J. Grenz and Roger E. Olson criticize Moltmann for underscoring "the perichoretic relationship between God and the world—a relationship of fellowship, mutual need and mutual interpenetration" by overemphasizing "God's immanence with history."[11]

For Moltmann, God is not merely "the Creator of the world" but also "the Spirit of the universe."[12] This means that God's transcendence is not debased by the immanence of God in His creation. "Through the powers of and potentialities of the Spirit, the Creator indwells the creatures he has made, animates them, holds them in life, and leads them into the

---

[5]Jürgen Moltmann, "Salm Eul Wooi Han Sinhak, Sinhak Eul Wooi Han Salm [Theology for Life, Life for Theology]," *Kukmin Ilbo*, May 12, 2009, available from *Kukmin Ilbo* database online, http://news.kukinews.com/article/view.asp?arcid= 0921286513, accessed October 26, 2011.

[6]Yonggi Cho, "New Year's Resolution" (Sunday sermon on January 2, 2005), available from the YFGC database on-line, http://www.fgtv.com/fgtv/F1/WF1_1_re.asp?aidnum=21162&page=1, accessed on 12 May 2012.

[7]Moltmann, "Salm Eul Wooi Han Sinhak, Sinhak Eul Wooi Han Salm [Theology for Life, Life for Theology]."

[8]Jürgen Moltmann, *The Source of Life: The Holy Spirit and the Theology of Life*, trans. Margaret Kohl (London: SCM Press Ltd., 1997), 115.

[9]Ibid.

[10]Ibid., 115-116.

[11]Stanley J. Grenz and Roger E. Olson, *20th Century Theology: God and the World in a Transitional Age* (Downers Grove, IL: InterVarsity Press, 1992), 184.

[12]Jürgen Moltmann, *God in Creation: An Ecological Doctrine of Creation*, trans. Margaret Kohl (London: SCM Press Ltd., 1985), 14.

future of his kingdom. In this sense the history of creation is the history of the efficacy of the divine Spirit."[13]

To Moltmann, God as the Creator and the world as His creation are inseparable. The presence of the world is in God, and the presence of God is in the world through the Holy Spirit.[14] The world created by God represents His divine nature and attributes. All things are from "God's living breath and that breath holds them together in a community of creation" and they are "mutually dependent; they live with each other and for each other, and often enough symbiotically within each other."[15] For this reason, "if they [all creatures] cut themselves off from that community, they lose the living Spirit."[16]

Moltmann's ecological theology is based on his understanding of God's immanence in creation and his pneumatology. "The theology of Pentecostal experience must lead to a theology of creation in the Holy Spirit."[17]

In contrast, Cho's ecological theology is based on his Christology. Referring to John 3:16, Cho understands "the world" saved by Christ on the cross to mean not only humanity but also the whole universe, including the ecosystem.[18] Cho says,

> Just recently I [Cho] found out many insufficiencies of myself in the forty-seven years of ministry. The Bible says, "For God so loved the world that He gave His one and only Son, that whoever believes in him shall not perish but have eternal life." However, I misinterpreted it; I understood that God so loved "humans," not "the world," that He gave His one and only Son. What is the world? In the world, there are all things such as people, society, sky, land, ocean, plants, insects and animals. The Bible says that God so loved "the world" that He gave His only Son; it does not limit and say that God so loved "human" [sic]

---

[13]Ibid.
[14]Ibid., 13.
[15]Moltmann, *The Source of Life*, 24.
[16]Ibid.
[17]Moltmann, "A Response to My Pentecostal Dialogue Partners," 62.
[18]Yonggi Cho, *Pastor! How Can I Be Healed?* (Seoul: Seoul Logos, 1997), 149-151; Young Hoon Lee, "Influence of Dr. Cho's God is so good-faith in the Korean Churches," 77.

that He gave His only Son. . . . When Jesus died upon the cross, he redeemed for nature also . . . the power of blood that Jesus shed on the cross saves nature.[19]

Regarding this change in Cho's soteriology, Lee states, "When Jesus died upon the Cross, He redeemed nature also." [20] This response recognizes the necessity of restoring the ecosystem that is being destroyed by the industrialization and urbanization of Korea during rapid economic growth.

Cho's changing perspective on soteriology offers the possibility that the scope of the Threefold Blessing can be expanded to include the salvation of society as well as the ecosystem. [21] Cho's social understanding about the Christian life is reflected in sermon themes like "the life of sharing," "the life of loving," and "the life of helping others."[22] Cho has often preached about showing love towards others.[23]

---

[19] Mun Cheol Shin, "Eco-theology of Young-san," *The Holy Spirit and Theology* 22 (2006): 115.

[20] Lee, *The Holy Spirit Movement in Korea*, 128.

[21] A. J. Swoboda approaches ecotheology in Pentecostal perspectives in his PhD thesis entitled "Tongues and Trees: Towards a Green Pentecostal Theology." He develops a Pentecostal ecotheology through dealing with "a pneumatology of the Spirit baptized creation," "the charismatic creational community," "the holistic ecological Spirit," and "the eschatological Spirit of ecological mission." See Aaron Jason Swoboda, "Tongues and Trees: Towards a Green Pentecostal Theology," (PhD thesis, University of Birmingham, 2011).

[22] Heung Kil Jang, "Youngsan Cho Yonggi Moksaeui Sahoi Goowonae Gwhanhan Shiyak Sungseo Yoonlijeok Pyungga [Ethical Critic for the perspective of Rev. Yonggi Cho about Social Salvation based on the New Testament]," 104.

[23] Some examples of recent sermons: Yonggi Cho, "Religion or Love?" (Sunday sermon, July 1, 1984), available from http://www.fgtv.com/fgtv/F1/WF1_1_re.asp?aidnum=20886&page=1, accessed March 24, 2012. Yonggi Cho, "Four Elements of Love"(Sunday sermon, September 22, 1996), available from http://www.fgtv.com/fgtv/F1/WF1_1_re.asp?aidnum=20510&page=1, accessed March 25, 2012. Yonggi Cho, "Life of Sharing" (Sunday sermon, July 18, 2004), available from http://www.fgtv.com/ fgtv/F1/WF1_1_re.asp?aidnum=21139&page=1, accessed March 28, 2012. Yonggi Cho, "Born to Give" (Sunday sermon, January 16, 2005), available from http://www.fgtv.com/fgtv/F1/WF1_1_re.asp?aidnum=21164&page=1, accessed March 25, 2012. Yonggi Cho, "Bonanza of Blessing" (Sunday sermon, August 6, 2006), available from http://www.fgtv.com/fgtv/F1/WF1_1_re.asp?aidnum=21239&page=1, accessed April 4, 2012. Yonggi Cho, "True Neighbour" (Sunday sermon, November 11, 2007), available from http://www.fgtv.com/fgtv/F1/WF1_1_re.asp?aidnum=21304&page=1, accessed March 28, 2012. Yonggi Cho, "Sharing Happiness and Love" (Sunday sermon, May 18, 2008), available from http://www.fgtv.com/fgtv/F1/WF1_1_re.asp?aidnum=21330&page=1, accessed April 4, 2012.

With the shift in his soteriology, he has focused more on society and the nation. Cho set the annual goal (2006) of YFGC as "Loving Neighbours and Loving Nature."[24]

In early 2008, Cho established the *Salangghwa Hangbok Nanoom Jaedan* (Sharing Love and Happiness Foundation) to assist low-income families with medical bills, basic living expenses, fixing house problems, and legal matters.[25] His new focus on social work has not yet been accompanied by a corresponding contemporary theological reinterpretation of the Threefold Blessing.

Kärkkäinen criticizes Cho's Threefold Blessing theology for placing too much emphasis on the victorious life and for neglecting social concern while promising physical and financial blessings.[26] Hwa Yung says that Cho's theology lacks "a deeper grasp of the sociopolitical implications of the gospel of Christ."[27] Dayton discusses Korean Pentecostalism in relation to early modernist-fundamentalist controversies, which polarized the church into two parties: one emphasizing "personal salvation of the individual" and the other "the social dimension of the gospel."[28] Dayton suggests that Korean Pentecostalism as well as Christianity has tended to emphasize personal salvation over the social gospel, but these need to be integrated.[29] For Moltmann, body and soul are inseparable because they are "embedded in nature."[30] These theologians agree that the theology of the Threefold Blessing needs to enlarge its scope to include an altruistic concern for neighbors, society, and the ecosystem.

---

[24]Shin, "Young San eui Saeng Tae Shin Hak [Yonggi Cho's Eco-Theology]," 398.
[25]Lee, "Youngsan Cho Yonggi Moksaeui Sahoigoowon Yihae [Understanding about Rev. Yonggi Cho's Social Salvation]," 67.
[26]Kärkkäinen, "March Forward to Hope," 255.
[27]Yung, *Mangoes or Bananas?*, 211.
[28]Dayton, "The Good God and the Theology of Blessing in the Thought of David Yonggi Cho," 53.
[29]Ibid.
[30]Althouse, *Spirit of the Last Days*, 189.

CHAPTER 25
RECONTEXTUALIZATION OF THE THREEFOLD BLESSING

Several dynamics need to be considered to recontextualize the Threefold Blessing for contemporary Korean Pentecostals. First, the context of Pentecostalism has changed considerably since its inception. In May 2012, South Korea joined Germany, France, Japan, the U.S.A., Italy, and the United Kingdom as the seventh member of the "20-50 Club." To be a member, the GDP per capita of the country must exceed $20,000, with a population of 50 million or more.[1] This reflects major changes since the post-Korean War context. Contemporary Pentecostals do not suffer from absolute poverty, although they may experience relative poverty.

Second, the demands of today's Korean Pentecostals have changed to more complex issues. With the rapid westernization of the complex societal structure of Korea, the values of Korea are changing. In a highly competitive society focused on material success, Koreans are losing their sense of communal responsibility and caring for others. Social problems, like the increasing gap between the rich and the poor and family breakdown, have deepened.

Third, Korean Pentecostals are struggling with new problems, including leadership succession. In many cases, the leadership of a church has been turned over to the son of its founder or senior pastor. Moral failure, financial misdemeanors, and sex scandals force pastors to resign and sometimes land them in prison.[2] The church also has other problems such as excessive competition between churches and an overemphasis on church growth.

Pentecostals prospered financially from Korea's economic prosperity until the early 90s. However, in November 1997, Korea received a bailout package from the IMF (the International Monetary Fund). During this crisis, many companies went bankrupt and many

---

[1] Park Sung Seek, "Korea in the 20-50 Club: Where Should It Go from Here?" *The Korea Herald*, June 11, 2012, available from http://view.koreaherald.com/kh/view.php?ud=20120611000997, accessed June 25, 2012.

[2] Lee, *The Holy Spirit Movement in Korea*, 121.

Koreans lost their jobs. The economy came under the supervision of the IMF and the polarization of wealth grew.

Increasingly, it is important for Korean Pentecostals to share their financial blessings with others rather than focusing on themselves. They must remember they were also marginalized financially after the Korean War, when the theology of the Threefold Blessing was first introduced. They need more concern toward neglected social groups, sharing their blessings with the poor, the needy, and the politically disadvantaged.

Korean Pentecostals sense the necessity of extending the scope of the Threefold Blessing to the whole of society. They also realize that non-believers are disappointed in Christians because of the immoral lifestyles of Christian leaders in the church and nation. In 2008, Christian president Myoung Bak Lee was elected with great support from Christian communities. Lee's election to the presidency demonstrates the increasing influence of Christianity.[3] His cabinet included many believers from SoMang GyoHoi [Hope Church], the church he was attending. In 2009, Christians made up 57 percent of his ministers, 50 percent of the Chong Wha Dae's [the Blue House] senior secretaries, and 39 percent of his secretaries.[4] Many of them had serious ethical problems and were involved in a series of corruption scandals. They were arrested and forced to step down, including his older brother Sang Deuk Lee, an elder in the church, who was suspected of having taken a bribe.[5]

The prosperity gospel without ethics can result in Christian materialism, encouraging Pentecostals to justify any means for the accumulation of wealth. Korean Pentecostals have not considered Christian ethics in handling wealth to be significant. Pentecostal preachers around the world, including Cho, preach that prosperity is the will of God without clarifying how Christians should deal ethically with financial matters. This can bring a dualistic fallacy that prosperity is

---

[3]Ibid., 120.

[4]Ho Woo Yoon, "Lee Myoung Bak Jeongkwon Seo Joongyong Doin Gidokgyo Shinja Deul [Christians appointed in President Lee's government]," *Joo Gan Kyoung Hyang* [Weekly Kyoung Hyang], April 7, 2009, available from *Joo Gan Kyoung Hyang* [database on-line];http://newsmaker.khan.co.kr/khnm.html?mode=view&dept=113&art_id=19621&fid=&sort=sym, accessed July 15, 2012.

[5]"South Korean President's Brother Lee Sang-deuk Arrested," BBC NEWS, July 11, 2012, available from http://www.bbc.co.uk/news/world-asia-18792840, accessed July 12, 2012.

good and the will of God for his people, while poverty is bad and not God's will. Due to their belief that prosperity comes entirely from God, many Pentecostals believe that it is the wealthy, rather than the poor, who are blessed by God.

In contrast, regarding the relation between Christianity and wealth, Methodists understand the sources of Christian wealth as diligence and frugality. [6] John Wesley says that "religion [Christianity] must necessarily produce both industry and frugality, and these cannot but produce riches."[7]

Korean Christianity, including Pentecostalism, has to admit that the church has stopped growing since the early 1990s.[8] A remarkable change took place in the YFGC at the beginning of the new millennium. It was anticipated that the YFGC would declined to around 400,000 members from 760,000 after the independence of its daughter churches.[9] Lee declared on January 7, 2010, that the process of independence for YFGC's twenty daughter churches was completed.[10] YFGC needs a new theological orientation in response to this change.

Unless hope renews itself in these new contexts, it will lose its function. Pentecostals need to recontextualize and reinterpret the Threefold Blessing theologically for today. If not, it cannot continue to give hope to Korean Pentecostals.

1. The Recontextualization of Spiritual Prosperity

The phrase in 3 John 2, "as your soul prospers," is the biblical basis for the spiritual blessing in the Threefold Blessing. Traditionally, the spiritual blessing is simplified as spiritual salvation. This raises two questions. First, does the phrase only refer to spiritual salvation? Second, is the salvation in the Threefold Blessing restricted to the spiritual

---

[6]Personal interview with Vinson Synan, Regent University, VA, August 16, 2011. See Appendix D. Interview with Dr. Vison Synan.
[7]Weber, *The Protestant Ethic*, 175.
[8]Lee, *The Holy Spirit Movement in Korea*, 120.
[9]Sung Shik Cho, "face to face with Young Hoon Lee," *Shin Dong A*, May 1, 2009, available from http://shindonga.donga.com/docs/magazine/shin/2009/05/08 /200905080500060/200905080500060_1.html, accessed June 27, 2012.
[10]Moon Hye Sung, "Yoido Soon Bok Eum Gyo Hoi, 20 Ga Jae Ja Gyo Hoi Dok Lip Seon Eon [Yoido Full Gospel Church, the Declaration of the Independence of 20 YFGC's Daughter Churches]," *Holiness Newspaper*, January 7, 2010, available from http://www.kehcnews.co.kr/news/articleView.html?idxno=6211, accessed June 27, 2012.

dimension? One of the major concerns of classical Pentecostals was how to define sanctification and the baptism in the Spirit. They agreed that sanctification and salvation should be separated or combined together as one experience. To them, salvation was not the ultimate goal but marked the beginning of their faith. In fact, the spiritual blessing does not merely refer to spiritual salvation, but also to the empowerment by the Spirit for service as well as for daily life. While liberation theology understands salvation as having social implications, conservative evangelical Christians have traditionally understood it as referring to "soul-salvation." Some Pentecostals, on the other hand, have extended the understanding of "God's work of the atonement" to include health and prosperity in this life.[11] Cho's Threefold Blessing reflects this perspective.

Cho has recently begun to recognize the importance of social and ecological redemption. Cho's holistic soteriology is based on the Threefold fall of Adam which corresponds with the triple corruption of humankind: "the spirit, the body and the environment."[12] Thus, one would expect Cho's theology of the redemptive work of Christ to have addressed these three categories, including environmental redemption. However, until 2005, his soteriology was restricted to the spiritual and individual aspects.[13] To him, Christ's salvation saves the soul and changes the way human beings live "from being a curse to being a blessing."[14] In other words, before 2005, it seems that he did not think that Christ's redemption could be applied to society and the ecosystem, even though Cho's understanding of salvation had been extended to include existential matters for believers.

When Christianity arrived in Korea, the most urgent theme of mission was to save souls. Spiritual salvation gave the hope of the Kingdom of God to Koreans who used to practice Shamanism or indigenous high religions. Theologically, however, it is questionable whether redemption only refers to spiritual salvation in the Bible. Dayton insists that redemption needs to include "social redemption that

---

[11]Dayton, "The Good God and the Theology of Blessing," 54.

[12]Lee, *The Holy Spirit Movement in Korea*, 129.

[13]Moon Chul Shin, "Young San eui Saeng Tae Shin Hak [Yonggi Cho's Eco-Theology]," in Gook Jae Shin Hak Yeon Goo Won [International Theological Institute], *Young San eui Mokhoiwya Shin Hak I* [Younggi Cho's Ministry and Theology], 398.

[14]Cho, *Salvation, Health, and Prosperity*, 16.

eradicates social depravity and environmental redemption for the sake of the whole groaning creation (Romans 8:22)" since the redemption of Christ is holistic.[15]

If Christ's redemption is restricted to spiritual salvation for individuals, the Kingdom of God cannot be experienced in the here and now. The Kingdom of God can be only an eschatological hope to Korean Pentecostals. For Moltmann, the Kingdom of God is present through living in the hope for the Kingdom of God.[16] In this sense, his eschatological hope is both future and present. In contrast, for Korean Pentecostals, the Kingdom of God is not merely the subject of their eschatological hope. They believe that, alongside spiritual salvation, they are saved from the curse and from the evil causes of poverty and disease through the redemption of Christ. This means that salvation in the Threefold Blessing has both eschatological and practical implications for the present Christian life.

Thus, the salvation of the Threefold Blessing needs to be extended to include the social and ecological dimensions. Restricting it to the spiritual dimension is contradictory to Cho's holistic soteriology. Nevertheless, it seems that Korean Pentecostals mostly understand the spiritual blessing as referring to the experience of Spirit baptism and the reception of spiritual gifts.

This raises another question of whether the phrase "as your soul prospers" refers only to the experience of Spirit baptism and spiritual gifts, without concern for the ethical dimension or the fruit of the Spirit (Gal 5:22-23). Korean Pentecostals place more emphasis on spiritual gifts than on producing the fruit of the Spirit for Christian maturity.

The spiritual gifts and fruits cannot be simply equated. According to William and Robert Menzies, "Paul's fruit of the Spirit or his ethical language" cannot be linked to "Luke's Pentecostal baptism in the Spirit" in a causal relationship.[17] According to them, compared with Luke, Paul includes a larger spectrum of activities within the ministry of the Spirit. To Paul, the Spirit is more than simply "the source of inspired speech

---

[15] Jun Hee Cha, "The Anthropology of Rev. Yonggi Cho's Threefold Blessing Theology: In the Light of the Old Testament," in *Dr. Yonggi Cho's Ministry and Theology I*, ed. Young San Theological Institute (2008), 155.
[16] Moltmann, *The Source of Life*, 29.
[17] Menzies and Menzies, *Spirit and Power*, 205.

and charismatic wisdom" and brings "ethical transformation" and "life-changing power into every believer."[18] For Luke, the spiritual gifts relate to "the missiological dimension of the Spirit's work," but for Paul, they are concerned with the ethical dimension and the regeneration of the Christian believer.[19] Regarding the relationship between the fruit and gifts of the Spirit, Parks says that they are "the two wings of a bird. The wings must work in harmony if the bird is to fly."[20] Dunn says that "through the washing of regeneration and renewal effected by the Spirit" Christians are saved and can be transformed into "the very image of the Lord."[21] As a branch can bear fruit when it remains on the vine (John. 15:5), the spiritual fruit will be produced when people are led by the Spirit.

Korean Pentecostals seem more concerned about being baptized in the Spirit than about producing the fruit of the Spirit. The spiritual life of Korean Pentecostals is based on being filled with the Spirit repeatedly, which involves not only having a spiritual experience, but continuing to live in the Spirit. The work of the Spirit in Christians cannot only be assessed in terms of the reception of spiritual gifts. Similarly, living in the Spirit does not merely mean practicing spiritual gifts on a daily basis but involves individual transformation into the image of Christ.

How then can this change in lifestyle through the Spirit be realized? The concept of spiritual blessing in the Threefold Blessing has to be reinterpreted and recontextualized from an ethical perspective to include a focus on the fruit of the Spirit alongside Spirit baptism. The cultivation of the fruit of the Spirit should follow the baptism in the Spirit. Thus, it is necessary to reconsider the meaning of spiritual prosperity, whether it only involves Spirit baptism or whether it includes ongoing life in the Spirit leading to Christian maturity.

---

[18]Ibid., 205-206.
[19]Ibid., 206.
[20]H. Parks, "Charisma: What's in a Word?" *Renewal* 52 (August/September 1974): 21; Paul Elbert, "Calvin and the Spiritual Gifts," *Journal of the Evangelical Theological Society* (September 1979): 237-238.
[21]James D. G. Dunn, "Spirit and Kingdom," *The Expository Times*, January 1970, 37.

2. The Recontextualization of Healing

Early faith-healing ministers such as E. W. Kenyon believed that people were not healed because of a lack of faith or hidden sins that blocked divine healing.[22] Cho mostly agrees but provides several reasons why people are not healed and how they can overcome obstacles to healing: 1) they need to wait for God's time, 2) healing may be hindered by sin, 3) they need to wait for *rhema* words from God, and 4) sometimes there is a higher purpose than healing.[23]

It is clear in the New Testament account that not all the sick were healed. The Apostle Paul prayed three times for the removal of his "thorn in the flesh" (2 Cor 12:7), which many scholars think may have been a physical weakness. Instead of receiving divine healing, he was told, "My grace is sufficient for you, for My strength is made perfect in weakness" (2 Cor 12:9, NKJV).

This raises pastoral questions about how to help Pentecostals who are not healed after extended periods of prayer. How can the Threefold Blessing give hope to those who are disabled, suffer from an incurable disease, or those who have never received material blessings despite praying for the Threefold Blessing? Korean Pentecostalism has failed to provide satisfactory theological responses to those who do not receive healing or blessings. James emphasizes that prayer for healing is not only the responsibility of the sick person but also that of the elders of the church (James 5:14-15). The sick person needs the help of the church as the body of Christ. The role of the church in healing is based on sacrificial love on behalf of others.

Pentecostal ministers and leaders tend to be silent about those in the church who have not received divine healing. However, these people need even more pastoral care as well as prayers instead of being criticized that sin or unbelief may be hindering their healing. The disabled suffer their physical or mental handicap as well as social prejudice and discrimination, which may cause more hardship than their

---

[22] D. R. McConnell, *A Different Gospel: A Historical and Biblical Analysis of the Modern Faith Movement* (Peabody, MA: Hendrickson, 1988), ch. 9; and C. Peter Wagner, *How to Have a Healing Ministry in Any Church: A Comprehensive Guide* (Ventura, CA: Regal, 1998), 110.

[23] Cho, *The Fourth Dimension*, 100-104.

disability. The ultimate goal of healing for the disabled may not be physical healing but rather healing of the social system which stigmatizes them. Amos Yong says that it is a problem to pray for the disabled with Down syndrome "to be healed of their chromosomal aberration" and also a problem when people fail "to recognize the human person in the image of God" beyond their physical difficulties.[24]

Healing in the Threefold Blessing has been considered only in its personal and physical dimension. Its scope needs to be enlarged to include society, the family, and the church. The suffering of the disabled cannot be alleviated without addressing the issue of social prejudice.[25] Disability and incurable sicknesses are still mainly perceived in "biological, medical and individualized terms" rather than in the social dimension.[26]

Richard Shaull points out that Pentecostal theology has not made many efforts to develop "a theology of social responsibility clearly integrating the personal and the social, a number of things are happening in their communities in which this integration is a reality."[27] The social dimension of healing in the Threefold Blessing has also not been considered. Moltmann says, "The modern concept of person is the social concept: 'person' no longer means the all-sufficing, self-sufficient, universal and reflective figure."[28] Thus, "person" cannot be understood outside relationships with others and healing should not be limited to personal matters. In the synoptic gospels, people encountered Christ as "the healing power of the divine Spirit." Jesus met people not as sinners but as those who were "sick, suffering, and in need of help."[29] Healing occurred in "the interaction between Jesus and expectation, a person's faith and His will."[30] To Moltmann, healing is "the sign of the new

---

[24] Amos Yong, "Disability and Gifts of the Spirit: Pentecost and the Renewal of the Church," *Journal of Pentecostal Theology* 19 (2010): 77.
[25] Personal interview with Amos Yong, Regent University, VA, August 16, 2011. See, Appendix C. Interview with Dr. Amos Yong.
[26] Yong, "Disability and Gifts of the Spirit," 81.
[27] Richard Shaull and Waldo Cesar, *Pentecostalism and the Future of the Christian Churches: Promises, Limitations, Challenges* (Grand Rapids, MI: Eerdmans, 2000), 214.
[28] Moltmann, *The Spirit of Life*, 251.
[29] Ibid., 189.
[30] Ibid., 190.

creation and the rebirth of life,"[31] and, furthermore, healing consists of "the restoration of disrupted community, and the sharing and communication of life." [32] To European theologians like Barth, Moltmann, and Tillich, the Kingdom of God is an agent "to heal social evils as well as disease" in the present.[33]

As physical and mental illnesses are often related to social and environmental circumstances, healing has to be understood from a broader perspective. Doctors believe many diseases are caused by stress in contemporary society; those who are cured from a disease may relapse if their stress remains. Healing not only concerns physical and mental illness but the individual circumstances with which people struggle, the communal society in which they are involved, and the natural ecosystem.[34] Healing is incomplete unless it addresses these areas.

In 2002, Korea ranked second behind the USA in its divorce rate.[35] Many victims, including children, suffer from family breakdown rather than poverty or disease. Inner emotional healing may be the preferred approach for family problems between spouses and between parents and their children.

Healing in the Threefold Blessing has focused more on physical than inner healing, so healing in the Threefold Blessing remains narrow in scope. Anderson says that "healing is more than curing": it must be holistic for today's suffering world.[36] Yong also distinguishes between the terms "healing" and "curing," preferring to use curing for physical healing since healing's broader and more holistic meaning includes the social and psychological dimensions.[37] Curing is not normally used when broken relationships in the family and society have been resolved.

---

[31]Ibid., 189.
[32]Ibid., 191.
[33]Dayton, "The Good God and the Theology of Blessing," 55.
[34]Kim, "Paul Tillich and Dr. Yonggi Cho," 360.
[35]Caroline Gluck, "Koreans Learn to Live with Divorce," BBC NEWS, May 8, 2003, available from http://news.bbc.co.uk/1/hi/world/asia-pacific/3011119.stm, accessed June 25, 2012. See also "The Statistics Korea," http://kostat.go.kr/portal/korea/kor_nw/2/2/1/index.board?bmode=read&aSeq=246945, accessed June 25, 2012. According to Statistics Korea, in February 2011, there were 23,600 marriages and 8,300 couples divorces.
[36]Allan Anderson, "Pentecostals, Healing and Ecumenism," *International Review of Mission* 93 (July/October 2004): 494-495.
[37]See Appendix C. Interview with Dr. Amos Yong.

Yong also insists that healing for the disabled goes beyond improving their physical conditions to bring about conceptual change in society on their behalf.[38] The healing of social prejudices and discrimination, which they face daily, is important to them. These can be resolved when ordinary people show concern towards them.

Can the theology of healing in the Threefold Blessing sufficiently respond to people's suffering in today's world? Cho's understanding of healing does not only mean physical curing, but is related to Christ's redemption and good news for suffering people.[39] Healing has been accomplished through the event of the crucifixion of Christ.[40] Physical healing is included in the healing ministry of Christ, but his healing should be understood as embracing all his creation. Thus, healing needs the broader sense of integrating social and ecological aspects.

To Moltmann, "healing and salvation are related."[41] Similarly, Cho makes no distinction between healing and salvation. The crucifixion of Christ was intended to bring about the holistic recovery of the whole universe, addressing not only physical illness but the whole of humanity, the ecosystem, and the universe. Healing in the Threefold Blessing needs to be extended likewise.

Urbanization, industrialization, and modernization bring environmental problems, family breakdown, human rights abuses, gender discrimination, and the increasing gap between the rich and the poor. Pentecostals have to consider if the focus on individual healing can give hope to Korean society. Pannenberg says, "Christians do not hope just for themselves, which would mean only too often the hope of one would be at the cost of the hopes of others. In Christ they share in a universal hope for humanity." [42] Indeed, it is questionable whether healing in the Threefold Blessing can continue to give hope to society and church if it remains limited to the physical and personal dimensions.

---

[38]See Appendix C. Interview with Dr. Amos Yong.
[39]Allan Anderson, "Pentecostal and Charismatic Theology," in *The Modern Theologians: An Introduction to Christian Theology since 1918*, ed. David F. Ford and Rachel Muers (Malden, MS: Blackwell Publishing Ltd., 2005), 601-603.
[40]Cho, *Fivefold Gospel and Threefold Blessing*, 128-129.
[41]Moltmann, *The Spirit of Life*, 189.
[42]Pannenberg, *Systematic Theology vol. 3*, 177.

The issue of *Han* also needs to be addressed. As already discussed, Koreans are people of *Han*,⁴³ the national sentiment with implications for every aspect of Korean life. *Han* is normally accumulated through external factors and will not be resolved unless these external elements of *Han* are removed. Korean shamanic rituals were focused on releasing people's *Han*,⁴⁴ and this is one of the primary reasons why Shamanism has survived.⁴⁵

Koreans experienced the *Han* of poverty and sickness, which left them frustrated because they could not handle it themselves. Dong Soo Kim insists that if Pentecostalism had been unable to release *Han*, it could not have grown so rapidly and quickly.⁴⁶ The Threefold Blessing, with its message of divine blessings, effectively responded to the *Han* of Koreans, so it was very appealing.

The Threefold Blessing focused on individual *Han* in the life of ordinary people rather than the collective *Han* of society. To address this collective *Han*, the meaning of healing in the Threefold Blessing has to be expanded to give hope to Koreans regarding change in their current circumstances through reinterpreting healing for contemporary society. Previously focused on individual and physical *Han* due to poverty and illness, the Threefold Blessing now needs to consider healing the collective *Han* caused by social factors such as injustice, inequality between the rich and poor, gender and racial discrimination, inequality of opportunity, and capital exploitation.

The healing of relationships between the oppressor and the oppressed, and the wrongdoer and the wronged, cannot be achieved without reconciliation through forgiveness. The division of the Korean peninsula is a major cause behind the *Han* of the Korean people. Both sides of Korea have been antagonistic towards each other. How can Korean unification come about? It cannot happen without each side extending the hand of forgiveness. Without healing wounded hearts, this political and diplomatic matter cannot be solved.

---

⁴³Dong Suh Nam, "Towards a Theology of *Han*," in *Minjung Theology: People as the Subjects of History*, ed. Commission on Theological Concerns of the Christian Conference of Asia (London: Zed Press, 1981), 50.

⁴⁴Suh, "Liberating Spirituality in the Korean *Minjung* Tradition," 33.

⁴⁵Kim, "The Healing of *Han* in Korean Pentecostalism," 127.

⁴⁶Ibid., 124.

A new understanding of healing must be accompanied by a new theological perspective. Forgiveness between social and political groups, and between individuals, has to precede the healing of *Han*. The biblical precedence in Matthew 5:23-24 and 6:12 teaches that the inner healing of those who are wronged cannot take place unless they offer forgiveness to the wrongdoer. Previously, healing focused on physical curing. Now it must include inner healing for individuals, healing of communal discord, recovering of the ecosystem, and even reconciliation between North and South Koreans.

3. The Recontextualization of Prosperity

The theology of the Threefold Blessing developed within a context of poverty. As already mentioned, Cho regards poverty as "a curse from Satan."[47] He was a victim of poverty and remembers what it means to have nothing to eat.[48] Most early members of the YFGC were extremely poor, so Cho's message of prosperity through Christ gave them hope.[49] Few members of YFGC today feel they suffer from poverty. They have received financial blessings and their hope for prosperity has been realized.

Pentecostals need to think about what prosperity means to them, taking into account their obligation to their neighbors. Vinson Synan say that in every generation, there will be the poor and the sick, just as Jesus said "you will always have the poor among you" (John. 12:8), and they will need the gospel of the Threefold Blessing.[50] Moltmann is not opposed to the prosperity of Christians but is strongly critical of rich Christians who further impoverish the poor or cheat others for their personal benefit.[51] In the New Testament, the tax-collectors were Jews who knew about the God of Israel. As they oppressed their powerless compatriots and abused their power in order to accumulate wealth, their god became Mammon, an unjust god.

---

[47]Cho, *The Fourth Dimension II*, 137.
[48]Ibid., 137-38.
[49]Cho, *Salvation, Health and Prosperity*, 11; Cho, *The Holy Spirit, My Senior Partner*, 8.
[50]Personal interview with Vinson Synan, Regent University, VA, August 16, 2011.
[51]Moltmann, *The Way of Jesus Christ*, 99-100.

To early Korean Pentecostals, prosperity in the Threefold Blessing was not the selfish pursuit of wealth but a source of hope in desperate situations. This hope has turned into a self-centered desire for more prosperity without a willingness to help others. Young Hoon Lee says Koreans suffer not from financial poverty but from symptoms of spiritual poverty such as spiritual malaise, emptiness of life, and lack of love.

To be relevant today, the Threefold Blessing must emphasize loving concern for others. Pentecostals need to discover a new hope based on sharing "blessings" with others in the wider society.[52] Lee also notes that Pentecostal churches have focused on the spiritual manifestations of the Spirit described in the book of Acts, but they should not overlook their responsibility for charitable works on behalf of their neighbors as these were also part of the early church's ministry.[53]

Korean Pentecostals need to think theologically about what the Kingdom in the here and now means in the contemporary Korean context and how they can participate in that Kingdom. Pursuing a more prosperous life on earth when they already have enough blessings is not the way to be a part of the Kingdom. Instead, they can participate in God's Kingdom by sharing their blessings and caring for the needy with the love of Christ.

Theological controversies arose in past decades about the Threefold Blessing, its emphasis on prosperity, and its relationship to Shamanism. These controversies continue because Pentecostals have not applied Christian values to their emphasis on prosperity. They have not reflected upon the purpose of prosperity in the contemporary Korean context. Pentecostals believe that blessings come from God. From a biblical and theological perspective, there is nothing wrong with that belief. However, by persistently asking God to provide financial prosperity when they already have enough, their concept of God becomes similar to the god of Shamanism.

The prosperity of Christians needs to be understood in terms of the community and responsibility to society in the same way that Moltmann points out that the concept of "person" needs to be understood in social

---

[52]Email from Young Hoon Lee, November 15, 2012. See, Appendix B. Interview with Dr. Young Hoon Lee.

[53]See, Appendix B. Interview with Dr. Young Hoon Lee.

terms.⁵⁴ Althouse insists that Moltmann's political theology is deeply engaged in the fulfillment of basic human needs and the protection of human dignity and rights.⁵⁵ The new Threefold Blessing has to deal theologically with those same social and political matters. Theologically and biblically, blessing does not mean to have more than others. If the Threefold Blessing does not theologically embrace the fulfillment of basic human needs for neighbors, sharing blessings with the poor and altruistic love for others, it can no longer give hope to Koreans.

Korean Pentecostals need to focus on sharing instead of receiving and to recognize that blessings are for the welfare of the community. The understanding of prosperity has to be changed to include a communal dimension where Pentecostals share community burdens and make sacrifices on behalf of others. Althouse says, "A revision of Pentecostal theology can revitalize the social-political dimensions of the Pentecostal message as a prophetic call to church and society."⁵⁶

Love without sacrifice is deficient. The love of God for humanity was made manifest in the sacrifice of Jesus on the cross: sacrifice is an essential element of Christian love. The new theological basis for prosperity in the Threefold Blessing must likewise focus on love for neighbors and the wider society. Althouse declares, "The dialectic of cross and resurrection is the moment of the inbreaking of eschatological future into the present."⁵⁷

How should the theological terms "hope" and "love" be understood in relation to each other? According to Pannenberg,

Hope and love belong together. Only those who hope with and for others, can also love them, not in the sense of egotistical desire to possess the one who is loved (*amor concupiscentiae*), but in the sense of a benevolent love that helps the other on the way to fulfilment of his or her specific human destiny (*amor amicitiae*).⁵⁸

To achieve "communal prosperity," hope's focus needs to shift from being self-centered to being community-oriented. Young Hoon Lee

---

⁵⁴Moltmann, *The Spirit of Life*, 251.
⁵⁵Althouse, *Spirit of the Last Days*, 181.
⁵⁶Ibid., 179.
⁵⁷Ibid., 178.
⁵⁸Pannenberg, *Systematic Theology vol. 3*, 182.

suggested that the Threefold Blessing needs a blessing which favors the distribution of wealth to marginalized people and balanced development that involves all of Korea's social classes.[59] As long as the hope of prosperity remains self-centered, it lacks a strong Christian ethical base.

The hope of prosperity for and with others will produce joy and fulfillment as Pentecostals pursue this hope in community. Moltmann says that hope must be forward looking, forward moving, and transforming the present.[60] His theology of hope helps to remedy the theological disadvantages of the Threefold Blessing. Cho writes,

> In order to live the life of true joy and happiness, we must love and sacrifice for our neighbours. If we would yield and sacrifice a little more sharing love for the happiness of our neighbours, the exploits of the love and sacrifice come back to us as joy and happiness like a boomerang. If we try to make others happy, then we also become happy. When freed from an egocentric mind, we live for the joy and happiness of our neighbours, greater joy and happiness come to ourselves.[61]

The emphasis of Cho's message has changed from a focus on personal blessing, especially prosperity and healing, to the pursuit of joy and fulfillment in Christ through sacrificial love for others. Commenting on this change in Cho's social theology, Anderson argues,

> The social theology of Cho is based on this concept of the love of God that fills the life of the Christian through the Holy Spirit and enables the Christian to share this love with others, thereby meeting Jesus in daily life through serving poor and disadvantaged people in the immediate society as well as in other countries.[62]

The Apostle Paul writes that the Kingdom is not "a matter of eating and drinking, but of righteousness, peace and joy in the Holy Spirit" (Rom 14:17). In the post-Korean War context, without resolving the

---

[59] See Appendix B. Interview with Dr. Young Hoon Lee.
[60] Moltmann, *Theology of Hope*, 16.
[61] Yonggi Cho, *Albeit We Shall Love* (Seoul: Seoul Logos, 2008), 267-291.
[62] Anderson, "A Time to Share Love," 167.

problem of eating and drinking, it was not easy to experience the Kingdom as "righteousness, peace and joy in the Spirit" in the here and now. However, in the contemporary context, the Kingdom is not a matter of eating of drinking for one's own benefit, but God's righteousness for an unjust society, and peace and joy with others in the Spirit through acts of love. In contrast to post-war Pentecostals, today's Pentecostals can act generously by sharing their financial blessings and resources with the marginalized and disadvantaged.

Prosperity in the Threefold Blessing must be recontextualized as prosperity for the whole of society rather than merely for individuals. Otherwise, contemporary Koreans without financial problems will lose interest in the message of the Threefold Blessing. As a result, the Threefold Blessing will no longer continue to function as a source of hope for them.

CHAPTER 26
OBSERVATIONS AND RECOMMENDATIONS FOR CONTEXTUALIZING THE THREEFOLD BLESSING INTO THE CURRENT KOREAN CONTEXT

Since the Threefold Blessing developed in the aftermath of the Korean War more than sixty years ago, life in Korea has changed significantly socio-politically, economically, and culturally. As Koreans have become westernized, their values and expectations have also changed.

The church and its responsibilities in society have entered a new phase. On the surface, Cho's social theology may not seem very active.[1] However, since the 1980s, the YFGC has undergone an ecclesiological change in relation to its social responsibility. The scale and budget of YFGC's social relief work around the world is larger than any social and religious organization in Korea. The YFGC has built hospitals, homes for the disadvantaged, nursing homes for senior citizens, a welfare town, and schools to help North Korean refugees. YFGC is also helping North Korea in various ways. Thus, it is clear that the YFGC is to some extent fulfilling its responsibilities in the nation and society.

In 2005, there was also a remarkable change in Cho's soteriology—a broadening in scope. He began to emphasize the necessity of a soteriology that embraces society, the ecosystem, and the whole universe.[2]

Nonetheless, the theology of the Threefold Blessing does not yet reflect these ecclesiological and soteriological changes nor the change in the Korean context. Scholars argue that the theology of the Threefold Blessing remains focused on the personal pursuit of a victorious and healthy life rather than social concerns[3] and has limited socio-political relevance.[4] Chan points out that Cho's "practical pneumatology" is in a danger of becoming a "pragmatic pneumatology."[5] Chan's concern will

---

[1] Anderson, "A Time to Share Love," 159.
[2] Shin, "Young San eui Saeng Tae Shin Hak [Yonggi Cho's Eco-Theology]," 398.
[3] Kärkkäinen, "March Forward to Hope," 255.
[4] Yung, *Mangoes or Bananas?*, 211.
[5] Chan, "The Pneumatology of Paul Yonggi Cho," 95.

become a reality unless the Threefold Blessing is recontextualized and reinterpreted for today's Korean Pentecostals. As Moltmann points out,

Pentecostalism originated as a result of the experience of the Holy Spirit. According to this experience, the Holy Spirit has to do with the soul and the body, with salvation and healing. Because people are linked bodily to the entire creation, it follows that the Holy Spirit has also related to all other creatures, in regard not only to their future salvation but also to their present preservation.[6]

The theology of the Threefold Blessing needs to enlarge its scope, allowing for practical expressions of altruism on behalf of neighbors, society, the ecosystem, and the universe for all, through sharing in the love of Christ.

After researching Cho's theology, Moltmann concluded that Cho's Christology was not developed.[7] In the Threefold Blessing, Jesus is the Savior, the Healer, and the dispenser of blessings. This raises a number of questions. First, does this mean that salvation in the atonement is limited to humanity or does it embrace all of creation? Second, is Christ's healing only for human beings or does it include the ecosystem? Third, is the message of prosperity only intended for the financial blessing of individuals or does it extend to the community, the nation, and beyond?

The message of the Threefold Blessing has been very influential among Korean Pentecostals as a source of contextual hope. However, for contemporary Korea, it needs to be reinterpreted and recontextualized from an emphasis on personal blessings to a focus on the community. This transition requires a new systematic theological foundation based on love and sacrifice.

Unlike Pentecostals in the post-Korean War context, the majority of today's Pentecostals neither belong to the lower socio-economic class nor struggle with absolute poverty or sickness. Their issues are not a matter of "having" but of "being" as Christians. Their complex dilemmas cannot be solved by receiving financial prosperity and healing for the body. Many suffer from social problems such as family breakdowns,

---

[6]Moltmann, "A Response to My Pentecostal Dialogue Partners," 62.
[7]Jürgen Moltmann, "Salm Eul Wooi Han Sinhak, Sinhak Eul Wooi Han Salm [Theology for Life, Life for Theology]," *Kukmin Ilbo*, May 12, 2009, available from *Kukmin Ilbo* database on-line; http://news.kukinews.com/article/view.asp?arcid =0921286513, accessed October 26, 2011.

broken relationships, sexual discrimination, inequality between the rich and the poor, environmental devastation, and the national emotion of *Han*. Healing in the Threefold Blessing must embrace not only the physical dimension but also "inner healing" and the healing of society and the ecosystem.

For continued future growth, Pentecostalism needs a new hope for new Korean contexts. Salvation and healing need to be understood in holistic terms. The atonement of Christ on behalf of humanity and the whole universe means the soteriology of the Threefold Blessing cannot remain limited to personal and spiritual dimensions. Healing has to be understood in broader terms to include not only the body but society and the ecosystem. Prosperity also must be reinterpreted with a cognitive change and theological foundsion based the theological references, "love" and "sacrifice," for communal prosperity. Such a theology would be hopeful, relevant, and helpful to Koreans today.

Bibliography

Books

Ahn, Byeong Mu. *Galilea ui Yesoo* [Jesus of Galilee]. Seoul: Hankook Sinhak Yeongooso, 2008.

Allen, Horace Newton. *Allen's Diary*. Seoul: Dankook Daehakgyo Chulpansa, 2008.

———. *Things Korean: A Collection of Sketches and Anecdotes Missionary and Diplomatic*. New York: Fleming H. Revell Company, 1908.

Althouse, Peter. *Spirit of the Last Days: Pentecostal Eschatology in Conversation with Jürgen Moltmann*. London: T&T Clark International, 2003.

Anderson, Allan. *Zion and Pentecost: Spreading Fires: The Missionary Nature of Early Pentecostalism*. London: SCM Press, 2007.

———. *An Introduction to Pentecostalism: Global Charismatic Christianity*. Cambridge: Cambridge University Press, 2004.

———. *African Reformation: African Initiated Christianity in the 20th Century*. Trenton, NJ & Asmara, Eritrea: Africa World Press Inc., 2001.

———. *The Spirituality and Experience of Pentecostal and Zionist/Apostolic Churches in South Africa*. Pretoria: University of South Africa Press, 2000.

Anderson, Allan, and Edmond Tang, eds. *Asian and Pentecostal: The Charismatic Face of Christianity in Asia*. Oxford: Regnum Books International, 2005.

Barnes, Albert. *Notes: Explanatory and Practical on the General Epistles of James, Peter, John and Jude*. New York: Harper & Brothers Publishers, 1875.

Barnes, Timothy David. *Tertullian: A Historical and Literary Study*. Oxford: Clarendon Press, 1971.

Barth, Karl. *Letters 1961-1968*. Translated by Geoffrey W. Bromiley. Edinburgh: T&T Clark, 1981.

———. *Protestant Theology in the Nineteenth Century: Its Background and History*. Translated by B. Cozens and J. Bowden. London: SCM Press, 1972.

Bartleman, Frank. *Azusa Street: The Roots of Modern-Day Pentecost*. South Plainfield, NJ: Logos, 1980.

Bauckham, Richard. *The Theology of Jürgen Moltmann*. London: T&T Clark Ltd., 1995.

———. *Moltmann: Messianic Theology in the Making*. Hant, UK: Marshall Pickering, 1987.

Bede the Venerable. *The Commentary on the Seven Catholic Epistles*. Translated by David Hurst. Kalamazoo, MI: Cistercian Publications, 1985.

Berkhof, L. *Systematic Theology*. London: The Banner of Truth Trust, First Edition, 1958, Reprinted 1960, 1963.

Bentz, Valerie Malhotra and Jeremy J. Shapiro. *Mindful Inquiry in Social Research*. London: SAGE Pulications, 1998.

Bevans, Stephen B. *Models of Contextual Theology*. Maryknoll, NY: Orbis Books, 1997.

Blair, William Newton, and Bruce F. Hunt. *The Korean Pentecost and the Sufferings Which Followed*. Edinburgh: The Banner of Truth Trust, 1977.

Brown, Arthur Judson. *The Mastery of the Far East: The Story of Korea's Transformation and Japan's Rise to Supremacy in the Orient*. New York: Charles Scribner's Sons, 1919.

Brown, Candy Gunther, ed. *Global Pentecostal and Charismatic Healing*. Oxford: Oxford University Press, 2011.

Bryman, Alan. *Quantity and Quality in Social Research*. London: Routledge, 1992.

Burgess, Stanley M., and Eduard M. Van der Maas eds. *The New International Dictionary of Pentecostal and Charismatic Movements*. Grand Rapids, MI: Zondervan Publishing House, 2003.

Burleigh, John H. S., ed. *Augustine: Earlier Writings*. Translated by John H. S. Burleigh. London: SCM Press Ltd., 1953.

Buswell Jr., Robert E., and Timothy S. Lee eds. *Christianity in Korea*. Hawaii: University of Hawaii Press, 2006.

Calvin, John. *Institute of the Christian Religion*. Translated by Henry Beveridge. Peabody, MA: Hendrickson Publishers Inc., 2008.

———. *Institutes of the Christian Religion*. Translated by Ford Lewis Battles. Grand Rapids, MI: Wm. B. Eerdmans Publishing Co., 1995.

Cartledge, Mark J., ed. *Speaking in Tongues: Multi-Disciplinary Perspectives*. Milton Keynes, UK: Paternoster Press, 2006.

Carwardine, Richard J. *Evangelicals and Politics in Antebellum America*. New Haven and London: Yale University Press, 1993.

Cho, Yonggi. *Albeit We Shall Love*. Seoul: Seoul Logos, 2008.

———. *Soon Bok Eum Ui Jin Ri* [The Truth of Full Gospel] I. Seoul: Young San Chul Pan Sa, 1979. Chong, Kelly H. *Deliverance and Submission: Evangelical Women and the Negotiation of Patriarchy in South Korea*. Cambridge, MA: Harvard University Press, 2008.

———. *Unleashing the Power of Faith*. Alachua, FL: Bridge-Logos, 2006.

———. *My Church Growth Stories*. Seoul: Seoul Logos Co., 2006.

———. *March Forward to Hope*. Seoul: Seoul Logos Co., 2002.

———. *Oh Jung Bok Eum Kwa Sam Jung Chuk Bok* [Fivefold Gospel and Threefold Blessing]. Seoul: Seoul Mal Sseum Sa, 2002.

———. *The Nature of God*. Lake Mary, FL: Charisma House, 2001.

———. *Successful Home Cell Groups*. North Brunswick, NJ: Bridge-Logos, 1999.

———. *How Can I Be Healed?* Seoul: Seoul Logos Co., Inc., 1999.

———. *The Story of Fivefold Gospel*. Seoul: Seoul Logos, 1998.

———. *Fivefold Gospel and Threefold Blessing*. Seoul: Seoul Logos, 1998.

———. *Sung Ryeoung Lon* [Pneumatology]. Seoul: Seoul Malsseum Sa, 1998.

———. *Pastor! How Can I Be Healed?* Seoul: Seoul Logos, 1997.

———. *Born to be Blessed*. Seoul: Seoul Logos Co., 1993.

———. *The Holy Spirit My Senior Partner*. Milton Keynes, UK: Word Ltd., 1989.

———. *Praying with Jesus*. Altamonte Springs, FL: Creation House, 1988.

———. *Salvation, Health and Prosperity*. Altamonte Springs, FL: Creation House, 1987.

———. *The Fourth Dimension vol. II*. Plainfield, NJ: Bridge Publishing Inc., 1983.

———. *Church Growth vol.3*. Seoul: Youngsan Press, 1983.

———. *More than Numbers: Principles of Church Growth*. Collins, Glasgow: Valley Books Trust, 1983.

———. *Solving Life's Problems*. Seoul: Seoul Logos Co Inc., 1980.

———. *The Fourth Dimension*. Plainfield, NJ: Logos International, 1979.

Clark, Allen D. *A History of the Church in Korea*. Seoul: The Christian Literature Society of Korea, 1971.

Coleman, Simon. *The Globalisation of Charismatic Christianity: Spreading the Gospel of Prosperity*. Cambridge: Cambridge University Press, 2000.

Cone, James H. *A Black Theology of Liberation*. Maryknoll, NY: Orbis Books, 1996.

———. *The Spirituals and the Blues*. Maryknoll, NY: Orbis Books, 1995.

Copeland, Kenneth. *The Laws of Prosperity*. Fort Worth: Kenneth Copeland Publications, 1995.

———. *Prosperity: The Choice is Yours*. Tulsa, OK: Harrison House, 1992.

Cotton, James, and Ian Neary, eds. *The Korean War in History*. Manchester: Manchester University Press, 1989.

Cox, Harvey. *Fire from Heaven: The Rise of Pentecostal Spirituality and the Reshaping of Religion in the Twenty-first Century*. Reading, MA: Addison-Wesley Publishing Co., 1995.

Cross, F. L. *The Oxford Dictionary of the Christian Church*, 3rd ed. Oxford: Oxford University Press, 2005.

Dallet, Charles. *Histoire de l'église de Corée* (Paris: Victor Palme, 1874). Translated by Eung Ryel An and Suk Woo Choi, *Hankook CheonJu GyoHoisa vol 1* [The history of Korean Catholicism]. Seoul: Hankook GyoHoiSa YeonGooSo, 2000.

Darlow, Thomas Herbert, and Horace Frederick Moule. *Historical Catalogues of Printed Editions of the Holy Scriptures in the Library of the British and Foreign Bible Society Vol. II (cont.)*. London: The Bible House Co., 1903.

Davis, George T. B. *Korea for Christ*. New York: Fleming H. Revell Co., 1910.

Dayton, Donald W. *Theological Roots of Pentecostalism*. Peabody, MA: Hendrickson Publishers Inc., 1987.

Dempster, Murray W., Byron D. Klaus, and Douglas Petersen, eds., *Called and Empowered: Global Mission in Pentecostal Perspective*. Peabody, MA: Hendrickson Publishers Inc., 1991.

Dunn, James D. G. *Baptism in the Holy Spirit: A Re-examination of the New Testament Teaching on the Gift of the Spirit in relation to Pentecostalism today*. London: SCM Press Ltd., 1984.

Dwight, Henry Otis, ed. *The Blue Book of Missions for 1907*. New York and London: Funk & Wagnalls Co., 1907.

Fabella, Virginia, Peter K. H. Lee, and David Kwangsun Suh, eds. *Asian Christian Spirituality: Reclaiming Traditions*. Maryknoll, NY: Orbis Books, 1992.

Fahlbusch, Erwin, Jan Milic Lochman, John Mbiti, Jaroslav Pelikan, Lukas Vischer, Geoffrey W. Bromiley, and David B. Barrett, eds. *The Encyclopedia of Christianity vol 2*. Grand Rapids, MI: William B. Eerdmans Publishing Co., 2001.

Fee, Gordon D. *God's Empowering Presence: The Holy Spirit in the Letters of Paul*. Peabody, MA: Hendrickson Publisher, Inc., 1994.

Ford, David F., and Rachel Muers, eds. *The Modern Theologians: An Introduction to Christian Theology since 1918*. Malden, MS: Blackwell Publishing Ltd., 2005.

Ga, Ok Myung. *Pneumatology*. Translated by Jae-yung Jung. Pyungyang: Pyungyang Presbyterian Bible School, 1931.

Gale, James S. *Korea in Transition*. New York: Eaton and Mains, 1909.

———. *A Korean-English Dictionary*. Yokohama: Kelly & Walsh Ltd., 1897.

Gidokgyo Daehan Hananim eui SeungHoi [the Korean Assemblies of God]. *Gyodan Heonbeob* [Denomination Constitution]. Seoul: Eumji, 2008.

Gil, Jin Ggyung. *Sun-joo Gil* [in Korean]. Seoul: Jongno, 1980.

Gook Jae Shin Hak Yeon Goo Won [International Theological Institute]. *Young San eui Mokhoiwya Shin Hak I* [Younggi Cho's Ministry and Theology]. Gunpo: Hansei University Press, 2008.

———. [International Theological Institute]. *Hananim euy Sunghoi GyoHoiSa* [Church History of Assemblies of God]. Seoul: Seoul Mal Sseum Sa, 1998.

———. [International Theological Institute]. *Yoido SoonBokEum Gyo Hoi Ui Shin Ang Gwah Shin Hak* II [The Theology and Faith of Yoido Full Gospel Church]. Seoul: Seoul Seo Jeok, 1993.

Gordon, A. J. *The Ministry of the Spirit*. Philadelphia, PA: American Baptist Publication Society, 1895.

Grayson, James Huntley. *Korea: A Religious History*. New York: Routledge Curzon, 2002.

Grenz, Stanley J., and Roger E. Olson. *20th Century Theology: God and the World in a Transitional Age*. Downers Grove, IL: InterVarsity Press, 1992.

Griffis, William Elliot. *A Modern Pioneer in Korea: The Life Story of Henry G. Appenzeller*. New York: Fleming H. Revell Co., 1912.

Gromacki, Robert Glenn. *The Modern Tongues Movement*. Philadelphia, PA: Presbyterian and Reformed Publishing Co., 1972.

Gu, Jee Byung. *Shamanism Gwha Hankook GyoHoi* [Shamanism and Korean Church]. Seoul: Sae Han Publishing House, 1996.Gutzlaff, Charles. *Journal of Three Voyages Along the Coast of China in 1831, 1832, & 1833*. London: Thomas Ward and Co., 1840.

Hagin, Kenneth. *How God Taught Me about Prosperity*. Tulsa, OK: Faith Library Publications, 1985.

———. *Redeemed from Poverty, Sickness, and Spiritual Death*. Tulsa, OK: Faith Library Publications, 1966

Hamilton, Angus. *Korea*. New York: Charles Scribner's Sons, 1904.

Hankook Gidockgyo Gyohoihyubuihoi. *Hankook Yoeksa Sokui Gidokgyo* [Christianity in Korean History]. Seoul: Giminsa, 1985.

Hansei University, ed. *2004 Young San International Theological Symposium*. Gunpo: Hansei University Press, 2004.

———. *2003 Young San International Theological Symposium*. Gunpo: Hansei University Press, 2003.

Hardy, Friedhelm, ed. *The Religions of Asia*. London: Routledge, 1990.

Hardy, Melissa, and Alan Bryman, eds. *The Handbook of Data Analysis*. London: SAGE Publication, 2009.

Harrington, Fred Harvey. *God Mammon, and the Japanese: Dr. Horace N. Allen and Korea—American Relations, 1884-1905*. Madison: University of Wisconsin Press, 1966.

Hollenweger, Walter J. *Pentecostalism: Origins and Developments Worldwide*. Peabody, MA: Hendrickson Publishers Inc., 1997.

Hoare, James, and Susan Pares. *Korea an Introduction*. London and New York: Kegan Paul International Ltd., 1991.

Hong, Harold S., Won Yong Ji, and Chung Choon Kim, eds. *Korea Struggles for Christ*. Seoul: Christian Literature Society of Korea, 1966.

Hulbert, Homer B. *The Passing of Korea*. New York: Doubleday, Page & Company, 1906.

Hunt, Everett N., Jr. *Protestant Pioneers in Korea*. Maryknoll, NY: Orbis Books, 1980.

Hurston, Karen. *Growing the World's Largest Church*. Kaduna, Nigeria: Evangel Publishers Ltd., 1994.

Jee, Byung Gu. *Shamanism gwa Hankook Gyohoi* [Shamanism and Korean Church]. Seoul: Sae Han Publishing House, 1996.

Jeon, Taek Bu. *The Faith Mountains of Natives*. Seoul: Christian Literature Crusade, 1993.

Jones, George Heber. *Korea: The Land, People, and Customs*. New York: Eaton and Mains, 1907.

Kang, W. Y., ed. *A Study on Pentecostal Movement in Korea*. Seoul: Korea Christian Academy, 1981.

Kaplan, Steven, ed. *Indigenous Responses to Western Christianity*. New York: New York University Press, 1995.

Kay, William K., and Anne E. Dyer, eds. *Pentecostal and Charismatic Studies*. London: SCM Press, 2004.

Kennedy, Nell L. *Dream Your Way to Success: The Story of Dr. Yonggi Cho and Korea*. Plainfield, NJ: 1980.

Kim, Heung Soo. *Hankook Jeonjaeng gwha Gibokshinang Hwaksan Yeongoo* [a Research for the Korean War and the Expansion of the Health and Wealth Gospel]. Seoul: Hankook Gidokgyo Yeoksa Yeongooso, 1999.

Kim, Ig Jin. *History and Theology of Korean Pentecostalism: Sunbogeum (Pure Gospel) Pentecostalism*. Zoetermeer, Netherlands: Uitgeverij Boekencentrum, 2003.

Kim, Yong Bock, ed. *Minjung Theology: People as the Subjects of History*. Singapore: The Commission on Theological Concerns of the Christian Conference of Asia, 1981.

Kitagawa, Joseph M. *Religion in Japanese History*. New York: Columbia University Press, 1966.

Kitamori, Kazoh. *Theology of the Pain of God*. London: SCM Press Ltd., 1966.

Kraft, Charles H. *Christianity in Culture: A Study in Dynamic Biblical Theologizing in Cross-Cultural Perspective*. Maryknoll, NY: Orbis Books, 1979.

Land, Steven. J. *Pentecostal Spirituality: A Passion for the Kingdom*. Sheffield: Sheffield Academic Press, 2001.

Latourette, Kenneth Scott. *A History of the Expansion of Christianity: The Great Century in Northern Africa and Asia A.D. 1800 – A. D. 1914 vol. VI*. London: Eyre and Spottiswoode Limited, 1944.

Lee, Jung Young, ed., *Ancestor Worship and Christianity in Korea*. New York: The Edwin Mellen Press, 1988.

Lee, Man Yel. *Hankook Gidokgyo wha Minjocktongil Woondong* [Korean Christianity and Reunification Movement]. Seoul: Hankook Gidokgyo Yeoksa Yeongooso, 2001.

Lee, Young Hoon. *The Holy Spirit Movement in Korea: Its Historical and Theological Development*. Oxford: Regnum Books International, 2009.

Longford, Joseph H. *The Story of Korea*. London: T. Fisher Unwin, 1911.

Lopez, Donald S., Jr., ed. *Asian Religions in Practice*. Princeton, NJ: Princeton University Press, 1999.

Luther, Martin. *Lectures on Romans*. Translated by Wilhelm Pauck. London: SCM Press Ltd., 1961.

Ma, Wonsuk, William W. Menzies, and Hyeon Sung Bae, eds. *David Yonggi Cho: A Close Look at His Theology and Ministry*. Baguio City, Philippines: APTS Press and Gunpo, 2004.

Martin, David. *Pentecostalism: The World Their Parish*. Oxford: Blackwell, 2002.

McConnell, D.R. *A Different Gospel: A Historical and Biblical Analysis of the Modern Faith Movement*. Peabody, MA: Hendrickson, 1988.

Menzies, Robert P. *The Development of Early Christian Pneumatology*. Sheffield: Sheffield Academic Press, 1991.

Menzies, William W., and Robert P. Menzies. *Spirit and Power: Foundations of Pentecostal Experience*. Grand Rapids, MI: Zondervan Publishing House, 2000.

Mills, Watson E., ed. *Speaking in Tongues: A Guide to Research on Glossolalia*. Grand Rapids, MI: William B. Eerdmans Publishing Co., 1986.

Min, Gyeong Bae. *Hankook Gidokgyo Gyohoi Sa* [the History of Korean Christianity]. Seoul: Yeonsei Chulpansa, 1993.

Moffett, Samuel Hugh. *A History of Christianity in Asia*. Vol. 2, *1500 to 1900*. Maryknoll, NY: Orbis Books, 2005.

Moltmann, Jürgen. *The Crucified God*. Translated by R. A. Wilson and John Bowden. London: SCM Press, 2001.

———. *Experiences in Theology: Ways and Forms of Christian Theology*. Translated by Margaret Kohl. London: SCM Press, 2000.

———. *The Spirit of Life: A Universal Affirmation*. Translated by Margaret Kohl London: SCM Press, 1999.

———. *The Way of Jesus Christ: Christology in Messianic Dimensions*. Translated by Margaret Kohl. London: SCM Press, 1999

———. *The Source of Life: The Holy Spirit and the Theology of Life*. Translated by Margaret Kohl. London: SCM Press Ltd., 1997.

———. *The Coming of God: Christian Eschatology*. Translated by Margaret Kohl. London: SCM Press, 1996.

———. *Theology of Hope: on the Ground and the Implications of a Christian Eschatology*. Translated by James W. Leitch. Minneapolis, MN: Fortress Press, 1993.

———. *The Trinity and the Kingdom: The Doctrine of God*. Translated by Margaret Kohl. Minneapolis, MN: Fortress Press, 1993.

———. *God in Creation: An Ecological Doctrine of Creation*. Translated by Margaret Kohl. London: SCM Press Ltd., 1985.

———. *Experiences of God*. Translated by Margaret Kohl. London: SCM Press, 1980.

———. *The Church in the Power of the Spirit: A Contribution to Messianic Ecclesiology*. Translated by Margaret Kohl. London: SCM Press, 1977.

Moltmann, Jürgen, and Karl Josef Kuschel, eds. *Pentecostal Movements as an Ecumenical Challenge*. London: SCM Press, 1996.

Munby, D. L. *God and the Rich Society*. London: Oxford University Press, 1961.

Myung, Sung Hoon, and Young Gi Hong, eds. *Charis and Charisma: David Yonggi Cho and the Growth of Yoido Full Gospel Church*. Oxford: Regum, 2003.

Nahm, Andrew C. *Korea: A History of the Korean People*. Seoul: Hollym International Corp., 1988.

Neill, Stephen. *A History of Christian Missions*. Middlesex: Penguin Books Ltd., 1964.

Newbigin, Lesslie. *The Gospel in a Pluralist Society*. London: SPCK, 1989.

Orr, J. Edwin. *Evangelical Awakenings in Eastern Asia*. Minneapolis, MN: Bethany Fellowship Inc., 1975.

Paik, George L. *The History of Protestant Missions in Korea 1832-1910*. Seoul: Yonsei University Press, 1980.

Pannenberg, Wolfhart. *Systematic Theology*, vol. 3. Translated by Geoffrey Bromiley. Grand Rapid, MI: Wm. B. Eerdmans Publishing Co., 1998.

Park, Andrew Sung. *The Wounded Heart of God: The Asian Concept of Han and the Christian Doctrine of Sin*. Nashville: Abingdon Press, 1993.

Park, Chung Hee. *Korea Reborn: A Model for Development*. Englewood Cliffs, NJ: Prentice-Hall, 1979.

Park, Myung Soo. *Hankook Gyohoi Booheung Woondong Yeongoo* [A Study on the Revival Movement in the Korea Church]. Seoul: Hankook Gidokgyo Ryeksa Yeongooso, 2007.

Pomerville, Paul A. *Introduction to Missions: An Independent-Study Textbook*. Irving, TX: ICI University Press, 1987.

Pratt, Keith, and Richard Rutt, *Korea: A Historical and Cultural Dictionary*. Richmond Surrey, U.K.: Curzon Press, 1999.

Rhie, Deok- Joo. *Chogi HankookGidokgyoSa YeonGoo* [A Study on the Early Christian History in Korea]. Seoul: The Institute for Korean Church History, 1995.

Rhodes, Harry A., ed. *History of the Korea Mission Presbyterian Church U.S.A.* Vol. I, *1884-1934*. Seoul: The Presbyterian Church of Korea Department of Education, 1984.

———. *The Fiftieth Anniversary Celebration of the Korea Mission of the Presbyterian Church in the U. S. A. June 30 – July 3, 1934*. Seoul: YMCA Press, 1934.

Rin, Ro Bong, and Marlin L. Nelson, eds. *Korean Church Growth Explosion: Centennial of the Protestant Church (1884-1984)*. Seoul: Word of Life Press and Asia Theological Association, 1983.

Roberts, Oral. *Expect a Miracle: My Life and Ministry*. Nashville: Thomas Nelson Publishers, 1995.

―――. *Holy Bible: With My Personal Commentary*. Tulsa, OK: Oral Roberts Evangelistic Association, 1981.

―――. *Better Health and Miracle Living*. Tulsa, OK: Oral Roberts Evangelistic Association, 1976.

Roe, James Moulton. *A History of the British and Foreign Bible Society 1905-1954*. London: The British and Foreign Bible Society, 1965.

Sapsford, Roger, and Victor Jupp, eds. *Data Collection and Analysis*. London: SAGE Publications, 1996.

Seo, Seon Kwang. *Hankook Gydokgyo Jeongchishinhak ui Jeon Gae* [the Development of Korean Christian Political Theology]. Seoul: Yewha Yeoja Dae Hak Chulpanboo, 1996.

Shaull, Richard, and Waldo Cesar, *Pentecostalism and the Future of the Christian Churches: Promises, Limitations, Challenges*. Grand Rapids, MI: William B. Eerdmans Publishing Co., 2000.

Shearer, Roy E. *Wildfire: Church Growth in Korea*. Grand Rapids, MI: William B. Eerdmans Publishing Co., 1966.

Sob, Zong In. *Folk Tales from Korea*. Seoul: Hollym Cor., 1970.

Sohn, Pow Key, Chol Choon Kim, and Yi Sup Hong. *The History of Korea*. Seoul: Korean National Commission for UNESCO, 1982.

Simpson, A. B. *The Four-Fold Gospel*. New York: The Christian Alliance Publishing Co., 1925.

Speer, Robert E. *Presbyterian Foreign Mission: An Account of the Foreign Mission of the Presbyterian Church in the U. S. A.* Philadelphia: Presbyterian Board of Publication and Sabbath School Work, 1901.

Sugden, Edward H., ed. *Wesley's Standard Sermons Vol. I*. London: The Epworth Press, 1951.

Suh, David Kwang Sun. *The Korean Minjung in Christ*. Hong Kong: The Christian Conference of Asia, 1991.

Synan, Vinson. *The Holiness-Pentecostal Tradition: Charismatic Movement in the Twentieth Century*. Grand Rapids, MI: William B. Eerdmans Publishing Co., 1997.

———. *The Old-Time Power: A History of the Pentecostal Holiness Church*. Franklin Springs. GA: Advocate Press, 1973.

Synan, Vinson, ed. *The Century of the Holy Spirit: 100 Years of Pentecostal and Charismatic Renewal 1901-2001*. Nashville: Thomas Nelson Publishers, 2001.

The Commission on Theological Concerns of the Christian Conference of Asia, eds. *Minjung Theology: People as the Subjects of History*. London: Zed Press, 1981.

Tillich, Paul. *Theology of Culture*. Oxford: Oxford University Press, 1964.

Underwood, Horace G. *The Call of Korea: Political-Social-Religious*. New York: Fleming H. Revell Co., 1908.

Underwood, L. H. *Fifteen Years among the Top-Knots or Life in Korea*. New York: American Tract Society, 1904.

Underwood, Lillias H. *Underwood of Korea*. New York: Fleming H. Revell Co., 1918.

Wagner, Peter. *How to Have a Healing Ministry in Any Church: A Comprehensive Guide*. Ventura, CA: Regal, 1998.

Weber, Otto. *Karl Barth's Church Dogmatic: An Introductory Report on Volumes I: 1 to III:4*. Translated by Arthur C. Cochrane. London: Lutterworth Press, 1953.

Webster, James. *The Revival in Manchuria*. London: Morgan and Scott Ltd., 1910.

Weber, Max. *The Protestant Ethic and the Spirit of Capitalism*. Translated by Stephen Kalberg. Los Angeles: Roxbury Publishing Co., 2002.

Williams, Cyril G. *Tongues of the Spirit: A Study of Pentecostal Glossolalia and Related Phenomena*. Cardiff: University of Wales Press, 1981.

World Missionary Conference (1910: Edinburgh), *Report of Commission I: Carrying the Gospel to All the Non-Christian World*. Edinburgh: Olphant, Anderson & Ferrier, 1910.

Yoo, Boo Woong. *Korean Pentecostalism: Its History and Theology*. Frankfurt am Main: Peter Lang, 1988.

Young San Theological Institue, ed. *Young San eui Mokhoiwya Shin Hak I* [Younggi Cho's Ministry and Theology I]. Gunpo: Hansei University Logos, 2008.

———. *Dr. Yonggi Cho's Ministry and Theology II*. Gunpo: Hansei University Logos, 2008.

———. *Dr. Yonggi Cho's Ministry and Theology I*. Gunpo: Hansei University Logos, 2008.

Yung, Hwa. *Mangoes or Bananas? The Quest for an Authentic Asian Christian Theology*. Oxford: Regnum Books International, 1997.

Zahl, Simeon. *Pneumatology and Theology of the Cross in the Preaching of Christoph Friedrich Blumhardt: The Holy Spirit between Wittenberg and Azusa Street*. London and New York: T&T Clark, 2010.

Zoh, Byoung Ho. *Democratization and Evangelization: A History of the Christian Student Movements in Korea, 1884-1990*. Seoul: Tanggulshi Publishing House, 2004.

Articles

Aker, Benny C. "Charismata: Gifts, Enablements, or Ministries?" *Journal of Pentecostal Theology* 11, no. 1 (2002).

Allen, Roland. "The Revelation of the Holy Spirit in the Acts of the Apostles." *The International Review of Mission* 7, (1918).

Anderson, Allan. "A Time to Share Love: Global Pentecostalism and the Social Ministry of David Yonggi Cho." *Journal of Pentecostal Theology* 21, (2012).

———. "Pentecostals, Healing and Ecumenism." *International Review of Mission* 93, (July/October 2004).

———. "The Contextual Pentecostal Theology of David Yonggi Cho." *Asian Journal of Pentecostal Studies* 7, no. 1 (January 2004).

Arrington, French L. "Indwelling, Baptism, and Infilling with the Holy Spirit: A Differentiation of Terms." *PNEUMA: The Journal of the Society for Pentecostal Studies* 3, (November 1981).

Avison, O. R. "In Memoriam: Dr. Horace N. Allen." *Korea Mission Field,* (May 1933).

Baird, W. M. "The Spirit Among PyengYang Students." *Korea Mission Field,* (May 1907).

Baker, Don. "*Hananim, Hanunim, Hanullim,* and *Hannolim*: The Construction of Terminology for Korean Monotheism." *The Review of Korean Studies* 5, no. 1.

Bonwick, Gerald. "The Year's Work of the British and Foreign Bible Society." *The Korea Mission Field* 8, no. 7 (July 1912).

Chan, Simon K. H. "The Pneumatology of Paul Yonggi Cho." *Asian Journal of Pentecostal Studies* 7, no. 1 (2004).

Chang, Christine Sungjin. "John Ross and Bible Women in the Early Protestant Mission of Northern Korea and Eastern China." *Rethinking Mission,* (March 2008).

Clark, Donald N. "Christianity in Modern Korea." *Education About Asia* 11, no. 2 (Fall 2006).

Cram, W. G. "Revival Fires." *Korea Mission Field,* (December 1905).

Dempster, Murray W. "Pentecostal Social Concern and the Biblical Mandate of Social Justice." *PNEUMA: The Journal of the Society for Pentecostal Studies* 9, no. 2 (1987).

Dunn, James D. G. "Baptism in the Spirit: A Response to Pentecostal Scholarship on Luke-Acts." *Journal of Pentecostal Theology* 3, (1993).

———. "Spirit and Kingdom." *The Expository Times,* (January 1970).

Elbert, Paul. "Calvin and the Spiritual Gifts." *Journal of the Evangelical Theological Society,* (September 1979).

Gaxiola-Gaxiola, Manuel. "Roundtable: Racial Reconciliation—From Azusa to Memphis: Where Do We Go from Here? Roundtable Discussion on the Memphis Colloquy." *PNEUMA: The Journal of the Society for Pentecostal Studies* 18, no. 1 (Spring 1996).

Hanan, Patrick. "The Bible as Chinese Literature: Medhurst, Wang Tao, and the Delegates' Version." *Harvard Journal of Asiatic Studies* 63, no. 1 (June 2003).

Hobbs, Thomas. "Pioneers." *The Korea Mission Field* 34, no. 5 (May 1938).

Hong, Ki Young. "Tochakhwa Ghajungeseo Barabon 1907 Pyongyang Dae Booheungwoondong [The Great Revival of 1907 in

Indigenization]." *Seongyo wha Shinhak* [Mission and Theology] 18, (2006).

Hong, Young Gi. "The Backgrounds and Characteristics of the Charismatic Mega-Churches in Korea." *Asian Journal of Pentecostal Studies* 3, no. 1 (2004).

Hunt, W. B. "Impressions of an Eye Witness." *Korea Mission Field*, (December 1907).

Jang, Heung Kil. "Youngsan Cho Yonggi Moksaeui Sahoi Goowonae Gwhanhan Shiyak Sungseo Yoonlijeok Pyungga [Ethical Critic for the perspective of Rev. Yonggi Cho about Social Salvation based on the New Testament]." *Journal of Young San Theology* 17, (2009).

Johns, Jackie. "Pentecostalism and the Postmodern Worldview." *Journal of Pentecostal Theology* 78, (1995).

Kalton, Michael C. "An Introduction of *Silhak*." *Korea Journal*, (May 1975): 31.

Kärkkäinen, Veli-Matti. "March Forward to Hope: Yonggi Cho's Pentecostal Theology of Hope." *PNEUMA: The Journal of the Society for Pentecostal Studies* 28, no. 2 (Fall 2006).

Kim, Andrew E. "Korean Religious Culture and its Affinity to Christianity: The Rise of Protestant Christianity in South Korea." *Sociology of Religion* 61, no. 2 (2000).

Kim, Dong Soo. "The Healing of *Han* in Korean Pentecostalism." *Journal of Pentecostal Theology* 15, (1999).

Kim, Sebastian C. H. "The Problem of Poverty in Post-War Korean Christianity: *Kibock Sinang* or *Minjung* Theology?" *Transformation* 24, no. 1 (January 2007).

Kim, Se Yoon. "Is *Minjung* Theology a Christian Theology?" *Calvin Theological Journal* 22, no. 2 (1987).

Korea Mission Field. "The Million Movement and Its Results." *Korea Mission Field*, (January 1911).

Landrus, Heather L. "Hearing 3 John 2 in the Voice of History." *Journal of Pentecostal Theology* 11, no. 1 (2002).

Lee, Bo Young. "5.18 Minjuhwa Woondong Gaheaja wha Phyheajaye Daehan Hyungsabumjeok Byungga [The Criminal Evaluation of

Those Responsible and Victim in the 5.18 Democratic Movement]." *Bubhakyeongoo*vol 27, no. 4 (1992).

Lee, G. "How the Spirit Came to Pyengyang." *Korea Mission Field,* (December 1907).

Lee, Jung Young. "Concerning the Origin and Formation of Korean Shamanism." *Numen* 20, (August 1973).

Lee, Sang Bok. "Youngsan Cho Yonggi Moksa euiSahoigoowon Ehae [An Understanding of Rev. Yonggi Cho's Social Salvation]." *Journal of Young San Theology* 14, (2008).

Lee, Young Hoon. "Dr. Yonggi Cho's Influence on the Korean Church in Relation to His Pneumatology" [in Korean]. *Journal of Youngsan Theology* 7, (August 2004): 138-39.

———. "Korean Pentecost: The Great Revival of 1907." *Asian Journal of Pentecostal Studies* 4, no. 1 (2001).

Macchia, Frank D. "From Azusa to Memphis: Evaluating the Racial Reconciliation Dialogue among Pentecostals." *PNEUMA: The Journal of the Society for Pentecostal Studies* 17, no. 2 (Fall 1995).

Ma, Wonsuk. "Toward an Asian Pentecostal Theology." *Asian Journal of Pentecostal Studies,* (January 1998).

McCune, G. S. "The Holy Spirit in Pyeng Yang." *Korea Mission Field,* (January 1907).

Miller, Hugh. "The History of Co-operation and the Federal Council." *Korea Mission Field,* (December 1934).

Moltmann, Jürgen. "The Blessing of Hope: The Theology of Hope and the Full Gospel of Life." Translated by Margaret Kohl. *Journal of Pentecostal Theology* 13, no. 2 (2005).

———. "The Hope for the Kingdom of God and Signs of Hope in the World: The Relevance of Blumhardt's Theology Today." *PNEUMA: The Journal of the Society for Pentecostal Studies* 26, no. 1 (Spring 2004).

———. "A Pentecostal Theology of Life." *Journal of Pentecostal Theology* 9, (1996).

———. "A Response to My Pentecostal Dialogue Partners." *Journal of Pentecostal Theology* 4, (1994).

———. "Political Theology." *Theology Today* 28, no. 6 (1971).

Moon, Chung In. "The Sunshine Policy and the Korean Summit: Assessments and Prospects." *East Asian Review* 12, no. 4 (Winter 2000).

Moore, J. Z. "The Great Revival Year." *Korea Mission Field,* (August 1907).

Mu, Han Goo. "Kookga Jochan Gidohoi Moouteul Namgyutna? [What did Kookga Jochan Gidohoi leave behind?]." *Gidockgyosasang* 48, (2004).

Parks, H. "Charisma: What's in a Word?" *Renewal* 52, (August/September 1974).

Pieters, Alex A. "First Translations." *The Korea Mission Field* 34, no. 5 (May 1938).

Reynolds, W. D. "Fifty Years of Bible Translation and Revision." *The Korea Mission Field* 31, no. 6 (June 1935).

Rhodes, Harry A. "Some Results of the Kim Ik Tu Revival Meeting." *Korea Mission Field,* (June 1921).

Sam, Lee Sŏng. "Gabshin Jŏngbyeon Gwa Kidokgyo [Gabshin Jŏngbyeon and Christianity]." *Kidokgyo Sasang* [Christianity Thoughts], (December 1973).

Seymour, William J. "Salvation and Healing." *Apostolic Faith,* (December 1906).

Sharp, C. E. "Motives for Seeking Christ." *Korea Mission Field,* (August 1906).

Shin, Mun Cheol. "Eco-theology of Young-san." *The Holy Spirit and Theology* 22, (2006).

Son, Annette Hye Kyung. "Modernisation of the System of Traditional Korean Medicine (1876-1990)." *Health Policy* 44, (1998).

The Edinburgh Review. "Corea." *The Edinburgh Review* 136, (October 1872).

Turner, Max. "Spiritual Gifts Then and Now." *Vox Evangelica* 15, (1985).

Underwood, H. G. "Bible Translating." *The Korea Mission Field* 7, no. 10 (October 1911).

Underwood, Horace G. "Division of the Field." *Korea Mission Field,* (December 1909).

Wagner, Ellasue. "Through the Hermit's Gate with Suh Sang Yun." *The Korea Mission Field* 34, no. 5 (May 1938).

Yong, Amos. "Disability and Gifts of the Spirit: Pentecost and the Renewal of the Church." *Journal of Pentecostal Theology* 19, (2010).

Yoo, Boo-Woong. "Response to Korean Shamanism by the Pentecostal Church." *International Review of Mission* 75, (January 1986).

Yoon, Gyoung Rho. "1900 Nyundae Chogi Janglogyohoieu Chili wa Chochanggi Gyoineu Sahoi Gyoungjaejeok Sunghyang [The socio-economic tendency of the early Korean Christians and the governance of the early Presbyterian church in 1900s]." *Hankook Gidokgyo wa Yeoksa* [Korean Christianity and its History], (January 1991).

Yonggi Cho's Sermons

Cho, Yonggi. "God's Blessing and Abraham." Sunday sermon, February 8, 2009, available from http://www.fgtv.com/fgtv/f1/WF1_1_re.asp?aidnum=21367&page=1, accessed December 21, 2012.

———. "Sharing Happiness and Love." Sunday sermon, May 18, 2008, available from http://www.fgtv.com/fgtv/F1/WF1_1_re.asp?aidnum=21330&page=1, accessed April 4, 2012.

———. "True Neighbour." Sunday sermon, November 11, 2007, available from http://www.fgtv.com/fgtv/F1/WF1_1_re.asp?aidnum=21304&page=1, accessed March 28, 2012.

———. "Bonanza of Blessing." Sunday sermon, August 6, 2006, available from http://www.fgtv.com/fgtv/F1/WF1_1_re.asp?aidnum=21239&page=1, accessed April 4, 2012.

———. "Born to Give." Sunday sermon, January 16, 2005, available from http://www.fgtv.com/fgtv/F1/WF1_1_re.asp?aidnum=21164&page=1, accessed March 25, 2012.

———. "New Year's Resolution." Sunday sermon, January 2, 2005, available from http://www.fgtv.com/fgtv/F1/WF1_1_re.asp?aidnum=21162&page=1, accessed May 12, 2012.

———. "Life of Sharing." Sunday sermon, July 18, 2004, available from http://www.fgtv.com/fgtv/F1/WF1_1_re.asp?aidnum=21139&page=1, accessed March, 28 2012.

———. "Three Calamities and Three Blessings." Sunday sermon, November 9, 2003, available from http://www.fgtv.com/fgtv/F1/WF1_1.asp?shType=1&code=2003&mm=11, accessed April 12, 2012.

———. "Four Elements of Love." Sunday sermon, September 22, 1996, available from http://www.fgtv.com/fgtv/F1/WF1_1_re.asp?aidnum=20510&page=1, accessed March 25, 2012.

———. "Is Poverty the Will of God?" Sunday sermon, June 11, 1989, available from http://www.fgtv.com/fgtv/f1/WF1_1_re.asp?aidnum=20341&page=7, accessed December 22, 2012.

———. "Religion or Love?" Sunday sermon, July 1, 1984, available from http://www.fgtv.com/fgtv/F1/WF1_1_re.asp? aidnum=20886&page=1, accessed March 24, 2012.

Dissertations

Cho, Chuong Kwon, "*HAN* AND the Pentecostal Experience: A Study of the Growth of the Yoido Full Gospel Church in Korea." PhD diss., University of Birmingham, 2010.

Jeong, Chong Hee. "The Formation and Development of Korean Pentecostalism from the Viewpoint of a Dynamic Contextual Theology." PhD diss., University of Birmingham, 2001.

Lee, Jae-bum. "Pentecostal Type Distinctives and Korean Protestant Church Growth." PhD diss., Fuller Theological Seminary, 1986.

Lee, Yvonne Young Ja. "Religion, Culture of *Han* and *Hanpuri*, and Korean *Minjung* Women: An Interdisciplinary Post-colonial Religio-cultural Analysis of the Indigenous Encounter with the Colonial Religions in Korea." PhD diss., University of Denver, 1999.

Myung, Sung Hoon. "Spiritual Dimensions of Church Growth as Applied in the Yoido Full Gospel Church." PhD diss., Fuller Theological Seminary, 1990.

Oh, Moon Tak. "The Impact of Korea Revival Movement on Church Growth of Korean Evangelical Christianity in 1903-1963." PhD diss., Southwestern Baptist Theological Seminary, 2000.

Swoboda, Aaron Jason. "Tongues and Trees: Towards a Green Pentecostal Theology." PhD diss., University of Birmingham, 2011.

Seminar Papers and Newspapers

Anderson, Allan. "Toward a Pentecostal Missiology for the Majority World." Represented in the International Symposium on Pentecostal Missiology at Asia-Pacific Theological Seminary in Baguio City, Philippines, January 29-30, 2003.

———. "The Gospel and Culture in Pentecostal Mission in the Third World." Represented at the 9th Conference of the European Pentecostal Charismatic Research Association, Missions Academy, University of Hamburg, Germany, July 1999.

BBC NEWS, "South Korean President's brother Lee Sang-deuk arrested." *BBC NEWS*, July 11, 2012, available from http://www.bbc.co.uk/news/world-asia-18792840, accessed July 15, 2012.

Cho, Sung Shik. "Face to face with Young Hoon Lee." *Shin Dong A*, May 1, 2009, available from http://shindonga.donga.com/docs/magazine/shin/2009/05/08/200905080500060/200905080500060_1.html, accessed June 27, 2012.

Gluck, Caroline. "*Koreans learn to live with divorce.*" *BBC NEWS*, May 8, 2003, available from http://news.bbc.co.uk/1/hi/world/asia-pacific/3011119.stm, accessed June 25, 2012.

Gregg, Donald. "Park Chung Hee." *Time*, August 23, 1999, available from http://www.time.com/time/world/article/ 0,8599,2054405, 00.html, accessed June 15, 2011.

Ma, Wonsuk. "Dr. Yonggi Cho's Theology of Blessing: New Theological Basis and Directions." 2003 Young San International Theological Symposiumat Hansei University, 2003.

Kidokshinmoon [Christian News Paper]. March 17, 2009, available from http://www.kidok.com/news/articleView.html?idxno=58701, accessed July 6, 2010.

Mokhoi wha Sinhak, "Interview with Yonggi Cho (1 September 2009)," in *Mokhoi wha Sinhak* [Ministry and Theology] October 2009.

Moltmann, Jürgen. "Salm Eul Wooi Han Sinhak, Sinhak Eul Wooi Han Salm [Theology for Life, Life for Theology]." *Kukmin Ilbo*, May 12, 2009, available from http://news.kukinews.com/article/view.asp?arcid=0921286513, accessed October 26, 2011.

Park, Sung Seek. "Korea in the 20-50 Club: Where Should It Go from Here?" *The Korea Herald*, June 11, 2012, available from http://view.koreaherald.com/kh/view.php?ud=20120611000997, accessed June 25, 2012.

Park, Young Hee. "The Great Revival Movement of 1907 and its Historical Impact on Korean Church." Presented to PCA (the Presbyterian Church in America) Korean-American English Ministry Pastor's Conference, January 29, 2008.

Sung, Moon Hye. "Yoido Soon Bok Eum Gyo Hoi, 20 Ga Jae Ja Gyo Hoi Dok Lip Seon Eon [Yoido Full Gospel Church, the Declaration of the Independence of 20 YFGC's Daughter Churches]." *Holiness Newspaper*, January 7, 2010, available from http://www.kehcnews.co.kr/news/articleView.html?idxno=6211, accessed June 27, 2012.

Yoon, Ho Woo. "Lee Myoung Bak Jeongkwon Seo Joongyong Doin Gidokgyo Shinja Deul [Christians appointed in President Lee's government]." *Joo Gan Kyoung Hyang* [Weekly Kyoung Hyang], April 7, 2009, available from http://newsmaker.khan.co.kr/khnm.html?mode=view&dept=113&art_id=19621&fid=&sort=sym, accessed July 15, 2012.

Encyclopedias and Archives

The New Encyclopaedia Britannica. "*Silhak.*" *The New Encyclopaedia Britannica.* The New Encyclopaedia Britannica: Macropedia 15 ed. 1987.

The New Encyclopaedia Britannica. "Park Chung Hee." *The New Encyclopaedia Britannica.* The New Encyclopaedia Britannica: Macropedia 15 ed. 1987.

ChosŏnWangJoShilLok [The Annals of the Chosŏn Dynasty]. "King Jŏng-Cho Year 15 (1791), November 8." *ChosŏnWangJoShilLok* [The Annals of the Chosŏn Dynasty].

ChosŏnWangJoShilLok [The Annals of the Chosŏn Dynasty]. "King Soon-Jo Year 1 (1801), October 3." *ChosŏnWangJoShilLok* [The Annals of the Chosŏn Dynasty].

ChosŏnWangJoShilLok [The Annals of the Chosŏn Dynasty]. "King Soon-Jo Year 1 (1801), October 5." *ChosŏnWangJoShilLok* [The Annals of the Chosŏn Dynasty].

ChosŏnWangJoShilLok [The Annals of the Chosŏn Dynasty]. "King Ko-Jong Year 13 (1876), February 3." *ChosŏnWangJoShilLok* [The Annals of the Chosŏn Dynasty].

ChosŏnWangJoShilLok [The Annals of the Chosŏn Dynasty]. "King Ko-Jong Year 21 (1884), 17 October." *ChosŏnWangJoShilLok* [The Annals of the Chosŏn Dynasty].

Interviews

Lee, Yong Hoon, email, November 15, 2012.

Moltmann, Jürgen, at his house in Tübingen, Germany, January 4, 2012.

Synan, Vinson, at Regent University, VA, August 16, 2011.

Yong, Amos, at Regent University, VA, August 16, 2011.

Appendix A

Interview with Dr. Jürgen Moltmann

Sang Yun Lee:
The first question sent to you is to know your general perspective of Korean Pentecostalism. About twenty or thirty years ago, Pentecostalism was still a kind of spiritual movement, which was not yet developed theologically. But now both many Pentecostal and non-Pentecostal scholars are studying Pentecostalism.

Dr. Moltmann:
It was some twenty years ago. One of my doctoral students, Park Jong Wha brought me to meet with Yonggi Cho from the Yoido Full Gospel Church. And I had a long conversation with him. It was theological one. And I spoke to his missionaries, male and female. Since that time, I came back to Yoido Full Gospel Church again and again, and talked to Yonggi Cho. And my general perspective is very positive, as the Evangelical Church in Korea. And I think the secret of his large church of six hundred thousand congregational members are the house churches, the family churches. He has fifty thousand house churches. With good congregations and communities, not all single members, but communities. And I have spoken at several conferences at Hansei University.

Lee:
I graduated from that school.

Dr. Moltmann:
So, Korean Pentecostalism as Pentecostalism in the United States of America and South America is coming theologically of age. It has the Journal of Pentecostal Theology in Sheffield. It's on the same level of other denominations [theologically]. Perhaps, they no longer have a movement but the Spirit is not only in movements. Sometimes, the Spirit is also resting in institutions. Yeah, I am trying to end up my perspective of Korean Pentecostalism. Yeah, this is my experience in

the Yoido Full Gospel Church. I don't know other churches, but I know Yonggi Cho very much.

Lee:
Many scholars say that there are some shamanic elements in Korean Pentecostalism. Some of them call it a sort of Korean Christian shamanism. What is the major difference and relation between Korean Pentecostalism and Shamanism?

Dr. Moltmann:
When I first came to Korea in 1975, I went to the Korean Shamans. It was on a mountain, where the Shamanist ceremony was. That was my experience of Korean Shamanism. There was a Shamanist ceremony going on for a woman. It was a memorial for her husband who died two years ago together with her family. If I compare this with the service in the Yoido Full Gospel Church, there is no comparison that can be made. I was attracted also to the writings of Harvey Cox. I don't agree with Cox's idea about the relation between Korean Pentecostalism and Shamanism. Yonggi Cho's appearance is more of a Confucian than of a Shamanist. That is an idea of sociologists but there is no a real relationship between Korean Pentecostalism and Korean Shamanism. Korean Pentecostalism is more related with the work of the Holy Spirit than Shamanism.

Lee:
The second question is that what kind of social works do Pentecostal churches have to get into?

Dr. Moltmann:
According to my limited experience, Latin American Pentecostalism is enthusiastic. And black Pentecostal churches in the United States of America are full of enthusiasm while Korean Pentecostalism is very disciplinary. Therefore, it is more Confucian and Shamanistic. During the military dictatorship while *Minjung* theology started in universities and taught about the Galilee community I went to Korea. At that time, Korean Pentecostals focused on saving souls of the lost but not to make political questions.

However, I don't know whether you know this, but Yonggi Cho's speech in the year of 2005. It is in the journal of the Yoido Full Gospel Church. He made a statement on Christ and social salvation. It has to do repentance because he only concentrated on salvation for the soul. Therefore, he claimed the year of 2005 for the year of social salvation and salvation of the earth, eco-theological salvation. I think this is very important. I did comment on this article. I wrote it in German and it was translated into Korean. I responded to the article in terms of social salvation and the salvation of nature. This is a real change of his message and his ministry. My comments are on the Newspaper of Full Gospel Family [which is the weekly newspaper of the Yoido Full Gospel Church]. This shows that there is a change in the Yoido Full Gospel Church for the socio-political engagement and also for the relationship between North and South Korea.

I think the main task for the Christian gospel is to form communities and congregations where people can meet without anxiety, without control but to learn and to trust. The dictatorial government can easily oppress individuals, but if they form a community it is more difficult to oppress them. Therefore, a community is a great help for individuals in a dictatorship and also in a capitalistic society.

In Seoul, the suicide rate is very high. In big cities of a capitalistic society, inequality of people is growing, thus we need equality in congregations and communities. I think this is most important for people because the family relationship is declining in big cities. Therefore, people need congregations and communities where they feel at home, accepted and loved by other people. This is my idea for capitalistic societies.

Okay, what is your next question?

Lee:
My next question is regards to the Threefold Blessing. In the Korean context I call it the, 'Pentecostal Hope.' What is the main difference between your hope and the Threefold Blessing?

Dr. Moltmann:
I found out at Hansei University that the theology of Yoido Full Gospel Church has grown and it is the theology of Cross, forgiveness

of sin, and the theology of Pentecost with many gifts of the Spirit. But it is very weak in the resurrection of Christ. Therefore, my theology of hope is on the resurrection of Christ. And I think the Pentecostal theology needs to develop the theology of resurrection of Christ, the resurrection of the Spirit, and the resurrection from death in the future. The resurrection of Christ is the cornerstone of Christian faith because without the resurrection of Christ we would know nothing about Jesus. And the resurrection of the Spirit is important to courage to live and to be. The resurrection of the Spirit came upon the Disciples of Christ and formed into a community of sharing in Acts chapter 4, incorrectly called early Christian communists. But the resurrection of hope brings people hope to form a community where there were no differences in gender, income and where they can accept each other as brothers and sisters. Therefore, the resurrection of hope is important for life. And it is also important for the ancestor cult in Asia. Ancestors are not dead in Shamanism. There are living death and the hope of the resurrection of dead. We are in a community of hope.

<u>Lee</u>:
How can I understand the difference in terms of hope in the German context after the Second World War and the Korean context after the Korean War?

<u>Dr. Moltmann</u>:
After World War II, the community happened. The Threefold Blessing, salvation of the soul, divine healing, and financial prosperity, all three are very individualistic. But, in common poverty, we [Germans] helped each other. Mutual help is more important than financial prosperity. If anyone is prosperous financially, he can help others. So, mutual help in a community is a key to salvation.

There is a growing of inequality in capitalistic societies. This is destroying the community feeling and mutual help. This is a danger because the growing inequality of people will destabilize a country. There are very rich people and poor people in Korea. The middle class is sinking down in my country. The cornerstone of democracy is not only freedom, but also equality. Therefore, we need a new social movement to form a community and equality in our society.

Lee:

Korea is separated in the North and the South. We expect that the unification of Korea may be possible in the near future. For the unification of Germany, what did the German churches do? What do Korean churches need to do for the unification of Korea?

Dr. Moltmann:

The separation of the two Germanys was never as strict as the separation of the two Koreas. There were open borders. We could visit our relatives in the other country. So for both sides the churches could communicate with each other. Therefore, the Protestant church had a stronghold of unity in the East and the West Germany. The Protestant church of Germany was an initiative for the unification of Germany. More than 300,000 people gathered and demonstrated the unification in the Nikolai Church. So, it is completely different with Korea. So, you must find your own way.

Appendix B

Interview with Dr. Young Hoon Lee

Lee:

The Threefold Blessing (salvation, divine healing and prosperity) was developed on the post Korean context. After the Korean War, most Koreans suffered from poverty and disease and Christianity was still not influential to them. At that time, the message of the Threefold Blessing gave hopes of healing and prosperity to the sick and the poor. However, the contemporary Koreans are under a good National Health Care which even the U.S.A government desires. There is the relative poverty but national poverty no longer exists in South Korea. In this today's context, what kinds of hope can the Threefold Blessing give to Korean people and Christians?

Dr. Young Hoon Lee:

First of all, I agree with your understanding with regard to the Threefold Blessing. As you pointed out, the message of the Threefold Blessing gave hope to Koreans who went through the hardship of the Japanese Rule and the Korean War. Indeed, the Threefold Blessing fulfilled spiritual and financial needs as well as needs for health. I think you also pointed out a good point that what kind of hope the Threefold Blessing can give to today's Koreans. This is a very important question for me related to the matter that what kind of message I need to preach today.

The Gospel is always unconditional and has never been changed. However, the ways to transfer the Gospel need to be various according to different contexts. As the Gospel cannot effectively transfer to people without cultural and contextual understandings, the messages of the Gospel needs to be contextualized. The theological background of the Threefold Blessing is the theology of Calvary. Our souls are saved through the sacrifice of Jesus on the Cross. We can have the victorious life because of His resurrection from death. In other words, our good God has removed spiritual death, sickness, curse and poverty due to the fall of humanity, by the sacrifice of His only begotten Son, Jesus

Christ. This is the biblical foundation of the Threefold Blessing. In contemporary Korean contexts, prosperity and health have to be reconsidered more among the Threefold Blessing. When the Koreans heard the message of the Threefold Blessing during the 1950s and the 1970s, they had a tendency to accept the triple blessings as personal blessings because of their hardship. However, today is different. Nowadays, material poverty has been reduced, but many people are struggling with spiritual desolation, emptiness of life, loneliness and apathy.

In this society, it is not enough to interpret prosperity and blessing only for personal sake. In fact, the Korean society is suffering from the after effects, which followed after Korea's rapid economic growth.

Therefore, prosperity in God has to be recontextualized for contemporary Korean Christians. In order to do that, the Threefold Blessing has to represent the model of blessing that practices the distribution of wealth for the marginalized people, and the balanced development between the social classes. We need to have a new vision for communal well-being to conduct the reconciliation and development of the society. Korea is experiencing a state of social pathology due to the economical high-speed growth. In extremely competitive society, many Koreans suffer from high stress, depression, despair, the loss of the will to live and so on. When we believe and share the message of the Threefold Blessing, we need to extend its horizon toward our neighbours and society. When we do this, the Threefold Blessing can be continuously effective to us as the promise of God's blessings.

Lee:
I think that the Threefold Blessing is very personal. Thus, its personal salvation has to be extended to the salvation for the whole ecosystem; personal prosperity needs to transfer to the prosperity for the whole society and community; and healing also has to have wider perspectives such as healing of the broken family, social corruption, the gap between the wealthy and the poor, and the destruction of ecosystem. What do you think about this? In the same vein, how does the Threefold Blessing need to be reinterpreted and recontextualized for contemporary Korean Christians?

Dr. Lee:

The Gospel is for both the individual and a society. The message of the Threefold Blessing needs to extend its boundary beyond personal salvation. It must embrace social salvation. When the triple blessing emphasises on personal prosperity, it can be in danger of the prosperous gospel. Based on the acknowledgment that personal salvation and social salvation are inseparable, Yoido Full Gospel Church (YFGC) carries out social participations and ministry in balance. We believe that salvation for the soul is the most important task that the Lord has given to our church. However, we believe that God's work for salvation is not limited in spiritual salvation but eco and social salvations are a part of it. Thus, the YFGC has trained and educated our church members to bear 'social sanctification' as born again Christians as much as 'personal sanctification.' For instance, the church has taught them the Threefold Blessing as the core message that they can realize the salvific grace of Jesus. At the same time, they learn the Fivefold Gospel (salvation, the fullness of the Spirit, divine healing, blessing, and the Second Advent) and the seven Full Gospel beliefs (belief of Calvary, belief of the fullness of the Holy Spirit, belief of evangelism to the ends of the earth, belief of the good God, belief of Jesus taking away illness, belief of the Second Advent, and belief of sharing). The seventh belief among them is 'the belief of sharing.' Through the belief of sharing, our church members are learning that God's blessing is to share with our poor and hungry neighbours. The church helps them practice the belief in their lives in various ways. For your better understanding, I want to tell you about our church ministries for the society.

In 1988, Elim Welfare Town which is the largest welfare town in Asia was built in Goon-po city by the church for elderly people with no one to rely on and for unfortunate youths. Since then, the Elim propagation, the vocational training institute, and the nursing home have established. From 1998, our ministries for the society have expanded. We are supporting welfares for the disabled, the churches not able to do self-supporting financially, and even the government programme named 'Anabada' practicing 'recycle,' 'reuse,' 'reduce,' and 'share.' In 1999, the Good People Foundation affiliated with NGO was formed. Through this foundation, we help the poor and the sick, the hungry, political refugees, and flood victims over the world. For the

North Korean people, we are sending food, medicines, corn seed, fertilizers and children's meals under humanitarian circumstances.

In order to help the North Korean refugees settling down in South Korea, the church has established the Free Citizen College to educate them. The church has also helped them start their own businesses in South Korea. As a result, there are 15 convenient stores being run by North Korean refugees.

The church is actively engaged in social and foreign relief works with operating mobile clinics, medical volunteers, children and the disabled care service, supporting for child breadwinners, and building up hospitals and schools in third worlds. In 2003, the Full Gospel Medical Centre was opened to help foreign workers in Korea, the disabled and doctor-less villages. In 2007, the Pyoungyang Cho Yong Gi Hospital specialized in heart disease was started to build in Pyoungyang, the capital city of North Korea. From February 2008, the social works such as fixing low income's houses, repairing the building of old local children centre, and counselling the multi-cultural families. About 4,500 children suffered from heart diseases had free medical operations since 1984. In 1982, the Sharing Movement Centre was opened and started raising funds to support orphanages, nursing homes, churches in the farming and fishing village, and the leper house in Sorok island. There are more social relief works operating by the church to help poor and marginalized neighbours through the fundraising campaigns; 'collecting used clothes (1992)' and 'Love-Loaf.' For the purpose of making the health society environmentally, the Full Gospel Holy City Eco Campaign Centre was founded in 2009. Through the centre, the campaigns such as 'using the public transportation' and 'energy saving campaign' have operated to make our environments clean and healthy. I am sure you could understand that the Threefold Blessing is applying to the social salvation and the healing of the community beyond personal blessings if you consider our social ministries. I think not only the YFGC, but all churches should have an active 'sharing and serving ministry.' Moreover, all Christians and churches have to try their best to be examples to the society.

Lee:

The transfer from the personal blessing to the social and communal blessing accompanies sacrifices such as pain-sharing and sharing own things. For this transition, the meaning of the blessing needs to be changed that the blessing is not to hold or have but to share with others. The orientation of the Threefold Blessing also has to be changed from 'I-oriented' to 'we-oriented.' This means that the new Threefold Blessing has to start in a different theological perspective. The Threefold Blessing has to rebuild up on the theological foundation of love. How do you think Korean Pentecostals and churches need to accept this transition?

Dr. Lee:

Personal blessings from God have to sublimate into sharing and serving for the neighbours. Surely not only Pentecostal churches, but also all other churches have to practice sharing God's blessings with others and serving our neighbours more. Those who have the salvation from the threefold punishment through the crucifixion and resurrection of Christ have already the holistic salvation, transferred from the children of the wrath to the children of God spiritually along with blessings as the soul is prosperous. The top priority among the Threefold Blessing is the spiritual blessing which is born again with the amazing love and grace of God. This means that having the prosperous life and a good health begins with spiritual salvation through God's grace and love. When believers understand this correctly, they can give thanks to God. Thanks to God will be expressed as love and sharing for neighbours. You can understand better if you consider how the YFGC is involved in the social activities and relief works I mentioned earlier. Furthermore, the Pentecostal churches, which considers the church growth by the works of the Holy Spirit as the model of the church growth, need to pay attention to the fact that the Early Church did focus on not only the ministries of the Spirit but also the relief works (Acts 2:44-45). In addition, you can have an advanced understanding about the Threefold Blessing if you consider that it leads believers to the faith which shares abundant grace and holistic blessings from God instead of redistributing limited sources generally called 'pain-sharing.'

Lee:
What kinds of roles do Korean churches including Pentecostal churches need to carry out for the reunification of Korea?

Dr. Lee:
Korean churches can learn a lesson from the West and from East German churches who made big contributions to the unification of Germany. Before the unification of East and West, Western and Eastern churches had spiritual and social leadership in each country. Especially, East German churches did not lose their faith under the Communist regime. The Communism of the East German oppressed the East German church for a long time. The Communists expected that the East German church could become nominal through persecutions. However, in the late 1980s, the East German churches remained as praying church and still had social influence with the spiritual leadership. The churches became the holy shelters where people, who were seeking freedom, could be protected. As the church continuously held prayer meetings for unification, the desire for the unification of Germany could be sustained. The West German church actively prepared the unification by doing the non-governmental exchange with the East. The Korean church has to work hard for the unification of Korea and, at the same time, prepare for it. Jesus came into the history of humanity and became the sacrificial offering for the reconciliation between God and human beings. Like Jesus, the Korean church has to play a significant role for the reconciliation between the North and the South Korea. First, I think that the role of the Korean church for the unification is to transfer the gospel of reconciliation through Jesus Christ to North Korea. The Gospel will empower us to rebind the North and the South in the love of Jesus Christ. Jesus Christ brought peace and reconciliation to all over the world. When the gospel of reconciliation transfers to North Korea, the North and the South can be reconciled with each other. For this, the South Korean churches have to work together. Regardless of differences between denominations, doctrines, theologies, and conservatives and progressives, the Korean churches have to cooperate for North Korea. All Korean churches have to do their best to let the Kingdom of God present in reunified Korea. Second, the important work of the Korean church for unification is to help North Koreans from a humanitarian point of view. As the Lord fed

the people who came to Him when they were hungry, the Korean church has to help poor and starved North Koreans with the love of Christ. Especially, North Korean children, who are suffering from malnutrition and complications, are needed emergency aid with medicines and foods for survival. The mission for North Korea should not be a one-time aid but rather consistent supports in order to construct infrastructure and social overhead capital through building up hospitals, schools, factories and so on. In this sense, the missions of the YFGC for North Korea such as 'Good People,' 'Pyongyang Cho Yonggi Heart Specialized Hospital,' and other humanitarian supports can be good examples for the unification of Korea in the love of Jesus.

Appendix C

Interview with Dr. Amos Yong

Lee: What is your definition of Pentecostalism?

Dr. Amos Yong:
I actually mention that in my book, *The Spirit Poured Out on All Flesh*, if you look in pages 18-19, you will be able to see my definition. I would define, Pentecostalism, as a spiritual movement which includes charismatic movements as well as other related movements. I would like to say that most spiritual movements practice the spiritual gifts in some way or just practice in the gift of tongues. But they may not call themselves Pentecostals, or see themselves as Charismatic. So, I have a phenomenological definition of this. I do not define Pentecostalism theologically in terms of a doctrine or anything like that. If it looks like a duck, if it quacks like a duck, if it smells like a duck, it's a duck . . . right? Have you read my book, *Theology and Down Syndrome*?

Lee: Yes, but not the whole book though.

Dr. Yong:
Then, you gotta read that book . . . ha ha ha. . . .
You read that book and I also have another book that is coming out in October. It is called, *The Bible, Disability and the Church,* where I look at biblical texts and Jesus' healing narratives.
In the book, *Theology and Down Syndrome*, there is a chapter on Salvation where I discuss healing quite a bit. I distinguish between the two concepts of curing and healing.

Lee:
What is the major difference between curing and healing?

Dr. Yong:
Curing involves in the fixing of some kind of physical problem. Healing could be involved in curing but that is not necessary. Someone could be healed but not necessarily cured.

Lee:
What do you mean by that? What are some examples you could give me?

Dr. Yong:
Healing is a New Testament word for Salvation. So, Salvation is healing.

Let's say someone is born without an arm. Technically, there is really nothing wrong with him. He can still be saved, but that doesn't mean God has to grow an arm out of his body.

There are all kinds of disabilities, that's why you have to read my book for more details on this.

Sometimes, disabilities are involved with something not being well with our body, like for example, chronic illness is a disability. Chronic illness is also a kind of physical condition, that if you're going to heal chronic illness then you have to cure that disability.

Disability is a social consciousness. Disability is when someone who has one arm and applies for a job, people will say 'I will keep your record and call you later,' but don't call him or never hire him. So, disability is a social construct. What I am saying is that for the disabled we need healing, not curing, healing for social constructions. When Jesus cured people, he usually restored them with their communities. That's where healing takes place.

Lee:
I have been dealing with divine healing as a hope for those who have diseases.

How would you respond to those who do not get healed despite hard prayed prayers over a long period of time? What can we as Pentecostal Preachers and Theologians say to them? How can we handle their disappointment?

Dr. Yong:

We can handle their disappointments by not setting up expectations that are inappropriate. Someone might say, "Well, one of the reasons why Pentecostalism has grown so much around the world is precisely because it is a faith message." In other words, we as Pentecostal Preachers need to continue to install faith in hearers. When we install faith in hearers, then they would believe and then they would be cured. So, when they are not cured, there would be two or three problems. First, they are not believing. Second, the preacher is building up faith properly or is not leading them to expect a miracle. This is the classic argument. You need to preach with enough enthusiasm so that people can really believe then they can get healed.

Lee:

Yes, but this is about Pentecostal Preachers, but what about Pentecostal Theologians?

Dr. Yong:

I think that a part of what we need to do is to expand our definition of healing to salvation. I talk about seven or eight different types of salvation in my book, *The Spirit Poured Out on All Flesh*. Have you read my book *The Spirit Poured Out on All Flesh*?

Lee: Yes.

Dr. Yong:

Okay. I did not define salvation individually, but relationally. I define it socially. I define it environmentally. Salvation, therefore, is relational, not just for individuals. It involves in a bodily dimension but not limited to that. In other words, when we preach the full gospel we need to expand our understanding of the full gospel. This is just an example. The full gospel needs to be expanded to all creation. Even in Romans Chapter 8, it says that the Spirit is groaning until the redemption of all creation.

Lee: All creation means even animals and all?

Dr. Yong:
What's the point? The point is that the first creation has value. This is the whole point of resurrection. It's the whole point of redemption.

Lee:
Then, how about the new heaven and the new earth? The Bible says the first heaven and earth will vanish.

Dr. Yong: Do you believe in the resurrection of the body?

Lee: Yes.

Dr. Yong:
What's the point of having the resurrected body? In other words, there is something in our present that is deserving of resurrection. This means that the first creation is not just to be disregarded.

Lee:
But animals do not have souls. There should be differences between human beings and other creatures in Salvation.

Dr. Yong:
I am not saying that we are same as animals. What is the new creation? The new creation is the resurrected body. I am not going to say the resurrected body is going to be exactly the same. But there is going to be discontinuity between the resurrected body and the present body, but there is also going to be some sort of continuity between them. If there is no continuity your resurrected body will never recognize you. So, there will be some kind of continuity.

What's the point? The point is that the first creation has value. This is the whole point of resurrection. It's the whole point of redemption.

Because to redeem means . . . what? To salvage, it means something old is going to be pulled forward, to renew, to make it again, right?

Lee:
For the present Korean context, I think Korean Pentecostalism needs to find a new paradigm.

Dr. Yong:
Korean Pentecostalism like any other Pentecostalism, needs to recapture a certain aspect of narrative, regarding the work of the Spirit. In the early 20th century, the mainstream church neglected the work of the Spirit. So, here is my point, I contextualize the emergence of Pentecostalism. Harvey Cox argues that one of the reasons of Pentecostalism's emergence in the 20th century is that it has captured the primal spirituality. I think that Pentecostalism was able to resonate with the spiritual hunger of people in the modern world. Now, here is my next challenge for the churches of Pentecostalism in the 21st century. Now all kinds of spirituality are accepted. You don't have to turn to Pentecostalism. You can chose other forms of spirituality in the post-modern Christian world. We, Christians in general and Pentecostals in particular, need to start some questions which are two-fold. What is our situation? Like you said, South Korean Pentecostals now have health care. It's a different situation. You preach the same old messages which originated fifty years ago. Who is going to get excited about that?

So, pay attention to the situation. Like what Charles Parham did, *"Let's go back to the Bible."* And we need to ask, "Holy Spirit, what do you want to do today?"

So, what does this mean as a theologian? I am not necessarily prescribing what to do or what to believe for the future, but the more important thing is that we as Pentecostals really need to ask ourselves the question, "Holy Spirit, what is thing that you really want to do today in our time?" South Korean context will be different from Chile's or Zimbabwe's; it will be different from that of North America. Can we just export a certain gospel either from Seoul or Springfield to Birmingham and assume that the gospel is going to work? If we try to do that, I would say we are not being Pentecostal, because being a Pentecostal means to follow the wind of the Spirit. If we develop an institution for the previous successful movement by using a paradigm, and once we develop the institute and when next movements come along the established institutions reject those movements. It's kind of like Classical Pentecostals rejecting Neo-Pentecostals, the third wave and prosperous gospel and so on. Once the classical Pentecostals got in power, they established institutions. These institutions are based on the paradigm of the success from the 20th century. These institutions rejected new movements. If you see the church history the established institutions normally are not meeting the need of the contemporary situations, right? So, we need a new theology of the Holy Spirit.

<u>Lee</u>:
Thank you so much.
I am inspired by you for the future of Korean Pentecostalism.

Appendix D

Interview with Dr. Vinson Synan

Lee:
What is Pentecostalism?

Dr. Synan:
From what I know, Great Catholic theologians refer Pentecostalism to Christians who emphasize the baptism of the Holy Spirit and the gifts of the Spirit with the proclamation that Jesus Christ is the Lord to glorify God the Father.

Emphasizing on the baptism of the Spirit and the manifestations of the gifts with the proclamation that Jesus Christ is the Lord to glorify God the Father is the broad theological definition of Pentecostalism.

Lee:
What is your definition of Pentecostalism?

Dr. Synan:
Pentecostalism can be defined in many ways. I've been thinking about it recently. Pentecostalism is almost like a mood and openness to the spontaneous work of the Holy Spirit, rather than a big theological system. It is kind of like an attitude toward God and toward the work of God.

Historically, Pentecostalism is a movement that comes out of the Holiness Movement; which comes from John Wesley who taught the second blessing in term of sanctification. However, John Fletcher defines the Second Blessing as the baptism of the Holy Spirit. That sentence is very Wesleyan in the idea of separate and subsequent Christ experience. And now, modern Pentecostalism inherited most of teachings from the earlier evangelical, protestant, holiness movement and even Catholic misterical tradition.

Generally, before the Pentecostal Movement started, you had the teaching of the four-fold gospel: salvation; sanctification as the baptism in the Spirit; divine healing and the second coming. Then, when

Modern Pentecostalism came in, the second blessing was divided into two. Sanctification was separated from the baptism in the Spirit and tongues were seen as the evidence of receiving the baptism of the Holy Spirit. This is the Classical Pentecostalism. Then there is the Charismatic Movement; the neo-charismatic movement; the third wave movement, and many other new movements. But basically all of them believe in an experience of the baptism in the Holy Spirit. That's how we have defined Modern Pentecostalism.

Lee:
What about Korean Pentecostalism? There was no report on the tongue event in the Pyongyang Revival. Because of that, Classic Pentecostals say it was not a Pentecostal Movement, but an Evangelical Movement.

Dr. Synan:
Well, you had . . . I'm trying to remember the names but . . . Pyongyang and Wonsan had revivals before the Pentecostal Movement started . . . there were evangelists who had tongues speaking before a Pentecostal came from America . . . so . . . that was already there, but not taught as the evidence of the baptism in the Holy Spirit. I think you need to read more about the Pre-Pentecostalism of Korea. I don't remember but I think there were speaking of tongues in the Pyongyang and Wonsan Revivals.

Lee:
How should I deal with the relationship between David Yonggi Cho and the American Evangelists, not only Oral Roberts but I mean other evangelist who influenced Cho very much?

Dr. Synan:
Well, I think Cho became a very much Assemblies of God person theologically, especially when he went to seminary. And he was taught generally what the Assemblies of God have been teaching. He became the superintendent of the Korean Assemblies of God. In more recent years, he was the chairman of the World Assemblies of God Fellowship. So, he clearly identifies with the Assemblies of God, which is a version of American Pentecostalism.

Lee:
But didn't he leave the Korean Assemblies of God later?

Dr. Synan:
Cho took a lot from Oral Roberts who was not in the Assemblies of God, but he was in the Pentecostal-Holiness Church. His doctrine of healing is a part of the Assemblies of God's heritage, but I think he was more influenced by Oral Roberts as well as Roberts' prosperity doctrine. I think he got his emphasis on healing and prosperity more from Oral Roberts than regular Assemblies of God missionaries.

Lee:
Next question, I gave you before is about the contribution of Korean Pentecostalism on the socio-economic change of Korea after the Korean War. What would you think?

Dr. Synan:
Well, I think the prosperity of Korea changed Pentecostals more than how the Pentecostals changed Korea. Korea was extremely poor right after the Korean War and then it became very prosperous. Cho grew with the prosperity of South Korea. I think that influenced him because he saw prosperity. And his church became prosperous as well he had very rich members in his church. But I think, on the other side, Cho being the pastor of the largest church in the world with a newspaper and he is also well known in Korea. He teaches prosperity (I am sure) and healings that have affected all the churches in South Korea, Methodist, Presbyterian, Holiness churches and even Catholic churches. So I think it's two-way thing; the prosperity of South Korea influenced Cho because his church prospered and his people prospered and then he began to teach strongly on prosperity. I think this affected the Korean society for the good.

Lee:
How about social engagements? He has not been involved in social matters.

Dr. Synan:
Well, in the beginning he was like most Pentecostals. He did have a

social consciousness because . . . you've heard about the holy rice. Everybody brings rice to his church and puts it into a big bin, where poor people come and receive the rice for free. He has always reached out to the poor. That is a social consciousness, but it is not like the socialist who want to change governments and laws.

I don't think he is really a part of politics, although he has influenced government circles. I think his church probably has been a big influence in changing laws for the better, as well as, bringing Christian influences with his newspaper into Korean life. I don't think he's been an anti-reform, but it is known that spiritual things are far more important than material things.

Lee:

My next question is regards to the Threefold Blessing. The Threefold Blessing has been significant for the church growth and even the theological development of Korean Pentecostalism. But, I am in doubt that the Threefold Blessing would be as influential to contemporary Korean Pentecostals; as it was to the Korean Pentecostals after the Korean War. So, I would like to hear your perspective about the Threefold Blessing for the next generation of Korean Pentecostalism.

Dr. Synan:

Well, of course it was a big transition from being a poor church with very poor people who didn't have money and couldn't afford doctors. Thus, healing was extremely important in those circumstances, but Korea has prospered and now you have health care. Yet, there are a lot of sicknesses that doctors cannot cure. So, still there will be people who really need healing beyond what medicine cannot do. There will always be that need. The Threefold Blessings are salvation, healing, and prosperity. People still need salvation whether they are rich or poor, this will not change. Many people still need supernatural healing where medicine cannot heal. So, there will always be a demand for prayer for healing not as much as before. But still there are a lot of people who need a prayer. Material prosperity is still needed for poor people. There are still a lot of poor people in Korea. But the prosperity teaching is more than to try to get people who get wealthy. It's a trust to make them feel good about their wealth and to justify their wealth. It says that God gave them wealth. Most Christians in Christian history glorify poverty. Poverty has been looked down in virtue for thousands of years, especially in the Catholic world. Now people have this idea that poverty is not very good spiritually. It is more materialistic of course. But often when you have a prosperous society, wealthy people want to have preachers who say it's good to be rich and justify their wealth. Christians in Christian history glorify poverty. Poverty has been looked down in virtue for thousands of years, especially in the Catholic world. Now people have this idea that poverty is not very good spiritually. It is more materialistic of course. But often when you have a prosperous society, wealthy people want to have preachers who say it's good to be rich and justify their wealth.